Personal Politics

PERSONAL POLITICS

The Roots of Women's Liberation in the Civil Rights Movement and the New Left

by Sara Evans

Alfred A. Knopf · *New York* 1979

Copyright © 1979 by Sara Evans

All rights reserved under International and Pan-American
Copyright Conventions. Published in the United States by Alfred
A. Knopf, Inc., New York, and simultaneously in Canada by
Random House of Canada Limited, Toronto. Distributed by
Random House, Inc., New York.

Grateful acknowledgment is made to the following for permission
to reprint previously published material:
Beacon Press: An excerpt from *SNCC: The New Abolitionists* by
Howard Zinn. Beacon Press, Boston, 1964.
Liberation Magazine: For their kind permission to reprint "Sex and Caste," a
memo by Casey Hayden and Mary King. Published in April 1966.
McGraw-Hill Book Company: An excerpt from *Letters from Mississippi* by
Elizabeth Sutherland. Copyright © 1965 by McGraw-Hill, Inc. Used with
permission of McGraw-Hill Book Company.
The New Republic: "Of, By and For the Poor: The New Generation of Student
Organizers," by Andrew Kopkind, *New Republic,* vol. 152, June 19, 1965;
"Raising the Question of Who Decides," by Casey Hayden, *New Republic,* vol.
153, January 22, 1966. Reprinted by permission of *The New Republic,* © 1965,
1966, The New Republic Inc.
Southern Exposure: "We Started from Different Ends of the Spectrum," by
Cynthia Washington, *Southern Exposure,* IV, 4, Winter 1977. Special issue
entitled "Generations: Women in the South," p. 14 and p. 15.
Studies on the Left: "Newark Community Union," by Jesse Allen from *Studies
on the Left,* V, Winter 1965 and "Chicago: JOIN Project," by Richard
Rothstein from *Studies on the Left,* V, Summer 1965.
Viking Press: An excerpt from *Freedom Summer* by Sally Belfrage. New York,
Viking Press, 1965.

Library of Congress Cataloging in Publication Data

Evans, Sara.   Personal politics.

Bibliography: p. Includes index.
1. Women—United States—Social conditions.
2. Radicalism—United States.   3. Feminism—United
States.   4. Civil rights—United States.   I. Title.
HQ1426.E9   1979   301.41′2′0973   78-54929
ISBN 0-394-41911-1

Manufactured in the United States of America

FIRST EDITION

For my mother

Maxilla Everett Evans

Contents

Acknowledgments

When I began this study I knew the outlines of a story that was waiting to be told. As a newcomer to Chicago in October 1967, I fortuitously joined one of the earliest women's liberation groups. In that group and others then forming I first became aware of national new left networks and began to see the impact of women's experiences in the southern civil rights movement and in community organizing. My previous experience had been primarily as a local participant in a few civil rights marches, a drive to organize nonacademic employees at Duke University, and as North Carolina coordinator for Vietnam Summer (1967).

I remember myself that year as a quiet but passionate participant in what we all believed was a historic undertaking: the creation of a new, radical feminist movement. The following summer I returned to North Carolina with missionary zeal to spread the word (and to engage in a style of community organizing that I later learned was distinctly out of fashion in the new left). In the fall of 1969 I entered graduate school at the University of North Carolina determined to study women's history. I did not know then that hundreds of women all over the country were doing the same thing; but I was reassured by the example of my former teacher Anne Firor Scott, who had been studying women when I met her in 1963. The idea for this study emerged some years later as I cast about for a dissertation topic. In a conversation with Peter Filene I described the new left origins of contemporary feminism as a history that "someday" I hoped to write. He urged me not to wait and throughout the project provided the kind of painstaking criticisms and suggestions that one expects but too seldom receives from teachers and colleagues. Armed with further ideas from a sociologist friend, Paula Goldsmid,* about how such an investigation might be pursued, I got support from my advisor, George Mowry, to proceed.

From the outset I was aware that my own background—southern, white, activist, feminist—would profoundly influence this work. The influence could, I knew full well, amount to distortion—the substitution of my own experience for that of others (autobiography for history) and the failure to ask questions that could lead to information and interpretations which would challenge my assumptions. At the same time, my own participation and experience, used rigorously and self-consciously, might provide the kinds of intuitions and empathetic leaps that inform all historians as they come to know their material intimately. Fortunately, I had neither met nor heard of most of the people I interviewed before I began this research, nor was I present at the main events described here. As was the case with thousands of other women, my experiences were a local variant of a national story from which I could sometimes draw empathetic resonance but little more. Yet the rapport that developed in many interviews resulted in part from my own and my informants' confidence that my prior research and my personal experience together allowed me to comprehend what they had to say in a way that no "outsider" could. The results, time

---

* I met Paula in the Hyde Park (Chicago) women's liberation group in 1968. That fall she too moved to North Carolina to teach at the University of North Carolina School of Social Work. Together she and I organized a consciousness-raising group that evolved into a children's book publishing collective, Lollipop Power, Inc.

after time, were extraordinary. I only hope I have done justice to the histories with which I have been entrusted.

There is not time or space to describe the anxious, ecstatic summer of my oral research. I prepared for it by attending Lawrence Goodwyn's inspiring seminar on oral history methodology and by extensive research in traditional literary and archival sources. I set out with a growing file of names, most without addresses, and a list of people with whom I might stay. The research grew as I traveled. I had not imagined the subtle complexity, both positive and negative, of women's experiences in various parts of the new left, or the intricacy of a network of relationships that stretched across the country and over nearly a decade. None of the written sources gave more than the barest hint of what I would find. To all those I interviewed I owe an enormous debt. Most of them accepted my probing questions with surprising trust. Many shared files of movement literature, personal correspondence, and names and addresses. They encouraged me—I particularly remember Jo Freeman, who was just finishing her own fine study of the women's movement, assuring me that it could be done. They reshuffled schedules to accommodate me on a day's notice, meeting me in a variety of probable and improbable settings: kitchen tables, clattering restaurants, a Cape Cod beach, Mary Baker Eddy's tomb, a city park bench, a busy women's center. They, and others who housed me as I traveled, lent me cars and shared their food.

I could have interviewed dozens more. There were names for which I never found addresses, people who were not available when I was, cities I never visited. I finally stopped, however, believing that the structure of the analysis I have presented would be altered more in detail than in substance with further information. This is a collective story concerning patterns more than a set of individuals. While there are many more names that could appear here, I hope that many of the women not mentioned will feel spoken for. And I know that there are many other stories yet to be written.

Throughout this long process I have relied on the critical judgment and warm support of colleagues and friends too numerous to name. In particular, however, I want to thank William H. Chafe, Jacquelyn Dowd Hall, Donald Mathews, Jane DeHart Matthews, Sandra Powers, James O'Brien, and Pamela Oliver. A grant from the University of Minnesota gave me time for rewriting and additional research. In revising the manuscript I received useful criticisms from Ames Sheldon Bower, Charlotte Bunch, Casey Cason, David Lelyveld, John Modell, and Mary Rothschild; and from my editors at Knopf, Alice Quinn, Ellen Mastromonaco, and Ann Adelman. The Charlotte Perkins Gilman group and its predecessor sustained and nourished me before and during this work. My parents, Maxilla Everett Evans and Joseph Claude Evans, Sr., contributed in myriad ways, as they know. Craig Chatten Evans Boyte kept me rooted in the real world.

Intellectually and materially I owe the most to Harry C. Boyte. He did more than his 50 percent of child care, transcribed tapes, and typed and edited the dissertation. The ideas in the last chapter are part of an ongoing conversation between us.

The errors—of omission and commission—are all mine. But where there is truth here, I can claim only partial credit.

Sara M. Evans

Minneapolis, Minnesota
July 4, 1978

Personal Politics

1

Prologue:
Cracks in the Mold

Of the accomplishments of the American woman, one she brings
off with the most spectacular success is having babies.
—*Life* magazine,
December 24, 1956

In the mid-1950s Betty Friedan wrote and edited articles entitled "Millionaire's Wife," "I Was Afraid to Have a Baby," and "Two Are an Island" for *Cosmopolitan, McCall's,* and *Mademoiselle.* Robin Morgan was a child-actress playing Dagmar on the popular TV series, "I Remember Mama." Thousands of other future feminists lived in middle-class homes, growing up to be bright, popular, and good. Everything appeared to promise them a future of happy domesticity. Who would have guessed that within a decade they would rise up to challenge that promise, to name it fraud, and to demand fundamental changes in American society under the banner of women's liberation? Feminism had been dead for over thirty years. Even the word had become faintly embarrassing. Feminists were seen as unfulfilled, neurotic, grasping women.

When *Life* magazine produced a special issue on women in December 1956, Mrs. Peter Marshall charged in her introduction that "many of woman's current troubles began with the period of her preoccupation with her 'rights.' " She advised women to turn instead to the most satisfying and "completely fulfilling" moments of their lives: the first formal dance, the first embrace, the first baby. In the same issue Cornelia Otis Skinner denounced the "shrill ridiculous war over the dead issue of feminism." "Ladies," she appealed, "we have won our case, but for heaven's sake let's stop trying to prove it over and over again."

The odor of embarrassment surrounding women's changing roles lingered as a reminder of the acrid attack that had been launched more than a decade before when Philip Wylie had blamed "Mom" for all the evils of American society. Modern industrialization, the critics argued, had undermined the basic functions of the traditional home. Such changes induced severe neurosis in women, they said. According to Wylie, it transformed them into narcissistic "Moms" who devoured their sons and husbands, robbing them of independence and ego strength. Freudians like Marynia Farnham and Ferdinand Lundberg pointed to another "pathological" response in modern women: feminism. They recommended massive use of psychotherapy, government propaganda and awards for good motherhood, cash payments to mothers, and the restoration of such traditional home tasks as cooking, preserving, and decorating. Only through a return to the traditional home, "a social extension of the mother's womb," could "women's inner balance" be reclaimed and the level of hostility in the world reduced.[1]

By the mid-fifties such worries seemed a bit misplaced. Women were marrying younger, having three and four children, and apparently loving it. The vast majority of American women identified themselves as housewives whether they worked outside the home or not. Although growing numbers of them attended college, educators assured the public that they were simply preparing to be better mothers and wives, nothing more. If pickling and preserving had become the province of automated canneries, the work of the suburban housewife expanded in other ways. *Life* described a "typical" housewife under the banner: "Busy Wife's Achievements: Marjorie Sutton is Home Manager, Mother, Hostess, and Useful Civic Worker." No longer a household drudge, Marjorie the housewife had become a glamorized "superwoman" whose husband made $25,000 a year. Married at sixteen, she managed her household with the help of a full-time maid, worked with the Campfire Girls, the PTA, did charity fund raising, and sang in the choir. She cooked, sewed clothes for her four children, entertained 1,500 guests a year, and exercised on a trampoline "to keep her size 12 figure."[2]

While alternative images of womanhood never disappeared altogether, for most people they scarcely existed. The mass media proclaimed the triumph of domesticity. Women's magazines displayed "feminine" fashions with cinched waists, billowing petticoats, and accented bustlines. The movie industry promoted blond, buxom, sexy-but-innocent stars like Marilyn Monroe and Jayne Mansfield. Advertisers pedaled a host of new appliances and household products to improve the housewife's ability to serve her family with cleaner, whiter clothes, odor-free kitchens, and "Poppin' Fresh" breads. The family as firmament of a stable social order received a stream of paeans from noted figures who encouraged women to center their energies in the home. Adlai Stevenson, liberal hero and two-time Democratic Party nominee for president, exhorted Smith College graduates in 1955 to remember that marriage and motherhood gave them a unique political duty. A woman could "inspire in her home a vision of the meaning of life and freedom . . . help her husband find values that will give purpose to his specialized daily chores . . . [and] teach her children the uniqueness of each individual human being." Studies indicated that most young women intended to do just that.[3]

How, then, shall we explain the fact that by the early

1960s Betty Friedan had issued her famous denunciation of
the "feminine mystique"—her term for the identification of
womanhood with the roles of wife and mother? Or that
Robin Morgan would grow up to organize a demonstration
against Miss America in 1968 and use her powerful skills as
writer and poet to proclaim herself a radical lesbian feminist
in the early 1970s? Or that newspapers would be filled with
news of a revival of feminism while feminist organizations
and projects sprouted in every city in the country? The feminist resurgence in the 1960s and the 1970s makes sense only
when one looks deeper under the surface of the apparent
placidity of the 1950s, for there lay a dramatically changed
reality for women, one that the old ideologies about women's
place could not explain. The "feminine mystique" in operation offered a modernized version of the Victorian notion of
women's sphere sharply separated from the public (male)
realms of paid work, politics, and "historic" action. As an ideology it shaped women's and men's perceptions of reality,
but its life was limited at the outset.

This undercurrent of change provoked Wylie's rage and
Farnham and Lundberg's assault. And it prompted Adlai Stevenson to preface his remarks about the political power of
homemakers with an acknowledgment that many women in
that role "feel frustrated and far apart from the great issues
and stirring debate for which their education has given them
understanding and relish. Once they wrote poetry. Now it's
the laundry list."[4] The reassertion of domesticity and its apparent hegemony in the 1950s constituted an attempt to ignore and contain the altered conditions of the twentieth
century that had begun to culminate in new life patterns for
women. But women's lives could no longer be encompassed
by the older definitions of a "woman's place."

Within the home women with more and more education
found that they had less and less to do. Despite the baby

boom, their families were smaller than their grandmothers' had been. Technology abbreviated the physical labor of housework while consumer items complicated and, in effect, expanded it again. Laundry could be done by an automatic machine, but it required the appropriate detergents, bleaches, and rinses to meet changing standards of cleanliness. Children spent their days in school and afternoons at the playground, but a model mother had to be constantly available, both physically—to drive car pools, lead Scout troops, entertain bored children—and emotionally to avoid inflicting irreparable psychic damage. The suburban supermom, as illustrated by Marjorie Sutton, fulfilled a complex round of community activities and enhanced her husband's career opportunities with her well-kept home and lavish entertaining. Other women attempting a similar burden with less money and no full-time maid felt anxious, guilty, and inadequate. For all their busyness, little of what they did felt like work. Women's function in the home had shifted from producing food and clothing for family use to maintaining the family as an emotional community, making sure that everyone was healthy and above all happy. Led to fantasize that marriage would provide them with total emotional and intellectual fulfillment, more and more women experienced acute disappointment and then guilt when it fell below the mark. In particular, educated suburban housewives, the women who attempted to live out the mystique in its fullest form, found that their goal had become a trap.

Large numbers of them now attended college, where they performed to intellectual standards that made no allowances for sex. Although educators defensively proclaimed that they were educating women to be better wives and mothers, they nonetheless offered women essentially the same training as that which prepared men for future careers in professions and business. Thus women entered marriage

with heightened expectations of companionship and fulfillment and with a growing knowledge of their own diverse capabilities. Yet they arrived to find that suburbia had become
a female ghetto. Their husbands worked miles away; parents
and relatives lived in other cities. The social isolation of modern housewives and the automation of housework, combined
with a rising awareness of what they were missing "out
there," produced, inevitably, a high degree of loneliness and
boredom. Life seemed to be passing them by: shopping trips
became forays into the outside world, and husbands, who had
less and less time to spend with their families, were now their
major link to the public realm.

Even more important than these changes in the home
was the fact that many housewives were also leaving home
for up to eight hours a day to shoulder additional jobs as secretaries, social workers, teachers, sales clerks, stewardesses,
and waitresses. These were not the dreaded "career women."
They had jobs, not professions. But the fact that most of them
were older, married women shattered the notion that work
outside the home was a male preserve, to be shared only with
young, single women filling in a gap between childhood and
marriage. Furthermore, they were not all victims of grinding
poverty. Throughout the fifties women from middle-income
families entered the labor force faster than any other group
in the population.[5]

If Harvard seniors in 1955 were concerned to limit the
boundaries of their future wives' aspirations, then they had
reason to worry. "She can be independent on little things, but
the big decisions will have to go my way," said one. "The
marriage must be the most important thing that ever happened to her." Another would permit his wife to work until
she had children, after which she must stay home. A third
wanted an "Ivy League type," who "will also be centered in
the home, a housewife." Writers like Ashley Montagu be-

moaned women's failure to understand that homemaking was the world's most important occupation and exhorted them to look to the model of European women, who focused their lives on the happiness of their husbands and children. Such women, he noted wistfully, "seem to behave as if they love their husbands." The fear of female competition with men had become a thread running through contemporary fiction, while the funny pages featured strong-minded Blondies married to foolish, ineffectual Dagwoods.[6]

Yet few of the women entering the labor force saw themselves engaged in a challenge to tradition. They were simply doing what they could to help their families. And the jobs open to them were generally accepted as appropriate "women's work," requiring attributes similar to those expected of women at home. A changing economy created new jobs in such fields as health care, education, child care, clerical work, social work, and advertising—many of them labeled "female" from the beginning. If there were not enough young single women available for them, employers would have to relinquish their prejudices against married women and women with children. And they did. Thus millions of families achieved their "middle-class" status in the surge of postwar prosperity because of the additional income brought in by women. By 1956, 70 percent of all families in the $7,000 to $15,000 annual income range had at least two workers in the family, and the second was most often a woman.

Such participation in the labor force widened women's horizons. It gave them new skills and a paycheck that enhanced their role in family decisionmaking. But the blessing was a mixed one. A woman's work was likely to be threatening to her husband. It implied that he was not being a "good provider." Her guilt required that she avoid planning, training, or high aspirations. As a result she could not challenge discrimination according to sex. The only jobs logically open to most women were repetitious and boring. This structural inability to take oneself seriously induced a deep insecurity and a negative self-image. The lack of seriousness with which women and their employers viewed their work reflected itself in their paychecks. In 1966 women received a smaller income relative to men than in 1939; and as the percentages of women in certain occupations rose, their incomes relative to men in the same occupations fell.[7]

In this context it seems logical that between 1940 and 1960, while the overall percentage of women working outside the home was climbing rapidly, there should have been a "slight but persistent decline in the proportion of professional, technical, and kindred workers that were female."[8] Professional women could not pretend that their work was secondary and inconsequential. They pursued their careers with drive and determination.

These professional women were the most unmistakably "deviant," and often harbored among themselves the few remnants of feminism left in the 1950s. Many found it difficult to accept their performance of formerly "male" roles and went out of their way to assure themselves and others that they were still truly "feminine." A study of female executives found that all of the women surveyed placed home and family ahead of business, but felt that they could do both jobs, "if they want to badly enough." Frances Corey, a senior vice-president at Macy's, argued that women were "equal-but-special." "My attitude is that I can contribute something as a woman," she said. "My reaction is much more emotional—and emotion is a necessary commodity. There are places where I can't fill the bill as well as a man and I don't try."[9]

The next generation, daughters of the fifties, grew up with the knowledge that their identifying roles should be those of wife and mother, but they knew that they would probably have a job at some point as well. They frequently observed their mothers shouldering the double burden of work outside the home and continuing responsibility for housework. Many knew that their mothers worked hard and were good at what they did—running day-care centers and shops, working in factories or offices, as lawyers or musicians. But their pay stayed low and their jobs offered few independent rewards. The feminine mystique had not obliterated the reality of working women. Rather, it had absorbed them. In 1956, alongside its "typical housewife," *Life* magazine included six pages of pictures bearing the title: "Women Hold 1/3 of U.S. Jobs." The accompanying photographs showed masses of women in various occupations. None of the jobs was portrayed as inviting; none seemed in the pictures to imply creativity or excitement. For example, hundreds of nurses in identical uniforms sat in a large auditorium listening to a male doctor; 104 middle-aged teachers stared impassively into the face of a man lecturing them on mental tests given to girl students; a typing pool of 450 pounded away in one enormous room. The only lively picture of the lot showed scantily clad chorus girls. This dulling mosaic contrasted sharply with other articles describing the "rich experience" of having a baby, the "achievements" of the busy housewife, and the glistening kitchen of a "Housewife's House."

Both in the home and outside it, women experienced themselves in new ways, discovering their capacities; yet they remained enclosed in the straitjacket of domestic ideology. To challenge it openly would be too frightening. In a rapidly changing world, clouded with the threat of nuclear warfare and the early brushfires of racial discontent and urban decay, where corporate behemoths trained their bureaucrats into interchangeable parts, few were ready to face the unnerving necessity of reassessing the cultural definitions of femaleness and maleness. If the world was changing, at least men could know that they were men and women were women. But that could happen only if women continued to maintain the home as a nurturing center, a private enclave, symbol of security and stability.*

Yet even in that most intimate arena, newly recognized female potentials generated tremors. Alfred Kinsey let the cat out of the bag in 1953. A sexual revolution had been going on for most of the twentieth century. Women, it turned out, had orgasms; they masturbated, engaged frequently in heavy premarital petting and not uncommonly in premarital intercourse; they committed adultery; they loved other women, and as Kinsey pointed out, "heterosexual relationships could . . . become more satisfactory if they more often utilized the sort of knowledge which most homosexual females have of female sexual anatomy and female psychology." One commentator noted that "the criticism here implied of heterosexual relationships on the average in our society is, to say the least, devastating to the male ego." Now the "togetherness" of the home required achievement of the simultaneous orgasm as proof of its felicity.[10]

However, this too could be contained, at least temporar-

---

* The resurgence of domestic ideology in the 1950s had complex roots. In the broadest context it meshed with a national mood that denied change in all aspects of American life. In foreign policy the rhetoric of the cold war held out the threat of nuclear annihilation as the price for violation of the status quo. Domestically McCarthyism was only the most extreme form of "rooting out subversion from within," as even moderate arguments for change in areas like race relations, labor, and education were treated as serious threats. The permission granted by government leaders and mass media to ignore or deny threatening changes was received gratefully by the American middle class, which after a generation of depression and war wanted nothing more than security and stability. And nothing represented these more clearly than home and family.

In addition, the feminine mystique may have represented the projected needs of middle-class men unable to accept their own changing roles. Within the burgeoning corporate and governmental bureaucracies, the work of these "organization men" had become increasingly technical, specialized, rationalized, and separated from any tangible "product." Bureaucracy suppressed emotion and passion, training its members into "interchangeable parts." Bureaucratic values

ily. The romantic fantasy life fostered by popular culture reemphasized passivity rather than power in female sexuality. The seductive but innocent woman remained a child. Beauty pageants stressed the competitive display of women's bodies and jealously guarded the purity of the chosen queens. *Life* preceded its "typical housewife" and working women with a thirteen-page display on "The American Girl at Her Beautiful Best." Yet most of the ten "girls" were married and over twenty. Advertisements made sex itself a commodity and women's bodies the medium for an array of beauty-enhancing products. Titillation and suggestion were "in," but direct discussion of sexuality remained a (faltering) taboo.

The entire special issue of *Life* provides an interesting study in the contrasts and blandly unresolved ambivalences of the mid-fifties. In praising beauties and babies, the primacy of sex-stereotyped roles went largely unquestioned. Beyond the "housewife's house," however, lay an article entitled "My Wife Works and I Like It." Here a multitude of commentators examined, defended, and criticized women's status. Emily Kimbrough, prolific writer of witty travelogues and former editor for the *Ladies' Home Journal,* defiantly challenged those who urged women to return to the home.

---

emphasized "female" traits of cooperation, passivity, and security. "Getting along" and being well-liked became new life goals. Yet the older definitions of masculinity remained, and few could recognize the contradictory fact that what one part of their consciousness valued, another part judged unmanly. Thus, if women would stay within their traditional role, men could receive reassurance both that the emptiness in their own lives would be cared for and that their "manhood" had not changed. In one last realm, the home, the man could maintain the illusion of control. See William Hollingsworth Whyte, *The Organization Man* (New York: Simon and Schuster, 1956); Auguste C. Spectorsky, *The Exurbanites* (Philadelphia: Lippincott, 1955); Maurice R. Stein, *The Eclipse of Community: An Interpretation of American Studies* (Princeton, N.J.: Princeton University Press, 1960); Vance Packard, *The Hidden Persuaders* (New York: D. McKay, 1957), pp. 89–91; David Riesman, "The Saving Remnant: An Examination of Character Structure," in *Years of the Modern: An American Appraisal,* ed. by John W. Chase (New York: Longmans, Green and Co., 1949); Filene, *Him/Her Self,* pp. 169–202.

"All the Canutes in the world, lined up shoulder to shoulder, could not turn back this tide now." *Life* staff writer Robert Coughlan railed at length against that "fatal error" of feminism, "that common urban phenomenon known as the 'career woman.'" He found hope, however, in the reappearance of the three- to five-child family in upper- and upper-middle-class suburbs. This somewhat more optimistic replay of Farnham and Lundberg appeared in a magazine whose cover was graced by the profiles of a young mother and a five-year-old child, gazing fondly into each other's eyes. The caption read: "Working Mother."

Clearly the feminine mystique was already in the process of erosion, even as it reached its zenith. Emily Kimbrough was correct. The traditionalists could not win. But their temporary hegemony in the continuing domination of the feminine mystique laid the basis for the more explosive readjustment of a feminism reborn. The dilemma went underground and gathered force. It did not disappear.

Eventually the conflicts could no longer be contained. The feminine mystique's promise of "fulfillment" raised the expectations of middle-class women. Yet the social role of housewife as it shaped women's work both in the home and in the paid labor force generated disappointment as expectations continually fell short, and strain as large numbers of bored and restless women strove to meet the growing emotional demands placed upon them. Such pervasive unhappiness could not remain hidden. The illusion of the "happy housewife" began to crack along with the rest of the illusory equilibrium of the 1950s. Its solidity was undermined as on every level changing realities came crashing through old assumptions to expose the uncertainty and anxiety that lay beneath. Internationally, the upsurge of third world nationalism undermined the earlier cold war certainty of American superiority and "goodness." Domestically, a few Beatnik young people with disheveled lifestyles and writings on the problem of "meaninglessness" challenged the lives and dreams of middle Americans. Invisible to the general public, a much larger mass of affluent youth yearned for something they couldn't define, a purpose and goal beyond the material security their parents had achieved. More visibly, black Americans began to express their discontent with the barriers to full participation in the "mainstream." Signs of racial unrest began to multiply: in 1956 the Montgomery Bus Boycott; in 1957, Little Rock; and then early in 1960, the sit-in movement, which was to initiate directly that mass protest reverberating through the decade.

The election of John Fitzgerald Kennedy in 1960 marked a shift in the public mood. Change became a positive rather than a negative value. Together with the southern civil rights movement, programs like the Peace Corps and VISTA sparked a resurgence of idealism and active involvement in social change. The child-mother no longer fit the times. She was too static, too passive, maybe even too safe. A rising number of voices in the late 1950s urged the abandonment of outmoded myths, though usually with a qualifying clause about the importance of mothers to very young children and the primacy of the family. Many social scientists moved from using "role conflict" as an argument for women to refuse outside work, to a more realistic appraisal of the problems of the "working wife," who could not and would not evade such conflicts by returning to the home. Thus such observers had finally achieved the level of adjustment to changing reality accomplished already by millions of American families. Jobs for women were becoming legitimate as extensions of the housewife role.[11]

With the growing public acceptance of women's work outside the home, the mass media suddenly discovered the "trapped housewife." Betty Friedan pointed out that in 1960 the housewife's predicament was examined in *The New York Times, Newsweek, Good Housekeeping, Redbook, Time,*

Harper's Bazaar, and on CBS Television. *Newsweek* entitled
a Special Science Report and cover story: "Young Wives with
Brains: Babies, Yes—But What Else?" The editors reported
that the American middle-class woman "is dissatisfied with a
lot that women of other lands can only dream of. Her discontent is deep, pervasive, and impervious to the superficial
remedies which are offered at every hand."[12] Both seriously
and superficially, most articles in the issue treated women's
problems of boredom, restlessness, isolation, over-education,
and low esteem.

Educators also responded to the changing mood. Beginning in about 1960, a series of educational experiments and
innovations appeared to meet the newly recognized malaise
of the middle-class housewife. The "continuing education
movement" focused on shaping the educational system to
meet the demands of women's "dual role." Educational and
career interruptions due to marriage and children were presumed inevitable. The problem, therefore, was to allow middle-class educated women to reenter the work force either
full or part time without being forced into low-skilled, low-
paid work.[13]

Even the federal government began to treat women's
roles as a public issue and to explore public policy alternatives to meet changing conditions. On December 14, 1961,
President Kennedy established the President's Commission
on the Status of Women, chaired by Eleanor Roosevelt. The
purpose, in fact, may have been to quell a growing pressure
for an Equal Rights Amendment, but unwittingly the government organized its own opposition. The existence of the
commission and in subsequent years of state commissions on
the status of women provided a rallying point for professional
women. Such commissions constituted a tacit admission that
there was indeed a "problem" regarding women's position in
American society, that the democratic vision of equal opportunity had somehow left them out. Furthermore, they fur-

nished a platform from which inequities could be publicized and the need for women's rights put forth. The President's Commission's report, entitled *American Women* and published in 1963, was moderate in tone. Yet despite obeisance to the primacy of women's roles within the family, it catalogued in great detail the inequities in the lives of women, the discrimination women faced in employment, and the need for proper child-care centers.[14]

The importance of the report and the commission itself lay less in the specific changes they generated directly than in the renewed interest in "women's place in society" which they reflected. The following year women's rights advocates gained a crucial legal victory in the passage of Title VII of the Civil Rights Act, which prohibited discrimination by private employers, employment agencies, and unions on the basis of sex as well as race, color, religion, and national origin. Though introduced by a southern senator in a facetious gesture of hostility to the entire act, Title VII provided women with a legal tool with which to combat pervasive discrimination in hiring and promotion in all aspects of the economy.

The renewed discussion and activism took place primarily among professional women, who did not see themselves as housewives. Precisely because these professional women thought their work important and because they resented being patronized as if they had fled housework to get a little excitement, they felt even more acutely the discrimination leveled against them. Having openly admitted a certain level of drive and ambition, they were far more likely to experience discriminatory hiring, training, promotion, and pay rates as unfair. Other women could justify their unwillingness to fight against such barriers by saying, "I wouldn't be here if I didn't have to be," or "I'm only doing this for my family, not for myself." But for professional women, long-term careers were involved. Discrimination could close off opportunities they had invested years of training and hard work to attain. And it could deny them the positive reinforcement of respect from their colleagues. Since they took their work seriously, they were more vulnerable to the contempt that underlies patronage.

In general such women embraced the American ideology of equal opportunity, believing in advancement according to individual merit and achievement. Between 1940 and 1960, while the numbers of professional women declined relative to men, they also grew in absolute numbers by 41 percent. With more and more women in professional jobs, there were more examples to prove that women could excel at any occupation they chose. The individual professional woman was not a fluke or a freak of nature. On the other hand, there were also multiplying examples of blatant discrimination as their salaries and promotions increasingly lagged behind those of men with the same training and experience.[15]

The new public attention to women's roles finally generated an overtly feminist position in 1963 in Betty Friedan's book, *The Feminine Mystique.* In a brilliant polemic she declared that housework was intrinsically boring, that the home had become a "comfortable concentration camp" which infantilized women. She took dead aim at the educational establishment, Freudians, women's magazines, and mass advertising, which she believed had combined to limit women's horizons and to force them back into the home. More academic but equally critical reassessments of women's traditional roles soon followed.[16]

By the mid-sixties these angry professional women were developing an oppositional ideology and a strong network within governmental commissions on the status of women. As participants and consultants, they articulated the discrepancy between the ideals of equal opportunity and the actual treatment of women by employers. They mobilized to press for the passage of Title VII and then for its enforcement. A growing circle of women, including Friedan, Rep. Martha

Griffiths, and the lawyers Mary Eastwood and Pauli Murray, urged the creation of an action group to pressure a government that continued to issue provocative reports but showed little sign of taking effective action. When, at a national conference of state commissions on the status of women in 1965, activists were informed that they could pass no resolutions and take no action in their capacity as state commissioners, a group broke away to resolve to found the National Organization for Women (NOW). These women had become convinced that, for real change to occur, a new civil rights group must be formed that could pressure the government to enact and enforce laws against sexual discrimination. Thus NOW became the "women's rights" branch of a renewed feminism.[17]

In general, the professional women who created NOW accepted the division between the public and private spheres and chose to seek equality primarily in the public realm. Betty Friedan's devastating critique of housewifery ended up with a prescription that women, like men, should be allowed to participate in both realms. In effect she urged women to do it all—to be superwomen—by assuming the dual roles of housewife and professional. She made no serious assault on the division of labor within the home. For Friedan it was easier to imagine a professional woman hiring a "professional housewife" to take her place in the home than to challenge the whole range of sex roles or the division of social life into home and work, private and public, female and male domains.

In contrast, however, the oppression of most American women centered on their primary definition of themselves as "housewife," whether they worked solely inside the home or also outside it. Although they could vote, go to college, run for office, and enter most professions, women's primary role identification created serious obstacles both internally and in the outside world. Within themselves, women were never

sure that they could be womanly when not serving and nurturing. And such doubts were reinforced by a long series of
experiences: the advice and urging of high school and college
counselors; discrimination on the job; pressure from family
and friends; a lack of social services such as child care; and
social expectations on the job that continually forced women
back into traditional roles. Somehow women in every position from secretary to executive all too often ended up making the coffee.

→   At the same time that women acknowledged the social
judgment that their work counted for very little—by accepting lower pay and poor jobs outside the home, or describing
themselves as "just a housewife"—they also felt uncomfort-
able in any role other than that of the housewife. To admit
discontent was to face a psychic void. The choices were there
in a formal sense, but the price they exacted was a doubled
workload and loss of both self-approval and public approval.
Thus, though the *Newsweek* article on "Young Women with
Brains" generated a storm of response from women, many
who responded in writing denied the existence of a problem
altogether. Others advised volunteer work and hobbies to fill
the time, or else criticized women for their unhappiness.
Only a few women echoed the article and discussed their
distress.[18]

If women found housewifery unfulfilling, they also on
some level believed it was their own fault, thus turning their
guilt and anger back in upon themselves. In a culture that offered no support for serious alternatives, women clung to the
older definitions. If such roles did not reflect changing options or their real desires, at least they were familiar.

The tenacity of traditional roles and their internalization
by most women meant that any successful revolt that drew
on women's discontent would finally neither accept a traditional view of "female nature" as particularly suited to home

and motherhood nor restrict itself simply to a critique of inequities in the public realm. For this reason, the emergence
of the National Organization for Women did not provoke a
massive grass-roots feminist movement. As a civil rights lobbying group, it could and did raise the public policy issues of
discrimination in education, employment, and media in ac-
cordance with its stated purpose:

> . . . to take action to bring women into full participation
> in the mainstream of American society *now*, exercising
> all the privileges and responsibilities thereof in truly
> equal partnership with men.

But while the professional women in NOW's constituency
militantly demanded equality in the public realm, they were
not prepared to question the mainstream itself, nor to carry
their critique into the operation of sex roles in every aspect of
life.

Yet the initiation of a mass movement required that the
problem be addressed at its core. The pressures on most
women were building up not on the level of public discrimination but at the juncture of public and private, of job and
home, where older structures and identities no longer suf-
ficed but could not simply be discarded either. The growing
emotional strains of providing nurture for others with no-
where to escape to oneself, of rising expectations and low
self-esteem, of public activity and an increasingly private,
even submerged, identity required a radical—in the literal
sense—response. A new movement would have to transform
the privacy and subjectivity of personal life itself into a political issue.

Once such issues were raised by the radical young feminists in the late sixties, the challenge to traditional roles pen-

etrated the mainstream of American society within a few years. Outrageous assaults on such cultural icons as Miss America, motherhood, and marriage caught the attention of the mass media. Americans were both shocked and intrigued by the sudden questioning of fundamental assumptions. As ever-widening circles of women joined in the process, a range of institutions—from corporations to families—began to experience angry insurgency from within. The *Ladies' Home Journal*, its offices seized by female journalists, agreed to print in August 1970 a special section written and produced by feminists; soon afterwards, women at *Newsweek* and *Time* staged their own rebellions. No institution, it seemed, was sacred or safe. Nuns organized within the Catholic Church; female seminary students began to agitate for full equality within Protestant churches. In 1975 they wracked the Episcopal Church with controversy, when eleven women defiantly joined in an unauthorized ordination service. And in the privacy of thousands of bedrooms and kitchens across the country, revolutions over housework, child care, family decisionmaking, and sexuality raged on or reached quiet resolution.

The young are prominent in most revolutions. In this case in particular it seemed logical and necessary that the initiative should come from young women who did not have marriages and financial security to risk or years invested in traditional roles to justify. Within the context of cultural unrest and the attack on tradition made by women like Friedan, the catalyst for a profounder criticism and a mass mobilization of American women proved to be the young female participants in the social movements of the 1960s. These daughters of the middle class had received mixed, paradoxical messages about what it meant to grow up to be women in America. On the one hand, the cultural ideal—held up by media, parents, and school—informed them that their only true happiness lay in the twin roles of wife and mother. At the same time they could observe the reality that housewifery was distinctly unsatisfactory for millions of suburban women and that despite the best efforts of *Ladies' Home Journal,* most American women could expect to work outside the home a substantial part of their lives. Furthermore, having grown up in an era that commoditized sexual titillation while it reasserted repressive norms, they found themselves living on the ambiguous frontiers of sexual freedom and self-control opened up by the birth control pill. Such contradictions left young, educated women in the 1960s dry tinder for the spark of revolt.

The stage was set. Yet the need remains to unravel the mystery of how a few young women stepped outside the assumptions on which they had been raised to articulate a radical critique of women's position in American society. For them, a particular set of experiences in the southern civil rights movement and parts of the student new left catalyzed a new feminist consciousness. There they found the inner strength and self-respect to explore the meaning of equality and an ideology that beckoned them to do so. There they also met the same contradictory treatment most American women experienced, and it spun them out of those movements into one of their own.

2

Southern White Women
in a Southern
Black Movement

We have given great offense on account of our womanhood,
which seems to be as objectionable as our abolitionism. The
whole land seems aroused to discussion on the province of
woman, and I am glad of it. We are willing to bear the brunt
of the storm, if we can only be the means of making a break
in that wall of public opinion which lies right in the way of
woman's rights, true dignity, honor and usefulness.[1]
                                        —Angelina E. Grimke,
                                        July 25, 1837

   Twice in the history of the United States the struggle for
racial equality has been midwife to a feminist movement. In
the abolition movement of the 1830s and 1840s, and again in
the civil rights movement of the 1960s, women experiencing
the contradictory expectations and stresses of changing roles
began to move from individual discontents to a social movement in their own behalf. Working for racial justice, they
gained experience in organizing and in collective action, an
ideology that described and condemned oppression analogous to their own, and a belief in human "rights" that could
justify them in claiming equality for themselves. In each case,
moreover, the complex web of racial and sexual oppression
embedded in southern culture projected a handful of white
southern women into the forefront of those who connected
one cause with the other.

The lessons of the NAACP and its legal defense arm were not lost on the women who founded NOW: to adult professional women in the early 1960s the growth of civil rights insurgency provided a model of legal activism and imaginative minority group lobbying. But the relationship between feminism and civil rights was deeper than that. While advocates of women's rights took cues from one branch of the civil rights movement, the sweeping critique of sexual roles that characterized the more radical women's liberation movement of the late sixties first developed from within the ranks, and the revolt, of young southern blacks.

In the 1830s and again in the 1960s the first voices to link racial and sexual oppression were those of southern white women. Within southern society, "white womanhood" provided a potent cultural symbol that also implied little practical power for women. The necessity of policing the boundaries between black and white heightened the symbolic importance of traditional domestic arrangements: white women in their proper place guaranteed the sanctity of the home and the purity of the white race. As long as they remained "ladies," they represented the domination of white men. Thus the most brutally repressed assault upon white authority became a sexual liaison between a black man and a white woman—culturally defined as "rape" regardless of the circumstances. And the polar opposition of the "pure white woman," rigidly confined to her domestic sphere, and the animalistic black man, violently pressed into subservience, represented classic elements in the psychosis of southern racism.[2] The rebellion of either necessarily reverberated into the position and self-image of the other.

When Sarah and Angelina Grimke began to speak out against the sin of slavery in the 1830s, they did so as devout Quakers and daughters of a Charleston slaveowning family. No one in the antebellum south after 1830 could speak against slavery and remain there—least of all a woman. Not

only was opposition to slavery suppressed, the separation between public (male) and private (female) was so sharp and so
total that for a woman to express herself publicly on a con-
troversial social issue was unthinkable. Thus the Grimke sisters were exiles both as women and as abolitionists. At the
same time, their activity, defined entirely in religious and
moral terms, exposed the weak link in the image of the Victorian southern lady. Ultimately it made no sense to place
women in charge of piety and morality and then deny them
access to the public sphere where immorality held sway. On
this basis Sarah Grimke urged women to participate in moral
and social reform movements: "Whatsoever it is morally
right for a man to do, it is morally right for a woman to do."

As female, southern abolitionists, the Grimke sisters
were uniquely sensitive to the subjective realities of racial
prejudice that undergirded the objective evil of slavery.
When they were forced to assert their rights as women in
order to continue speaking on behalf of slaves, the two issues
of race and sex were fused:

> They [the female slaves] are our countrywomen—*they
> are our sisters*; and to us as women, they have a right to
> look for sympathy with their sorrows, and effort and
> prayer for their rescue. . . .
> Women ought to feel a peculiar sympathy in the col-
> ored man's wrong, for like him, she has been accused of
> mental inferiority, and denied the privileges of a liberal
> education.

In the antebellum era Sarah and Angelina Grimke were
so exceptional that there is literally no one to compare them
with. Anne Firor Scott has demonstrated that there were
many southern "ladies" who abhorred slavery and compared
their situation to that of the slaves, but they expressed such

beliefs only in the private pages of their diaries. Public activity in the name of social change was not in the province of the southern woman. By the end of the century, however, a growing number of white women were tentatively emerging from the confines of the domestic sphere. Among working-class whites, bitter economic necessity forced women and children alike to work long hours in the proliferating cotton mills. For middle- and upper-class white women the pathway out of the home lay—as it had for the Grimkes—through expanding their roles in the Church. In the 1870s women all over the south began to organize missionary societies. Within such societies and the YWCA, women created semi-autonomous arenas in which to learn organizational skills, gain in self-confidence, and experiment with new patterns of behavior. Although reluctant to challenge overtly cultural definitions of either race or sex, they nonetheless began to act on their religious values in a way that drew them inexorably into social action. Their initial involvement had simply extended the expected piousness of a southern lady. But the missionary impulse, when carried beyond the home, brought these women face to face with the grinding poverty of the south and personalized the horrors of racial discrimination. In response, they founded Home Missions to provide basic services to the poor despite the continuing opposition of ecclesiastical hierarchies. Thus they initiated the settlement house movement and the social work profession in the south. As they built their own organizations, battling with Church authorities to do so, these women evidenced an early flickering of feminist consciousness, tied to an awareness of the cultural centrality of race in the south.

Through this process a number of southern white women in the 1920s and 1930s became active in the women's committee of the Commission on Interracial Cooperation (CIC) and in the southern women's campaign against lynch-

ing. The historian of those movements concluded that "both
the CIC and [the] subsequent women's anti-lynching campaign drew their constituency as well as their language and
central assumptions from this network of women's church
auxiliaries and YWCA branches."[3]

Yet the reformers in the 1920s and 1930s remained in
many senses within the confines of their culture. The bonds of
white womanhood had stretched enough to allow a growing
level of public activity and social concern, but they were far
from broken. Though pushed initially by black women in the
YWCA to confront the issues of racism and lynching, white
women's responses were crucially limited by the boundaries
of class and caste that they were unable to transcend. Working in behalf of blacks, rather than side by side with them,
they could not cross the line between patronage and social
equality. Indeed, burdened with the deepest fears and anxieties about sex between black men and white women, any
possibility of such relationship brought their liberalism up
short. They could take a stand against racial abuses—for their
time a courageous one—without being forced to confront the
culture as a whole.

By the late 1940s and 1950s a few isolated women actively opposed the segregated culture of the south—Virginia
Durr in Alabama; Anne Braden in Louisville, Kentucky; Lillian Smith and Paula Snelling in Georgia. Lillian Smith in
particular offered a pioneering analysis of the intertwined racial and sexual repression in the south. But such rebels remained few—shunned and persecuted by the white
community, excoriated in the southern press.

A new set of circumstances in the late fifties and early
sixties forced a few young southern white women into an opposition to southern culture comparable to that of the
Grimke sisters and made them key figures in the articulation
of a new feminist impulse. Their youth and a particular religious subculture on southern campuses prepared them to re-

spond to the revolt of young southern blacks in 1960. For them, as for hundreds of women in the past, southern Protestantism opened a pathway into insurgency that was peculiarly appropriate.

Although southern Protestantism in the 1950s was in general as segregated and racist as the rest of southern society, it also nourished elements of egalitarian idealism, especially among college-educated young people. Anne Braden described her childhood church in Alabama as the scene of her greatest childhood joys. Years later, facing a possible jail sentence for opposing segregated housing in Louisville, Kentucky, she returned to that church where she "had first learned that all men are One." She pondered the fact that those who had taught her "had not mentioned what this concept did to their society's fetish of the color line. . . . But I am sure that the seed that was planted in my mind and heart here was the thing that made me able to seek a larger world later." Despite its worldliness, its fashionable silence on social issues, "this staid little church . . . was the most far-reachingly decent influence in my walled-in childhood—and probably the most radical in my life."[4]

While Anne Braden pondered the unintentional radicalism of her childhood church in 1954, students active in southern campus ministries and the YWCA encountered a community that fostered, in the language of existential theology, a radical critique of American society and southern segregation. Such groups were among the first in the white community to respond to the burgeoning movement among blacks in the late 1950s.

The Methodist Church, like the Baptist, Presbyterian, and Episcopalian churches, sponsored elaborate programs complete with special buildings for meetings and worship and staffed by ordained ministers on most major campuses. Such campus ministers tended to be recent graduates of divinity school; they frequently were ambivalent about assuming a traditional pastorate and preferred to remain in the less tradition-bound atmosphere of the campus. The Methodist Student Movement (MSM), with officers at the campus, state, and national levels, represented the organized expression of student involvement in these religious programs and a revitalization of the Methodist tradition of social action and concern. From the vantage point of a semi-autonomous structure within the institutional Church, students could, and did, criticize the rest of Christendom for its shortcomings. At state and national conferences and particularly through its journal, *motive* magazine, published in Nashville, Tennessee, the MSM had become by the mid-fifties a kind of institutionalized insurgency of youth within the Church and an increasing source of unease for its sponsors. In the late fifties, throughout the south, the MSM harbored the most radical groups on most campuses.

Allan J. Burry, assistant Methodist chaplain at Duke University and national chairman of the Methodist Student Movement, described the problem of the contemporary student in revealing terms. "The basic threat he faces," Burry wrote, is "the loss of meaning in an impersonal and destructive world." In the same issue of *motive,* Finly Eversole, an Alabama native and graduate of Vanderbilt, wrote on "Existentialism: A Christian Philosophy?": "The existential attitude is also one of passionate *concern* about one's world and oneself. . . . In choosing what he will be, man is free." Eversole further maintained that there was such a thing as "Christian" existentialism, but that the extremes of individualism and nihilism must be firmly rejected as un-Christian.

Given the involved Protestant students' preoccupation with the problem of meaninglessness, and their concomitant focus on action as an avenue to freedom, many young people—especially Methodists—sharply rejected the bland, trendy conformity of the fifties. The editors of *motive* decried the general assumption of meaninglessness as the underlying force in life. They solicited articles on subjects like ecumenism, internationalism, and nuclear warfare. And they sought to express the search for meaning through artistic expression. Each issue reproduced a rich display of prints and original woodcuts, with occasional special issues devoted to art, dance, or drama.

A magazine with such a critical stance, published in the south in the 1950s, could not avoid the issue of segregation: the Supreme Court decision in *Brown* v. *Board of Education*, the revival of the Ku Klux Klan, the violence in Little Rock, and the agitation in communities throughout the south spawned by resistance to school integration—everything combined to make race relations the foremost moral issue in the region. In the late fifties a rising number of articles on race, segregation, and integration accompanied the crystallization of a sternly activist theology.

In 1958 the national committee of the MSM on socio-political concerns issued a statement entitled "Prologue to Involvement." It consisted of an intense, if obscurely worded, attack on the institutional Church for its pious complacency. Written as a confession ("we the church have failed") it concluded: "The Christian faith calls us to proclamation." In the same issue of *motive*, a pamphlet by the Study Committee of the United Student Christian Council entitled *Theses for Study and Debate* was reprinted, offering the positive, progressive side of confession—the exhortation to act: "The Christian group on campus which does not promote involvement in political affairs denies [God's] authority in that area of life." Additional theses explained the nature of that involvement:

. . . to permit division within the church is to live in sin, and FURTHER, any form of segregation, discrimination, or privilege within the church is an abomination. . . . The Christian group which fails to question

both its own activity, and the society in which it finds itself, is failing to do the thing for which it exists.

Such words declared a youthful anger with the Church and
the university, the former for failing to live up to its professed
ideals and the latter for encouraging self-satisfaction in a violently unjust world. The statements expressed a wilful determination to act, if with little clarity about when, where, or
what should be done.

Some hoped to provide direction. For example, William
Walzer, formerly a teacher at Scarritt College, a school that
had trained women Methodist missionaries for seventy years,
demanded that Christians "support all those movements
which open up opportunities for God's children to be their
very best selves. Anything less than this is a denial of God and
[the] Father of us all and a denial of the Christ through whom
he has redeemed us all." Walzer and others perceived in
African and Asian anti-colonial revolts a revolutionary upsurge that promised a different future, and called upon
Christians in this country to give them aid. But even those
who envisioned specific targets for Christian action had as
yet no positive vision for their own society. In general, the
exhortations from that period had a hollow sound. Like the
late-seventeenth-century Puritan clergy, they reflected a
constituency consumed by the problem of sin but helpless in
the face of rampant injustice. Only a vague hope for future
transformation, symbolized by the Resurrection, relieved
their paralysis. "The Christian Confidence," they reminded
themselves, "is that Christ is Risen."[5]

The longing for a new purpose in American society was
becoming intense. For at least some young Christians in the
south, the opportunity to act upon their faith and passionate
concern would be welcomed as a great relief. Moreover,
through conferences and meetings a small group in the south
had begun to develop contacts with black students unlike any

they had previously known. For deeply religious southern whites the discovery on a personal level that black people were human beings, "just like us," was an often startling and moving experience.[6]

A number of campus ministries provided particularly conducive environments for both soul-searching and social action, and many of these were modeled on the Christian Faith and Life Community at the University of Texas. Dorothy Dawson remembered the Faith and Life Community as "the most intellectually alive" place on the campus. Led by a charismatic Methodist minister, Joseph Mathews, the community had evolved an intensive internal life of study and worship. Consciously reacting to the bureaucratic, success- and status-oriented ethos dominating the campus, members sought the theological dimension in every aspect of their lives. Existential theology became, for them, a kind of social gospel, placing a premium on Christian witness at the "prophetic edge" of history. Their name asserted that Christianity was not only a "faith" but also a "life." The degree to which they had departed from the mainstream was reflected in the fact that the community was the only place on the Texas campus where black students were allowed to live at that time.

In 1958–9 Dorothy Dawson and Sandra Cason moved into the Christian Faith and Life Community. Both were seniors already active in the YWCA. Dorothy Dawson recalled that within the Faith and Life Community personal relationships with black students strengthened her already dissident position on race. Aspects of her southern religious upbringing, which had previously supported a traditional southern racism, provided a responsive background for the new, progressive ideas of the community. Her childhood church, as a pillar of the social order, had practiced segregation and reinforced the self-righteous superiority of whites, yet it had also preached love and forgiveness. Lillian Smith recollected that it took thirty years for her to recognize that "something was wrong with a world that tells you that love is good and people are important and then forces you to deny love and humiliate people."[7] For Dawson, living in an integrated, Christian group where community life rendered virtually every act symbolic forced a more sudden awakening. The racial segregation of the world outside the community became an outrage, "because if you wanted to go to the movies or go out it was pretty insulting to go where other students that we lived with couldn't go."

Sandra "Casey" Cason also grew up in a religious, small southern town, Victoria, Texas. But from early in her life she had felt "different." She had only one parent, her mother, divorced, self-supporting, intellectual, and liberal. Cason remembered her shock and outrage when, in her high school journalism class, she read a newspaper report that school segregation had been outlawed by the Supreme Court. It had never occurred to her that segregation was a function of law. Two years later, rejected by the sorority of her choice at the University of Texas, she gravitated to church groups, the YWCA, and the Christian Faith and Life Community. At a regional YM-YWCA meeting she encountered her first experience in human relations programming. The following year, elected to a national YWCA meeting, she found that two of the four areas of study were race relations and the changing roles of men and women. For her, then, it was a natural extension of intellectual and moral concerns to join an integrated community, which in turn catapulted her into activism. When the YWCA initiated a series of pickets at local restaurants, Cason and Dawson joined their friends, and Sandra Cason was transformed from a "lively bobby soxer" into one of the principal leaders of the interracial movement in Austin. A year later she was heavily involved in the emerging civil rights movement.

Similar circumstances brought Sue Thrasher into the fight for racial equality. As a student at Scarritt College in 1961 she felt increasingly disturbed by the refusal of local restaurants to serve black students. The final straw came when the wife of a black minister from Rhodesia was refused membership in the local Methodist church that had sponsored them in the United States. With several friends, Thrasher circulated a petition on behalf of Christian brotherhood, written verbatim from phrases in the Discipline of the Methodist Church. To her surprise, few would sign and she and her group were branded as radical hotheads. Soon afterwards, the missionary impulse that had taken her to Scarritt in the first place returned to her own culture. Instead of becoming a three-year missionary, she stayed in Nashville to work in civil rights.

At about the same time, Cathy Cade, a high school student in Memphis, Tennessee, experienced the shock of discovery that "we are all people" when her Unitarian youth group held a meeting with a black youth group. Her family believed in integration but she rarely saw a black person of her own age. The next year, as a student at Carleton College, she elected to join an exchange program with Spelman College in Atlanta because she "wanted to relate to black people as people."

Such a pattern repeated itself again and again. Most white women who participated in the early years of the civil rights movement tended to be southerners, and virtually without exception white southern women who joined the civil rights movement came to it first through the Church.*

---

* In the very early years of SNCC the only white woman with a northern background was Dorothy Miller, whose family had a tradition of radical activism. Every white woman from the south I have interviewed or learned about joined the civil rights movement through Church-related activities.

Even Mary King, who grew up in New York, was the daughter of a southern Methodist minister. And she first came to the south on a trip sponsored by the student "Y."

The ethos of the southern civil rights movement matched the spirit of renewed religious and moral idealism that motivated the group of young southern whites. Following the first wave of sits-ins in the spring of 1960, the Southern Christian Leadership Conference (SCLC), at the insistence of Ella Baker, called a conference of sit-in leaders at Shaw University in Raleigh, North Carolina, on Easter weekend. Jane Stembridge, the daughter of a southern Baptist minister, drove down from Union Seminary in New York. She arrived at the crowded, humid auditorium feeling "out of it except that I cared, and that I was a Southerner." There she joined over 100 young veterans of the sit-ins singing "We Shall Overcome." She felt "it was the purest moment." For her and for women like Sandra Cason, Mary King, Dorothy Dawson, Sue Thrasher, and Cathy Cade, the civil rights movement offered a vision of cultural transformation in terms that spoke directly to their own experience. They responded emotionally to the theological language of the first statement of purpose adopted by SNCC:

We affirm the philosophical or religious ideal of nonviolence as the foundation of our purpose, the pre-supposition of our faith, and the manner of our action. Nonviolence as it grows from Judaic-Christian traditions seeks a social order of justice permeated by love. Integration of human endeavor represents the first step towards such a society.

Through nonviolence, courage displaces fear; love transforms hate. Acceptance dissipates prejudice; hope ends despair. Peace dominates war; faith reconciles doubt. Mutual regard cancels enmity. Justice for all

overcomes injustice. The redemptive community super-
sedes systems of gross social immorality.[8]

The biblical cadences touched a moral spirit that had
been nurtured in southern womanhood for more than a century. The stern preachments of young theologians in the fifties could give way to a more visionary, loving, and joyful
theology, because now there was a focus for action and a
concrete goal. That goal, described as the "redemptive community," or more often as the "beloved community," constituted both a vision of the future to be obtained through
nonviolent action and a conception of the nature of the
movement itself. "Black and white together," as one verse in
"We Shall Overcome" put it, would demonstrate to the
world new possibilities for human relationships.

When black youth decided to form their own organization rather than affiliate with established civil rights organizations, Jane Stembridge returned to become the first "paid"
staff member of the Student Non-violent Coordinating Committee (SNCC). She spent the summer establishing an organization and a viable network of communication. Together,
Jane Stembridge and Bob Moses, a young black philosophy
student from Harvard, passed hours in deep theological discussion in a corner of the SCLC office they had been
allocated.[9]

SNCC organizers like Moses set the style and tone of the
grass-roots civil rights movement in the rural south and led
the movement into the black belt—the Mississippi Delta, Alabama, southwest Georgia. While older, established civil
rights organizations responded ponderously to the new wave,
youth in their own organization felt free of prior definitions
of what the problem was, how to go about changing it, and
who should begin to do so. In specific southern projects far
from the bureaucracy in New York, staff members of the

Congress of Racial Equality (CORE) shared SNCC's ideology and rhetoric. Ideas coming from SNCC such as "Let the people decide" sometimes took six months or a year to filter into CORE projects in Louisiana, but once there they were readily accepted. As an organization, however, CORE had a long history and an older, male-dominated bureaucracy. The Southern Christian Leadership Conference (SCLC) was an organization of southern black ministers, male by definition, and integrated into a powerful tradition of social relationships centering on the Church. In addition, SCLC was dependent on massive financing from northern liberals who responded to the image and philosophy of Martin Luther King. Nevertheless, some younger field secretaries working for SCLC identified with SNCC in their work style and ideology.

SNCC's idealism was matched by a spirit of adventure, daring, and commitment that involved southern women in activities in striking contrast to behavior appropriate for "southern ladies." Thus Cathy Cade had been at Spelman College only two days in the spring of 1962 when she joined Howard Zinn in a sit-in in the black section of the Georgia legislature. Never before had she so much as joined a picket line. Years later she testified, "To this day I am amazed. I just did it." She does not remember being afraid. Rather, she was exhilarated. With one stroke she undid much of the fear of blacks that she had developed as a high school student in Tennessee.

The elation of young blacks, finally striking out at the symbols of repression their parents and grandparents had endured for generations, communicated an optimism that infused the early demonstrations and the notion of the "beloved community." Robert Coles tells of a SNCC worker whose first act of protest, after seeing demonstrations on television, was a solitary refusal to sit in the back of a bus. "Actually, I didn't think I was going to do that," he recalled. "I just started for the rear as usual, and found I didn't get there, but had sat down in the front." From that point he actively joined in the sit-in movement with the belief that "we'd demonstrate and then they'd fold up before us."

Once seized by the "freedom spirit," young blacks experienced an intense need to become deeply engaged. Ruby Doris Smith, only seventeen years old and a sophomore at Spelman College in Atlanta, convinced her older sister that she should take her place in the sit-in at Rock Hill, South Carolina. She explained to her uncomprehending mother that she just "had to go." Once there, she spent thirty days in jail as part of the first group to act on the "jail-no-bail" tactic. Lucretia Collins made an instantaneous decision to drop out of school in order to continue the freedom rides after the brutality and violence of whites had convinced CORE to call them off. She packed at midnight and left on a bus at 3:45 A.M. As she boarded the bus, she pondered the meaning of her act. "I felt certain that we were writing history, pages for a history book, some history book, I hope. . . . We thought that some of us would be killed." Even death seemed worth the risk because history was being made in a transcendently just cause. Racism, once exposed, must crumble. The good people of America would call it to a halt. In such a spirit the movement spread like wildfire across the south. In the summer of 1961 the freedom rides kept the jails filled in Jackson and Hinds counties, Mississippi. From those experiences there emerged a group of leaders bound by imprisonment, violence, and brutality endured, victories won.[10]

Legends began to grow—oral traditions within the movement detailing incredible courage and audacity. Two of the earliest legendary figures were Diane Nash and Ruby Doris Smith. Nash, "a tiny, slender campus beauty queen at Fisk" University in Nashville, Tennessee, plunged immediately into the movement that erupted there in February 1960. Her militance and courage were unsurpassed as she found herself "part of a group of people suddenly proud to be called 'black.' " Two years later, having become the first paid field staff member of SNCC, although pregnant she announced her refusal to cooperate with the court system by either appealing her two-year sentence or posting bond:

> We in the nonviolent movement have been talking about jail without bail for two years or more. The time has come for us to mean what we say and stop posting bond. . . . This will be a black baby born in Mississippi, and thus where ever he is born he will be in prison. I believe that if I go to jail now it may help hasten that day when my child and all children will be free—not only on the day of their birth but for all their lives.

According to one historian, Nash was the leading candidate in the first election for chairman of SNCC, but she declined to enter her name.[11]

Equally remarkable was Ruby Doris Smith. Smith moved from the Rock Hill prison to the freedom rides and other demonstrations in Georgia, Alabama, and Mississippi, suffering the indignities of southern jails and numerous injuries. Her powerful personality made her a force to be reckoned with in SNCC meetings, and it was soon matched by the responsibility and power over others that she exercised as SNCC's executive secretary. She remained a key person in SNCC until her death of cancer in 1967. White female volunteer workers in the SNCC Atlanta office, where she became the administrative assistant in 1963, remember being "scared shitless" of her. Myrna Wood, a white volunteer and later feminist theorist, described her as the "heartbeat" of SNCC, who ruled "with an iron hand. . . . Ruby Doris was a

woman I had the greatest respect for, and in a way, loved."
Howard Zinn, who knew her as a student at Spelman, remembered her as someone whose strength was almost tangible, coming from "very deep inside of her."[12]

There were many legendary male leaders in SNCC as
well. They held more top positions, tended more often to be
public leaders and spokesmen, and were better known to the
public: James Forman, John Lewis, Stokely Carmichael, Ju-
lian Bond, Robert Moses. Their names were familiar to millions. Nevertheless, in comparison to the division of roles in
most of American society, the civil rights movement was
strikingly egalitarian. Rarely did women expect or receive
any special protection in demonstrations or jails. Frequently
direct action teams were divided equally between women
and men, sometimes on the theory that the presence of
women might lessen the violent reaction.

When SNCC moved into voter registration projects in
the deep south, civil rights work took on a new dimension.
The urban sit-ins had been in many ways attempts by middle-class blacks to gain access to the social rights and privi-
leges of the white middle class by integrating public facilities
such as restaurants, motels, bus stations. Direct action movements incurred risk, but the risks were specific and temporary. Often one could decide whether to face arrest by
engaging in civil disobedience or to use only legal modes of
protest. Voter registration, on the other hand, required
reaching out to the impoverished masses of rural southern
blacks and experiencing sustained violence and the constant
threat of death from local whites. With no authorities to turn
to—the sheriff was often active in the KKK—the war with
white society seemed total. In such a context, far from the
urban centers of "middle America," the early notions of "beloved community" fused with a deepening distrust of all authority and hierarchy, and a strong romanticization of the

poor. Early staff meetings developed a pattern of anarchic democracy. Without order, agenda, or acknowledged leadership, staffers would go on and on into the night focusing on whatever problems seemed most pressing until a consensus on future action could be reached. This increasingly radical egalitarianism both reflected and reinforced the SNCC workers' growing respect for the very poorest blacks. "Let the people decide" was about the closest thing to an ideology that SNCC ever developed. By the winter of 1961 the SNCC staff "had begun to walk, talk and dress like the poor black farmers and sharecroppers of rural Georgia and Mississippi."

Eating, sleeping, working side by side day after day, SNCC activists created a way of life more than a set of ideas. According to James Forman, "It seemed important then just to do, to act, as a means of overcoming the lethargy and hopelessness of so many black people. . . . Working in the rural south, facing constant death, trying to heighten consciousness seemed in itself an ideology around which all could rally." Out of such experiences the SNCC staff developed a deep sense of kinship. Even today those who were once at the center of the SNCC experience feel bound to each other, although their political beliefs and personal lives have since diverged widely.[13]

From the beginning, a cluster of young white women committed their lives to the revolt of black youth and shared most of that revolt's complexities: the exhilarating sense of "making history," which brought in its wake hard work, anxiety, fear, and comradeship. The civil rights movement of the sixties allowed white participants no license to cling to a patronizing self-image or to decide the movement's agenda. Young blacks, spearheaded by SNCC, demanded "freedom now," and the young whites who joined them were in no position, as earlier generations of white reformers had been, to suggest which freedoms should come first or how. Further-

more, participation in SNCC and in local movements modeled on SNCC meant beginning to see the south through the
eyes of the poorest blacks, a stark confrontation with the brutality of white racism that had been there all along. For
women, their new experiences and perceptions brought them
face to face with the tangled relationship between race and
sex, and with the fact that they, as white women, were walking symbols of racial domination. The confrontation was exceptionally lonely, for it shattered once-supportive ties with
family and friends. But as these young women stripped away
the social supports of white society, calling upon reserves of
strength they had not known they possessed, they developed
a sense of self that enabled them to recognize the enemy
within as well—the image of the "southern lady."

The process of breaking away from southern white society proved wrenching. One young woman had barely arrived in Albany, Georgia, when she was arrested along with
the other whites in the local SNCC voter registration project.
By the time she left jail after nine days of fasting, the movement was central to her life. But her over-worried father suffered a nervous breakdown. Though she was willing to
compromise on where she would work, she staunchly refused
to consider leaving the movement. That, it seemed to her,
"would be like living death." For other women, such tensions
could be compounded by the fact that parents and friends
might be in the same community. Judith Brown joined the
staff of CORE and was sent to work in her home town. She
wrote later of the anxieties she felt, "for that year I had to
make a choice between the white community in which I had
grown up and the black community, about which I knew
very little."[14]

The experiences of many white southerners, both male
and female, who became active in civil rights shared elements of such radical choice. Frequently parents made their

own acute embarrassment into a weapon: "How could you do this to me?"; "Your mother will have a heart attack." A traveling salesman charged, "No one will buy anything from me if you do this." A college professor announced that his daughter's activities might cause his university to lose its state funding. Where daughters were concerned, an undercurrent of sexual fear was also woven into the accusations. It was bad enough for a daughter to go off on her own without parental authority and put herself in a situation of extreme risk. It was even worse that she should do so with blacks. Within the cultural environment of many southern white parents, racial equality between white women and black men represented a breakdown in the social order. One of the most potent threats of the segregationist had always been, "But would you want your daughter to marry one?" And here were daughters who actually might. In many families such fears caused an unspoken, underlying tension. In others they surfaced vituperatively. The father of one white woman who announced that she wanted to leave school to work in a small-town black community accused her of being a whore and chased her out of the house in a drunken rage, shouting that she was disowned.

The common experience of being cut off from parents, friends, and fellow students drove one group of white southern activists to form an organization, the Southern Student Organizing Committee (SSOC), early in 1964. As Sue Thrasher put it, "I always thought that SSOC's existence sprang out of a need that people had . . . that they'd get involved in the civil rights movement and then be very isolated from people around them. . . . [They] needed to find other people like themselves." It became a means of reaching out to mobilize other young white southerners in the cause of racial justice. Moreover, the organization also functioned as a mechanism through which whites could claim for themselves the insurgent traditions obscured by conventional attitudes toward southern history. Whereas northern students could come in and out of the south, haughtily condemning its brutality, southern white students were in an important sense fighting for their own identities. Thus at its initiation on April 4, 1964, SSOC issued a statement entitled "We'll Take Our Stand," in an effort to assert a new southern identity, distinct from both the reactionary southern tradition and the dehumanizing northern industrial society:

> . . . The Freedom Movement for an *end* to segregation inspires us all to make our voices heard for a beginning of a true democracy in the South for all people. . . . We, as young Southerners, hereby pledge to take *our* stand now together here to work for a new South, a place which embodies our ideals for all the world to emulate, not ridicule. We find our destiny as individuals in the South in our hopes and our work together as brothers.*

Women were a distinct minority within SSOC. In 1964 they constituted one-third of the officers, one-seventh of the Executive Committee, and one-fourth of the Continuations Committee. But the women who participated were unusually strong and visible. Like Students for a Democratic Society (SDS) in the north, the intellectual leadership of SSOC consisted primarily of men. Unlike SDS, however, SSOC was not characterized primarily by intellectual activity in the early years. It had practical needs to meet—those of progressive white college students—and a clear-cut civil rights struggle

---

* "We'll Take Our Stand," quoted in Ron K. Parker, "The Southern Student Organizing Committee" (unpublished paper, January 5, 1965, in author's possession). The statement was written primarily by Robb Burlage, a Harvard student and early member of SDS. Its title refers to a manifesto of southern conservative agrarians in the late 1920s. In late 1963 Burlage married Dorothy Dawson.

to relate to. In the everyday work of organizing an office and traveling from campus to campus to talk to students and set up local groups, women proved very effective. Anne Braden asserted that "SSOC just wouldn't have happened without the women." Sue Thrasher was probably the key person in the creation and survival of SSOC. She was "the workhorse that pulled the founding conference together." Then, as the first executive secretary, Thrasher did the major work of building the organization. Other women who served as campus travelers included Cathy Cade, Cathy Barrett, Nan Grogan, and Lyn Wells.[15]

As in SNCC, women in SSOC tended to function autonomously, not as appendages to men in the organization. Their original involvement had required active self-assertion. Passivity was not an option. And as in SNCC, the basic skills required were interpersonal, organizational, and administrative ones—abilities that are commonly encouraged in women. At the same time, men in SSOC had not changed their more traditional views of women's place. A number of them were known for the frequency of their sexual conquests, their verbal condescension to women, and braggadocio in demonstrations. In the face of these assumptions, women often lost touch with their own strength and questioned their abilities. More frequently they fought back in lonely battles to keep from losing the ground they had gained.

In the long run such tensions produced a number of prominent leaders for the women's liberation movement. But SSOC did not provide an environment in which women could articulate their dilemma in those early years, partly because SSOC was a white organization and partly because the women in SSOC never formed a community among themselves. As whites in a white organization, the women did not confront the racial issue in its fullest ramifications. Where they did so, it was in the context of some other part of the civil rights movement—usually in SNCC. And because they had come into the movement after it had become a massive affair in nearly every major southern city, they were not thrown together with the same sense of being outcasts on a historic frontier that the tiny group of white women associated with SNCC in the earliest years developed. As a result, women in SSOC usually interpreted their problems as women in individualistic terms. Sue Thrasher had the recurrent experience of thinking that her fight for equality with men on the SSOC and SNCC staffs was a private one. "I could handle some of it . . . [but] in order to deal with that it made me into something I didn't want to be. I felt I could do battle . . . [but] that took a lot out of me personally." Thrasher recalled that she had felt critical of Cathy Barrett without knowing what Barrett was actually going through. Later on, when Barrett became a leading activist in the women's movement, Thrasher learned that Barrett's position in SSOC had also been difficult and lonely, and regretted that she had not understood or offered her support. "[It] didn't take me long to understand that if it hadn't been for the organization and the men between us, Cathy and I might have had a different relationship." Similarly, Nan Grogan and Lyn Wells each considered the other strong and self-confident, something that neither thought herself. According to Grogan, "we didn't have a lot of respect for ourselves. Both of us were trying to follow the lead of the other. Lyn thought of me as strong. I thought of her as real strong. Both [of us] felt untogether." These women would prove a responsive audience for the feminist message, but they were not the first to raise the issue.

From the beginning, young white women not only sought support and companionship from other young activists; they also looked for adult models among women who had made similar choices. But among white women such models were hard to find. Lillian Smith had been ill for years. They might draw courage and understanding from her writings, even visit her, but her heyday had been decades before. Activists in Birmingham, Alabama, knew Virginia Durr. The YWCA probably offered the largest number of socially concerned adult models. At the University of Texas the "Y" director, Rosalie Oakes, taught Sandra Cason and Dorothy Dawson that southernness was an identity to be claimed and used as one fought against racism. And Constance Curry, only a few years older than the college students, encouraged Cason, Dorothy Dawson, and Jane Stembridge away from solely local involvements toward working within a southern, even a nationwide, movement through the YWCA and National Student Association projects. She remained for them an important figure, but always in the background.*

Anne Braden was perhaps the most important adult white woman to young southern activists throughout the sixties. An Alabama native, born in 1924, Anne Braden was the daughter of an old southern family raised in the warmth and gentility of the small-town southern upper classes. While in college she had become convinced that segregation was wrong, a conviction that was reinforced when she went to work as a journalist after graduation. In her home town of Anniston, Alabama, and later in Birmingham, her deeply moral sense of justice was outraged by the brutality and blatant discrimination she observed on the "courthouse beat."

---

* Interviews with Sandra Cason and Dorothy Dawson Burlage. Curry came from North Carolina and had attended Agnes Scott College in Atlanta in the early fifties. She headed the National Student Association Southern Race Relations Project and later worked for the American Field Service Committee. Jane Stembridge was her roommate for a time. Through Curry, Cason and Dawson worked for NSA and came into close contact with Ella Baker. Curry worked closely with Baker in planning the early SNCC conferences. See Howell Raines, *My Soul Is Rested: Movement Days in the Deep South Remembered* (New York: Putnam, 1977), pp. 103–8.

Later, through her husband Carl Braden, a man equally committed to racial justice, she became involved in a wide range of liberal and labor causes. In the mid-fifties they bought a home in a white neighborhood and sold it to a black friend. Subsequently the local authorities in Louisville, Kentucky, branded them "communist agitators," the house of their friend was bombed, and they endured a series of indictments and trials on trumped-up charges of "sedition." Most of the Bradens' former liberal friends turned away from them in the witch-hunting atmosphere that ensued. Those who stood by them and backed them in their stand for principle were radicals. This searing episode in her life, during which she never flinched, radicalized Anne Braden and strengthened her resolve to continue fighting against segregation. It also convinced her that the greatest obstacles to racial equality and integration were the twin evils of race-baiting ("nigger-lover") and red-baiting ("commie sympathizer").*

Thus, for young whites in the 1960s, Anne Braden represented an apparently fearless radicalism. She had already been where they were afraid to go, taken stands they were summoning the courage to take, and done so in the fifties when there was no "movement" to back her up. Furthermore, for women Anne Braden provided a model of an adult woman, with three children, whose life was totally immersed in the struggle for racial equality. In 1960, when her children were nine, seven, and nine months, she described her day:

> I squeeze office work in when I can—after the house is
> cleaned up in the morning and before it's time to feed

---

* Anne Braden described a constant barrage of threats, intimidation, and Carl's jailing, which occurred after they sold their house to a black family in Louisville in 1954. Interview with Braden and Braden; Braden, *The Wall Between*, pp. 116–270. According to Clayborne Carson, Jr., "the Bradens, particularly Anne, became part of the small group of adults who gained the trust of most of the SNCC staff" ("Toward Freedom and Community," p. 132).

the baby again, after the older children get home from
school and I've talked to them a little and feel they are
settled for a while—and mostly late at night after everybody is in bed. I've sometimes counted up and I usually
manage well over 8 or 10 hours of actual office work in a
24 hour period, but I still don't catch up.[16]

As the primary staff people for the Southern Conference
Educational Fund (SCEF)—an organization that sponsored a
variety of interracial educational and organizing projects—
Carl and Anne Braden always remained in close touch with
the burgeoning civil rights movement. Once the sit-ins
began, the Braden household became a constant stopping
place for activists, with up to fifteen people to feed for
months at a time, and Anne Braden managed to attend most
of the major conferences connected with civil rights. She
consciously encouraged women to become involved wherever she went: "I always considered I had a mission in life to
get women out of the kitchen and involved in things. I've always done that. Any sort of movement that I've worked in
[my task] was to get past the husband to the kitchen and get
the woman out."

With Anne Braden's long history of courageous activism
and sympathy toward women, it was not surprising, then,
that young women in the movement turned to her when they
were lonely and needing support, or when fear and doubt
made them waver. Judy Brown wrote to her years later to say
that during the difficult years she spent organizing blacks in
her home town she had looked to Carl and Anne Braden as
surrogate parents, "until my own parents understood, which
they eventually did." In 1960 Jane Stembridge sat down in a
discouraged moment to describe "the hell of 'Am I scared?'
Have THEY silenced me with so little effort? Can I really just
stop and write a book? I am so tired, Anne . . . tired of try-

ing to know what to do in the whole thing. How to fight, when, where, and for what reason."[17] Cathy Barrett turned to Anne Braden during the breakup of a relationship with a man on the SSOC staff. "He thought I should leave SSOC. [Anne] raised the question of the broader context," which was the first time Barrett had heard the issue of women's equality put forward. Sue Thrasher consciously regarded Anne Braden as a model and spent many hours in conversation with her before launching into SSOC.

But Braden, Curry, and others were only a handful of women who were actively, immediately, and totally involved. The dearth of models was an indication of the unprecedented nature of this revolt led by black youth and of the sparseness of southern white women's participation in it.

In the ensuing search for others to emulate, these determined but uprooted young southern white women turned again and again to the examples of black women. There they found models that shattered cultural images of appropriate "female" behavior. "For the first time," according to Dorothy Dawson Burlage, "I had role models I could really respect."

In many communities civil rights workers drew their strongest support from local women. There is no doubt that women were crucial to organizing the black community. When volunteers wrote that they had met some of the "mamas" in the community, they indicated that they were in touch with the core of the local civil rights insurgency. SNCC staff member Charles Sherrod wrote the office that in every southwest Georgia county, "there is always a 'mama.' She is usually a militant woman in the community, out-spoken, understanding, and willing to catch hell, having already caught her share." "Mama Dolly" in Lee County was a seventy-year-old gray-haired lady "who can pick more cotton, 'slop more pigs,' plow more ground, chop more wood, and do a hundred more things better than the best farmer in the area."

Stories of such women abound. For providing housing, food, and active support to SNCC workers their homes were fired upon and bombed. Mrs. Marion King in Albany was shoved to the ground from behind by a police officer, kicked, and knocked unconscious. She was visibly pregnant at the time and had been taking food to children who were in jail. Several months later she gave birth to a stillborn child. Amelia Boynton in Selma, Alabama, Carolyn Daniels in "terrible Terrill" County, Georgia, and Fannie Lou Hamer of Sunflower County, Mississippi, were only a few. In the Atlanta offices of SNCC and SCLC, women like Ella Baker and Septima Clark, whose lives had been devoted to obtaining justice for black people, excited the love and admiration of young women like Dorothy Dawson, Mary King, and Sandra Cason.[18]

Many younger black women also gained considerable stature in their communities. In 1959 Patricia Stevens Due organized a CORE chapter in Tallahassee, Florida, by canvassing door to door through the women's dorms of Florida A & M College. As a movement developed, she became a symbol "head and shoulders above anyone concerned with human rights in that little southern city. To the Negro community she symbolized their greatest hope for the future." Cleveland Sellers described Gloria Richardson as *the leader* of the Cambridge, Maryland, Nonviolent Action Movement, and "one of the most outstanding leaders in the civil rights movement."

Throughout the south, music was a central element in the movement, and women often led the singing. In Albany, Georgia, Bernice Johnson Reagan helped sustain the music through her songs. James Forman describes the "spirit of Albany" in a passage in his autobiography addressed to Reagan:

Your voice echoes in my mind and your songs can sing what I felt in Albany better than the few words I put on paper. I remember seeing you lift your beautiful black head, stand squarely on your feet, your lips trembling as the melodious words "Over my head, I see freedom in the air" came forth with an urgency and a pain that brought out a sense of intense renewal and commitment to liberation.[19]

The daring of younger women, the strength and perseverance of "mamas" in local communities, the unwavering vision, energy, and resourcefulness of an Ella Baker, opened new possibilities in vivid contrast to the tradition of the "southern lady." Having broken with traditional culture, young white women welcomed the alternative they represented. For them these black women became "mamas" in the sense of being substitute mother figures, new models of womanhood.

All of the forces at work on young white women in the civil rights movement—the religious ethos of the movement, the sense of cultural alienation, the need for and discovery of new role models—impinged with greatest impact on those who became involved in SNCC at the very outset. The movement itself was small, and within it they formed a minuscule group, alienated from the culture in which they had been raised and also set apart inside the movement itself by both their race and their sex. Sandra "Casey" Cason, Dorothy Dawson, Jane Stembridge, and Mary King formed a tight network whose paths crossed and recrossed as they sought ways of working and living that would further their vision of an egalitarian society. SNCC itself was a tight band, which defined itself in the theological language of "beloved community" and "redemptive suffering." As they exercised their ingenuity to find ways of relating to the movement and of communicating to other whites the demonic nature of racial barriers, they also struggled to elaborate an understanding of community in which they could exist as equal persons, freed from both the passivity and the guilt of their internalized image as white southern women.

In the beginning of the movement black and white alike assumed that whites should work primarily in the white community. They had an appropriate place in urban direct action movements where the goal was integration. Their job after getting out of jail seemed to be to generate support for the movement within the white community rather than to organize blacks. In rural areas the presence of whites heightened the danger for everyone involved, a problem that multiplied when the whites were female. In addition, whites often frightened and confused the local blacks, who had difficulty transcending an ingrained sense of inferiority and fear in their presence. For the southern white women in SNCC, the knowledge that both their whiteness and their sex seriously endangered the people with whom they had cast their lot constituted a terrible reminder of the power of white culture and an acute consciousness of the changes in both sexual and racial attitudes required before they could participate as equals in the movement.

The few white women involved in the early years of SNCC defined their roles as primarily supportive. Since the movement itself was a diffuse and impoverished entity, they worked in whatever ways seemed available and valuable. In the process, they discovered in themselves new reservoirs of resourcefulness. Connie Curry, as director of the National Student Association Southern Student Human Relations Project, had recruited Casey Cason to participate in a six-week seminar in Minneapolis in the summer of 1960. Following the seminar, Cason attended the NSA convention, where she joined members of the recently formed SNCC in lobbying for support for the sit-ins. Curry also hired Dorothy Dawson

to head a voter registration project in Raleigh, North Carolina. Dawson insisted that women comprise at least 50 percent of the project staff, and one of the women who worked
with her there was Jane Stembridge. In the fall of 1961 Cason
worked for a YWCA human relations project headed by Ella
Baker. Cason had recently married Tom Hayden, a founder
of Students for a Democratic Society (SDS), and the two of
them worked in Atlanta to provide communications among
the growing number of activist students in the north and
south. When Dorothy Dawson lived temporarily in Cambridge, Massachusetts, she kept up a continuous correspondence with Casey and Tom Hayden about the developing
activities and ideology of SNCC. In Cambridge she organized
a support group for SNCC that became the first chapter of
the Northern Student Movement (NSM). In 1963 she returned south to work with a civil rights project in Atlanta,
where she developed an early voter registration freedom
school. Her marriage in late 1963 to Robb Burlage, another
founder of SDS, continued the links between the southern insurgency and the northern new left.

When Casey and Tom Hayden went to Michigan in September 1962, Mary King joined the staff of the human relations project headed by Ella Baker. Her position, as Casey
Hayden's had been, was funded by a special grant from the
Field Foundation for the purpose of broadening support for
racial equality among southern students. She worked with a
black woman graduate of Barnard organizing student support
for the movement. The tense racial atmosphere on white college campuses in the early sixties left students and professors
afraid to challenge the racial status quo. "So, we were trying
to find students and some way to help them bridge what was
a very great isolation." They used the campus "Ys" as their
"entry point." "In three cities, we organized secret groups of
black and white students who continued to meet together

without our support." In the meantime, Casey Hayden, bored with her church secretary job in Michigan, had returned to work full time with SNCC. King began to volunteer in the SNCC office on the weekends, and in 1963, when her grant ran out, she too joined the SNCC staff full time. Her work in the SNCC office followed the patterns set by Jane Stembridge and Casey Hayden. Although they did not work out "in the field," they assumed major responsibilities in first creating and then maintaining a viable organization. Mary King wrote a description of her work, which described a series of tasks from systematizing communications within SNCC to developing pamphlets, news releases, and other information that would publicize the struggle. Under the heading "Personal Testimony," she wrote:

> I enjoy this work, see great potential for SNCC in getting good and better propaganda out—and improving record-keeping. . . . I would appreciate open criticism of how I work. . . . I could work better, I am convinced, if I occasionally could take off a couple of days.[20]

By the summer of 1964 news gathering and distribution had literally become a matter of life and death for the movement. King knew that the field workers' only defense against racist brutality was the glaring light of publicity, and the work put her administrative talents to the test.

The commitment these women had made and the work that they did over a period of years reflected back on their strengthening perceptions of themselves. As Mary King put it:

> Well, it's this way too. . . . If you are spending your time thinking about how to expand the decision making process by enlarging the vote, by community organiza-

tion, by generally lifting or opening people's awareness to their own power in themselves, it inevitably strengthens your own conceptions, your own ability.

It was from this network of southern women, whose involvement dated from the beginning of SNCC and who understood their commitment in the theological formulas of ultimate commitment, that the earliest feminist response emerged. These women had recognized from the very beginning of their involvement in the movement that they, like their male associates, were at war with their own culture. Unlike the Grimke sisters, they did not leave the south; but like them, as they confronted the racial oppression of southern culture, they would be forced to challenge the most subtle assumptions behind their roles as southern whites who were also women. The sexual distinction was fraught with psychic and cultural torment. Unlike their male companions these young, driven, committed white women had also to challenge roles forced upon them by friends and enemies alike—assumptions about female behavior, goals, and responsibilities that were not only a part of the general culture, but naturally and painfully a part of themselves. Thus from within a movement led by southern blacks, young white women had of necessity to forge a new sense of themselves, to redefine the meaning of being a woman quite apart from the flawed image they had inherited. As a result they were being prepared (quite unbeknown to themselves) to play a significant role in articulating the intensifying dilemmas of a growing number of activist women.

Building on their new strengths, looking consciously to new models both black and white, southern white women in SNCC as early as 1960 sensed that the achievement of racial equality required fundamental changes in sex roles. To them the term "southern lady" was an obscene epithet. Dorothy

Burlage remembers long conversations with Jane Stembridge about the role of women in southern society. They believed that the struggle against racism was "a key to pulling down all the fascist notions and mythologies and institutions in the South." Racism "propped up notions about white women and repression," and turned the role of the Church, "as guardian of public morality, mostly women's morality," into a mechanism for keeping women "anti-intellectual, irrational about politics and economic questions." The defense of white women's sexual purity in a racist society held them separate from and innocent of the "real world" of politics. As their analysis deepened, these two women concluded angrily that "it wasn't just women, it was that all children were lied to, manipulated, brought up to be racist, fascists." They had heard many of those lies in Sunday School.

Again and again they came back to the Church. Religious conviction had nourished their own rebellion and provided the vocabulary to describe their mission and their vision. They understood its centrality in southern life and the paradoxical reality it presented, offering them the possibility of transcending the barriers of race and sex while formally exercising an opposite role in the society as a whole. Burlage thinks she may have discussed these issues with Casey Hayden as well, but she remembers most vividly the interchanges with Jane Stembridge because "we both came out of very religious kinds of backgrounds."

Before these conversations could take on significance to a broader group of women, hundreds more would have to share the experience of being "in the movement." Each individual reacted to a combination of factors reflecting events in her own personal history: How old was she in the fifties? Where did she grow up? What was her mother like? How had she come into the movement? And each reacted to the compelling events of the struggle of southern black people into which she had been swept. Their experiences had a far-reaching and contradictory impact on them. Sometimes they left scars. Sometimes they opened unexpected reservoirs of fear or anger. And sometimes they generated new vistas of possibility and a new sense of self.

3

Going South

June 27, 1964

Dear Mom and Dad,

This letter is hard to write because I would like so much to com-
municate how I feel and I don't know if I can. It is very hard to
answer to your attitude that if I loved you I wouldn't do this—
hard, because the thought is cruel. I can only hope you have the
sensitivity to understand that I can both love you very much and
desire to go to Mississippi. . . .

I hope you will accept my decision even if you do not agree
with me. There comes a time when you have to do things which
your parents do not agree with. . . . I think you have to live to
the fullest extent to which you have gained an awareness or you
are less than the human being you are capable of being. . . .

This doesn't apply just to civil rights or social consciousness
but to all the experiences of life. . . .

Love,
Bonnie[1]

The sit-in movement and the freedom rides had an elec-
trifying impact on northern liberal culture. The romance and
daring of black youth gave progressives an unassailable cause.
The good guys seemed so good—Martin Luther King made
them sound even better—and the bad guys seemed so horri-
fyingly bad. Many of those affected were former participants
in the "old left"—Communists, labor and religious activists,
pacifists—who had felt intimidated and isolated by the
McCarthyism of the 1950s. For them the new civil rights revolt came as a vindication of the ideals they had despaired of
realizing. Some among this older generation moved from
sympathy to action.

The children of northern liberals and radicals, however, were the most likely to join the new struggle with passionate commitment. Most had grown up with a naïve liberal faith in the nation's bland pronouncements of the fifties, accepting the cold war ideology that America had solved its social problems and was embarked on solving the problems of the rest of the world. For them the discovery of massive domestic poverty and discrimination inspired a simple desire to "make things right." Others from more critical families had knowledge of an activist past and the fears that accompanied its repression during the fifties.[2]

In the early sixties such white students from northern campuses slowly began to go south, and by the summer of 1964 their numbers had become a flood. Their experiences had an impact far beyond the borders of the south, moreover, for the white youth who joined the civil rights movement were crucial to the mobilization of the "new left." Their involvement in the south forced the northern student movement to shift from cerebral concerns to community organizing and direct action demonstrations. Students who had been to the south provided the leadership, tactics, and ideology for the developing movements against the Vietnam War, for "student power," and for women's liberation. Women, in particular, abandoned the limitations of the feminine mystique as they tested themselves and grew in self-respect.

In the quiescent atmosphere on campuses in the late fifties and early sixties, the few women who were politically involved tended to feel isolated and unhappy. When the civil rights movement appeared, it offered an outlet for their beliefs and the possibility of a community that shared them. Sharon Jeffry, daughter of a long line of union organizers in Detroit, described her search for "others who shared my values and politics" at the University of Michigan in 1959. When Al Haber of the Student League for Industrial Democracy called a meeting to design a conference on southern civil rights, she went and was "very turned on." Her excitement grew when, just before the conference, the Greensboro sit-ins occurred. Participants were flown up from the south, and the sit-ins immediately became the focal point of the conference. The following summer Sharon Jeffry worked with CORE in Miami. There she lived in the black community, provided training in nonviolent direct action, and participated in demonstrations.*

Similarly, Mimi Feingold had attended May Day parades in New York ever since she could remember and even organized a high school delegation to march for integrated schools in Washington, D.C., in the late fifties. At Swarthmore in 1959 she plunged into SANE (the Committee for a Sane Nuclear Policy), but the main activity of the group was discussion. When the sit-ins began she responded at once:

> Something was happening . . . after the fifties when everything was dead. And I had all this political consciousness and all this energy and really no place to focus it. . . . Here was something happening. . . . I wanted to go run south right away. . . . On the other hand I was scared to death.

An aunt told her about the founding meeting of SNCC but she found an excuse not to go, and immediately regretted it when she heard what had happened. From then on her wish to participate overrode her fears. She picketed Woolworth's in Chester, Pennsylvania, in 1960, and tried to unionize the

---

* Jeffry met another strong, northern white woman in Miami, Dorothy Miller, from an activist family in New York. Dottie Miller soon joined Casey Hayden, Jane Stembridge, and Mary King as members of the SNCC staff. Interview with Sharon Jeffry, Chicago, July 12, 1973.

black dining-room workers at Swarthmore. In 1961, the summer after her sophomore year, she volunteered to join the freedom rides sponsored by CORE. Her parents helped to finance her participation in the freedom rides and later her work with CORE in Louisiana.

As news of events in the south spread, the fears of the first women to become involved were further magnified, for it became clearer that to join the civil rights movement meant a conscious choice to confront violence and possible death. Kathie Amatniek, a Radcliffe activist, described the fears behind her refusal to go south in 1963:

I thought it would have been absolutely certain death to go to Mississippi. And a friend of mine, a black guy who went down, who was also a student at Harvard . . . I didn't want him to go. I begged him. I was sure he would be killed, because my vision of Mississippi was Richard Wright, *Uncle Tom's Cabin*, where everybody just got slaughtered, and I just felt it was certain death.

But her friend returned. He had survived and he communicated an excitement and a sense of commitment that was stronger than physical fear. She determined that she too could go. "It was no longer certain death. . . . It was a risk of death, but not certain."

In addition to their own fears, women had to overcome those of their parents. According to a study of summer volunteers in 1964 and 1965, "many more women than men spoke of the difficulties in getting parental approval and, unlike men volunteers, women were not allowed to work on any COFO [Council of Federated Organizations] or FDP [Freedom Democratic Party] project without parental approval if they were under 21 years old." As one volunteer explained, "most of . . . [my girlfriends] believe in what I'm doing! A lot of them would be here with me, but their parents won't let them." Another said that her parents had "looked askance" at her participation because "it was not a woman's place really."[3]

Frightened parents used every weapon they could muster: "We'll cut off your money" or "You don't love us!" Even activist parents, who themselves had taken serious risks for causes they believed in, were troubled. Mimi Feingold learned years later that when she joined the freedom rides her mother became ill with worry. Heather Tobis's uncle wrote that her work in Mississippi compared with the struggle against fascism in the 1930s and 1940s. "We are proud to claim you as our own," he said. But her parents asked angrily over the phone, "Did you know how much it takes to make a child?" Whether they kept their fears to themselves or openly opposed their children's participation, the messages from such parents, both overt and subliminal, were mixed: "We believe in what you're doing—but don't do it." Their parental love and concern could only heighten their daughters' ambivalences. In the face of pressures like these, women who volunteered to go south had to have the strength to handle the emotional fallout of strained relationships. The decision itself often represented a forceful act of self-assertion. Compared with male volunteers, the women tended to be more qualified and to have more political experience.[4]

For the young women who went south, the difficulties they faced in deciding to become involved were overridden by the moral excitement and vision that the civil rights movement generated. The rhetoric used reinforced the spirit of idealism that characterized northern middle-class student involvement, as it had the southern students' religious commitment. Phrases like "freedom," "equality," and "community" fired the imaginations of young people who believed they would participate in changing the course of history. "I have a dream," "We shall overcome." Again and again in their applications to come south they conveyed a sense of urgency, "I can't stand on the sidelines," "I can't sit by any longer." A generation steeped in ideas drawn from existential theology and philosophy translated the concept of "beloved community" into a belief in the power of transforming human relationships. "I've lost faith or interest in most of the things that a lot of people get absorbed in," wrote one applicant.

> About the only thing I really believe in is the ability of people to sometimes get through to one another . . . to make living easier for one another. I don't know exactly why it is [but] I feel more strongly about [the civil rights movement] than about, say, any other form of social injustice and misery. . . .

And Jane Stembridge said:

> . . . finally it all boils down to human relationship. . . . It is the question of . . . whether I shall go on living in isolation or whether there shall be a we. The student movement is not a cause . . . it is a collision between this one person and that one person. It is a *I am going to sit beside you.* . . . Love alone is radical.[5]

Although civil rights workers were continually frustrated by the depth of fear and passivity beaten into generations of rural black people, the movement's spirit was further nourished by the courage of people who dared to face the loss of their livelihoods and possibly their lives. A young volunteer wrote to her parents on June 23, 1964, after the disappearance of three volunteers in Mississippi, describing the awesome commitment of civil rights workers:

> Some of them put their lives up for grabs every day they spend in Mississippi—and yet they somehow stick it

out—not because they're exceptionally brave or fool-
hardy, not because they have any desire to lose their
lives—for a "cause" or for any other reason—but simply
and wholly because they wish fully to be allowed to
really live, to be treated as the real human beings that
they in fact are. And because they are human, they are
afraid—every time they walk into Mississippi, they're
afraid, just as I'm afraid and you're afraid for me. And
yet the wife of one of the three missing men was the one
to tell us of their disappearance—her calmness and
strength were a source of strength for us all.

Sandra Hard wrote her mother after one month in Mississippi: "It is so wonderful to witness what is happening
down here . . . [more and more people are] getting the
spirit of FREEDOM and are not going to be turned back." Another woman said that the Negroes in Holly Springs were incredibly brave, "the most real people" she had ever met. She
continued,

> I'm sure you can tell that the work so far has been far
> more gratifying than anything I ever anticipated. The
> sense of urgency and injustice is such that I no longer
> feel I have any choice . . . and every day I feel more
> and more of a gap between us and the rest of the world
> that is not engaged in trying to change this cruel system.

The songs of the movement constituted one of the strongest forces sustaining the spirit of insurgency in the south.
Vivian Leburg reflected years afterward, "I got a lot of my
politics from the songs." Sally Belfrage described "We Shall
Overcome" as

> the only song that has no clapping, because the hands
> are holding all the other hands. A suspension from color,

hate, recrimination, guilt, suffering—a kind of lesson in miniature of what it's all about. The song begins slowly and somehow without anticipation of these things: just a song, the last one, before we separate. You see the others, and the instant when it comes to each one to think what the words mean, when each nearly breaks, wondering, shall we overcome? The hands hold each other tighter. Mrs. Hamer is smiling, flinging out the words, and crying at once. "Black and white together," she leads the next verse, and a sort of joy begins to grow in every face; "We are not afraid"—and for just that second no one is afraid, because they are free.[6]

Once in the south, the movement's vision translated into daily realities of hard work and responsibility that allowed few sexual limitations. The young white women's sense of purpose was reinforced by the knowledge that the work they did and the responsibilities they assumed were central to the movement. Northern whites, like southern whites, found that the risks of a direct action movement and the intense relationships it generated became an exercise in self-discovery. Pam Parker, as an exchange student from Carlton College to Spelman College in Atlanta, Georgia, found herself "in a situation which is just extremely tense, and where you are constantly, every day, finding out new things about yourself and areas in which you have to change. Where you are the one who is realizing that you have some wrong conceptions." Throughout the spring of 1964 she could not escape—on picket lines, in dormitories, at meetings and conferences—a constant confrontation with her own beliefs, her willingness to take risks, and her capacity for empathy. In response she found in herself strength, courage, and the ability to change and grow.

From the very outset, involvement in direct action demonstrations frequently tested the women's physical courage and mental endurance. Mimi Feingold had jumped at the chance to join the freedom rides, but then found the experience more harrowing than she had expected. Her group had a bomb scare in Montgomery and knew that the last such bus in Alabama had been blown up. They never left the bus from Atlanta to Jackson, Mississippi. The arrest in Jackson was anticlimactic. Then there was a month in jail, where she could hear women screaming as they were subjected to humiliating vaginal "searches."

Experiences in jail varied greatly. White women in general were not subjected to the brutality that some black women and males of both races experienced. In Feingold's case, black and white women were not separated. In response to the noisy, crowded conditions, they organized silent periods and established rules about how many cells away one could yell. In the evenings they organized a radio station, and each cell contributed an act complete with commercials advertising the prison soap. Several years later another young woman found the jails in Jackson, Mississippi, less hospitable. The arrests had been terrifying: "They had dogs, police dogs. We thought we'd get killed. And we knew they killed people down there." White women were segregated into small cells, though eight people in a four-person cell was still better than the treatment others received. The group had arrived in the south only a few days earlier and lacked the sense of solidarity and community that sustained veterans of the movement. Tense and irritable with the crowding, heat, and boredom; frightened; strangers to one another and cut off from friends and families—they took out their feelings on each other. One woman "freaked out over the roaches" and refused to take her turn sleeping on the floor. Others complained incessantly about the food. When they began to make soap carvings, prison officials took away their spoons. When they became ill from the food, the prison doctor prescribed a very strong laxative which gave them all a case of "vicious diarrhea." Finally they began to fast in protest, only to discover that "food was the only source of conversation we had."[7]

When SNCC and CORE moved into voter registration projects in the deep south, the experiences of white women acquired a new dimension. The years of frustration finally convinced SNCC to invite several hundred white students into Mississippi for the 1964 "freedom summer," to try to dramatize and end the massive resistance civil rights workers continued to face.* For the first time large numbers of white women would be allowed to work "in the field" in the rural south. Previously white women had been excluded because they were highly visible in rural communities. Their presence, in violation of both racial and sexual taboos, provoked repression. According to Mary King, "the start of violence in a community was often tied to the point at which white women appeared to be in the civil rights movement." But the presence of whites also brought the attention of the national media, and in the face of the apparent impotence of the federal law enforcement apparatus, the media became the chief weapon of the movement against violence and brutality. Thus, with considerable ambivalence SNCC, along with CORE and SCLC, began to include whites—both men and women—in certain voter registration projects.[8]

Recruiters fanned out over the northern college campuses. One of the most effective was Casey Hayden, whose close contacts with the northern student movement suddenly paid off. One volunteer recalled that "Casey Hayden came to the University of Chicago and said, 'Mississippi is where it's at.' " Though she also warned students of the dangers, insist-

---

* The "freedom summer" was sponsored officially by COFO (composed of SNCC, SCLC, CORE, and the NAACP). In practice, however, with some help from CORE, SNCC played the dominant role in conceiving and running the project.

ing that they would have to raise their own money and then go through a rigorous selection process, she communicated such excitement and such a sense of the historic importance of the undertaking that many found themselves begging to be allowed to go. Those selected were trained in two separate orientation sessions at Oxford, Ohio. There they were introduced to the ideas that had been developing in the rural south for four years. The SNCC staff radiated belief in their cause and the strength that emerged from the suffering they had endured. For most volunteers their magnetism and charisma made them instant models to be emulated. Kathie Amatniek claimed that the first night of the orientation session in Oxford changed her life, "because I met those SNCC people and my mouth fell open. . . . They were so much more wonderful and exciting than anybody I had met in college. Anybody. And interesting and involved. . . ." Another volunteer described the SNCC leadership as "wise, caring, courageous, honest, and full of love. . . . The point is, I trust them and believe in them not only more than I expected to, but more than I trust any other group of organizers I can think of." Ruth Steward wrote her parents that her feelings were captured by a friend who said, "You can always tell a CORE or SNCC worker—They're beautiful."[9] Student volunteers only admired them more when SNCC workers began to express their distrust of whites and their anger at the insensitivity of students who had never known the brutality of a southern sheriff or lost a friend to a lynch mob.

In the projects women, like men, taught in freedom schools, ran libraries, canvassed for voter registration, and endured constant harassment from the local whites. Many women reached well beyond their previously assumed limits:

> I was overwhelmed at the idea of setting up a library all by myself. . . . Then can you imagine how I felt when

at Oxford, while I was learning how to drop on the ground to protect my face, my ears, and my breasts, I was asked to *coordinate* the libraries in the entire project's community centers? I wanted to cry "HELP" in a number of ways. . . .

Freedom schools challenged the failure of Mississippi's impoverished, segregated public school system. They set out to provide young blacks with a sense of their own past and their right to think and act for themselves, as well as remedial training in basic academic skills. Volunteers taught everything from black history to French, journalism, and adult literacy. Black Mississippians of all ages flocked to the classes, swelling them to more than double the original expectations. Pam Parker found that "the atmosphere in class is unbelievable. It is what every teacher dreams about—real honest enthusiasm and desire to learn anything and everything." She taught a class of girls who came willingly and responded eagerly. "They drain me of everything that I have to offer so that I go home at night completely exhausted but very happy."

And while they tested themselves they also experienced poverty and discrimination. As one volunteer realized, "for the first time in my life, I am seeing what it is like to be poor, oppressed, and hated. And what I see here does not only apply to Gulfport or to Mississippi or even to the South. . . ."[10]

Major projects like the "freedom summers" drew enough attention from the media to assure volunteers of the historic nature of their work simply by watching the nightly news. Sally Belfrage reported the "strange feeling" that " 'world news' appeared to be happening entirely from where we sat watching it." On the other hand, many projects had neither the reassurance nor the protection of national publicity, and the daily round of work bore more than its share of tensions and frustrations. In 1965 Carol Rogoff and Hazel Lee ran a voter registration project in Amite County where Rogoff described the daily routine as "boring, shitty" work. "It is canvassing from sunup to twilight, and then often a meeting in a church. There is nothing dramatic in the work. There are no emotional releases. The tension is constant." Added to boredom and frustration were the inevitable conflicts of large groups of people living in close proximity in an atmosphere of unrelenting fear. At midsummer Sally Belfrage wrote to a friend of her "battle fatigue." She explored the reasons: weariness, crowds, but mainly fear.

> There are incipient nervous breakdowns walking all over Greenwood. . . . I haven't had time enough for the full array of symptoms to immobilize me completely—I still *tell* myself to go to bed, though am far too tangled up to do it, while the negative feedback operating on the veterans has tired them out too disastrously for them even to know how tired they are anymore. It has something to do with fear. Fear *can't* become a habit. But there is something extra every minute from having that minute dangerous. . . .[11]

Middle-class women learned to live with an intensity of fear they had never known before. When local whites began to ride through the black community, Vivian Leburg found herself sleeping on a porch "next to a rifle which I didn't even know how to use." When she went to get a driver's license she was humiliated by hostile officials who sprayed all around her with air disinfectant. There were obscene phone calls, narrow escapes, highway chases at 80 to 90 miles an hour. One woman found it most difficult to accept the fact that the police were not on her side, that in effect she had no protection. Weariness and fear magnified small sounds:

Every shadow, every noise—the bark of a dog, the sound of a car—in my fear and exhaustion was turned into a terrorist's approach. . . . I tried consciously to overcome this fear. . . . Then I rethought why I was here . . . "We are not afraid. Oh Lord, deep in my heart, I do believe, We Shall Overcome Someday" and then I think I began to truly understand what the words meant.

The fears were no fantasy. By October 1964 there had been fifteen murders, four woundings, thirty-seven churches bombed or burned, and over 1,000 arrests in Mississippi. Every project had elaborate security precautions—regular communication by two-way radio, rules against going out at night or walking downtown in interracial groups.[12] Vivian Leburg summed up the feelings of hundreds when she explained, "I learned a lot of respect for myself for having gone through all that."

As they reached beyond cultural expectations, these white volunteers looked about for new role models, as had the southern women in the first years of the movement, and they found them everywhere. When three male volunteers disappeared in Philadelphia, Mississippi, early in June it was the wife of one of them, Rita Schwerner, who announced that fact to the students going through orientation at Oxford, Ohio. Suddenly two psychiatrists helping with the orientation found themselves working around the clock. A high incidence of minor medical complaints led them to conclude that "many students were quite doubtful of their strength—of body and mind—to face a continuation of what had happened in Philadelphia." But as these student volunteers struggled to face their own fear and anxiety, they referred again and again to the calm conviction of Rita Schwerner. At the end of the summer Mary Sue Gallaty wrote to her parents from Hattiesburg, "I keep remembering what Mrs.

Schwerner said a couple of days after they were reported missing—that it's exactly because this kind of thing can happen that we must work here, and that's why We'll Never Turn Back." Rita Schwerner's youth and small stature seemed to magnify her heroism:

> Standing on the stage [in Greenwood, Mississippi], alone and frail, she said, "I know what fear is, and I know it makes you think, 'I'm not going to do this, I'm not going to do that,' because the risk is too great. But I know that you can risk much more by doing nothing. It's not unnatural to be afraid, but you're cheating your children if your being afraid stops them from having something." A quiet, composed girl with a smile, and very pale, very thin, dressed in black.[13]

Veterans like Casey Hayden and Mary King whose involvement had pioneered the way for these young volunteers now served as experienced and capable models. Their easy access to the SNCC leadership made them seem very powerful, and their confidence in their own commitment and in the cause excited admiration and emulation. Cathy Cade lived with Casey Hayden when she went to work in the SNCC Atlanta office. "I was really awed by her; I was so impressed." Hayden seemed so knowledgeable, "together," influential and also beautiful.*

Young black women provided daring models of quite a different kind. Activists recounted early legends about women like Ruby Doris Smith Robinson and Diane Nash while they generated new ones. Students at Oxford knew Annell Ponder, a young woman on the staff of SCLC, as their

---

* Their very competence, however, left many volunteers feeling insecure about their own abilities. Mary Rothschild, tape, Tempe, Arizona, February 3, 1977.

teacher, very quiet and very poised. Many of them also knew that she had been brutally beaten in a Mississippi jail in 1963. A SNCC worker who visited her in jail reported, "Annell's face was swollen. . . . She could barely talk. She looked at me and was able to whisper one word: 'Freedom.' " Cynthia Washington moved into an Alabama county where no civil rights workers had ever been alone. Cars and trucks were always in short supply, and Washington decided that in rural areas cars were more trouble than they were worth anyway. She gave up the car she had and organized that county riding on the back of a mule. Sometime later, as patience with the methods of nonviolence wore thin among young blacks, several black women became known for their audacity in the face of provocation. In 1965 Annie Pearl Avery awed 600 demonstrators in Montgomery, Alabama. A white policeman who had beaten up several others approached her with his club aimed at her head. She reached up and grabbed his club and said, "Now what you going to do, mother-fucker?" Stunned, the policeman stood transfixed while Avery slipped back into the crowd.[14]

But the most important models for the young volunteers were the older black women in local communities. Living in their homes, eating from their tables, civil rights workers often became temporary members of the family, even to the point of being introduced to friends as "my adopted daughter." Volunteers knew that they brought danger to any black household in the deep south. "Our hostesses are brave women and their fear is not at all mixed with resentment of us, but that makes it none the easier for them." When the local radio station in Canton, Mississippi, announced that someone had offered $400 to bomb the homes where volunteers were staying, "it touched off the terror that must lie latent always in our sisters' hearts."[15]

In addition to their warmth and courage in taking in

civil rights workers, these black women also furnished the backbone of leadership in local movements. Volunteers wrote home of "Mama" doggedly attempting to register again and again or of a rural woman attending a precinct meeting, ". . . and no one showed up. With a neighbor as a witness, she called the meeting to order, elected herself delegate and wrote up the minutes."[16] Like the white southern women who had preceded them, female volunteers in the field found in these "mamas" vital examples of courage and leadership.

Yet new models conflicted with old ones; self-assertion generated new forms of anxiety; new expectations existed alongside traditional ideas about roles; and ideas like "freedom" and "equality" were often subordinated to assumptions about women as mere houseworkers and sexual objects. The civil rights movement was made up of children of the fifties whose beliefs had been shaped by the feminine mystique. Like their mothers who had left the home for paid work, these young women found that the social role of housewife had followed them even as they transcended many of their former expectations. Such contradictory experiences finally generated a feminist response from those who felt the reality of their new strength in an old world. The same women who explored new skills and talents and grew in self-respect also experienced a cultural undertow of expectations that they would perform traditional feminine tasks. Though both black and white women took on important administrative functions in the Atlanta office of SNCC, it was also true that virtually all the typing and clerical work was assigned to women. Very few women assumed the public roles of national leadership. In 1964 black women in the SNCC office held a half-serious, half-joking sit-in to protest these conditions.[17]

"In the field" there was a tendency to assume that

housework around the freedom house would be performed by women. As early as 1963 Joni Rabinowitz, a white volunteer in the southwest Georgia project, submitted a stinging series of reports on the "woman's role."

Monday, 15 April
. . . The attitude around here toward keeping the house neat (as well as the general attitude toward the inferiority and "proper place" of women) is disgusting and also terribly depressing. I never saw a cooperative enterprize [*sic*] that was less cooperative.

For the next four days she included a running commentary on the relegation of herself and other women to traditional female roles within the "freedom house." Another woman protested similarly: "We didn't come down here to work as a maid this summer, we came down to work in the field of civil rights."[18]

Women were found in disproportionately large numbers among the ranks of freedom school teachers, community librarians, and project office workers. Voter registration was considered more dangerous and male leaders sometimes imbued it with an air of macho derring-do. "The fastest guns in the South kind of thing," as Staughton Lynd put it. In many ways women were "protected" from dangers that men faced. Sometimes they were given preferential housing. Certain counties were considered too dangerous for women. Men did most of the driving, which was the most dangerous task of all. Women were consistently placed in less physical danger. Such echoes of chivalry proceeded from assumptions that were frequently only semiconscious. Perhaps they served to reinforce the men's sense of their own usefulness in an environment whose danger they could scarcely control—they were as protective of male egos as of female lives. The presence of white women provoked verbal abuse—"nigger-lovin' bitch"—but the violence generated was usually directed against men, a fact of which many were acutely aware.[19] The tenacity of tradition, then, could hardly have been more evident than here, in situations where a traditional division of labor continued while a more rational assessment would probably have resulted in placing a preponderance of women, as those least likely to be objects of violence, into voter registration work.

The presence of white women inevitably heightened the sexual tension that runs as a constant current through racist culture. For southern women this tension was a key to their incipient feminism, but it also became a divisive and explosive force within the civil rights movement itself. The entrance of white women in large numbers into the movement could hardly have been anything but explosive. Interracial sex was the most potent social taboo in the south. And the struggle against racism brought together young, naïve, sometimes insensitive, rebellious, and idealistic white women with young, angry black men, some of whom had hardly been allowed to speak to white women before. They sat in together. If they really believed in equality, why shouldn't they sleep together?

In many interracial relationships there was much warmth and caring. Several marriages resulted. One young woman described how

> . . . a whole lot of things got shared around sexuality—like black men with white women—it wasn't just sex, it was also sharing ideas and fears, and emotional support. . . . My sexuality for myself was confirmed by black men for the first time ever in my life, see. In the white society I am too large. . . . So I had always had to work very hard to be attractive to white men. . . . Black men . . . assumed that I was a sexual

person . . . and I needed that very badly. . . . It's a positive advantage to be a big woman in the black community.

Another woman echoed, "In terms of black men, one of the things I discovered . . . [was] that physically I was attractive to black men whereas I never had been attractive to white men." Thus, powerful, irresistible needs existed on both sides. For black men, sexual access to white women challenged the culture's ultimate symbol of their denied manhood. And some of the middle-class white women whose attentions they sought had experienced a denial of their womanhood in failing to achieve the cheerleader standards of high school beauty and popularity so prevalent in the fifties and early sixties. Both, then, were hungry for sexual affirmation and appreciation.[20] Furthermore, the insecurity and loss of emotional support from family and friends that volunteers sometimes experienced constituted an additional factor leading men and women into one another's arms for reassurance and support. Where such needs came together with genuine mutual regard, there was a sense in which the "beloved community" of black and white together took on concrete reality in the intimacy of the bedroom.

On the other hand, there was a dehumanizing quality to many such sexual interactions. One woman consciously avoided any personal involvement with people on the SNCC staff because she found them to be "chaotic" and "totally depersonalizing." She believed that it "had a lot to do with the fact that people thought they might die." They lived their lives at an incredible pace and could not be very loving toward anybody. "So you would go to a staff meeting and you would sleep with whoever was there."

Sexual relationships were not a serious problem until interracial sex became a widespread phenomenon in local

communities in the summer of 1964. The same summer that
opened new horizons to hundreds of women simultaneously
induced serious strains within the movement itself. Accounts
of what happened vary according to the perspectives of the
observers. Some paint a picture of hordes of loose white
women coming to the south and spreading corruption wherever they went. One male black leader recounted that white
female volunteers "spent that summer, most of them, on their
backs, servicing not only the SNCC workers but anybody else
who came. . . . Where I was project director, we put white
women out of the project within the first three weeks because
they tried to screw themselves across the city." He agreed
that black neighborhood youth tended to be sexually aggressive. "I mean you are trained to be aggressive in this country,
but you are also not expected to get a positive response."[21]
Others perceived the initiative coming almost entirely from
the males. According to Staughton Lynd, director of the
freedom schools,

> every black SNCC worker with perhaps a few excep-
> tions counted it a notch on his gun to have slept with a
> white woman—as many as possible. And I think that
> was just very traumatic for the women who encountered
> that who hadn't thought that was what going south was
> about.

The white women's guilt undoubtedly made them vulnerable to the charge of being racist. Nan Grogan, a white
woman who worked in Virginia for several years, explained
that white people came into the movement out of idealism,
but once in there was a lot of "gravitation" between white
women and black men. In part sexual relations developed
because they were forbidden fruit, but also because the
women found it "much harder to say no to the advances of a

black guy because of the strong possibility of that being taken as racist."

Clearly the boundary between sexual freedom and exploitation was a thin one. Many women consciously avoided all romantic involvements in intuitive recognition of that fact. Yet the presence of hundreds of young whites from middle- and upper-middle-class backgrounds in a movement primarily of poor, rural blacks exacerbated latent racial and sexual tensions beyond the breaking point. The first angry response came not from the surrounding white community (which continually assumed sexual excesses far beyond the reality) but from young black women in the movement. A black woman pointed out that white women would perform the domestic and more mundane tasks "in a feminine kind of way, while [black women] . . . were out in the streets battling with the cops. So it did something to what [our] femininity was about. We became amazons, less than and more than women at the same time." Another black woman, Jean Wiley, added, "If white women had a problem in SNCC it was not just a male/woman problem . . . it was also a black woman/white woman problem. It was a race problem rather than a woman's problem."[22] And a white woman, asked whether she experienced any hostility from black women, responded, "Oh! tons and tons. I was very afraid of black women, very afraid." Though she admired them and was continually awed by their courage and strength, her sexual relationships with black men placed a barrier between herself and black women.

Thus sexual relationships introduced a tension that was internal to the movement as well as a cause of opposition from the outside. The rising anger of black women would soon become a powerful force within SNCC, creating a barrier that shared womanhood could not transcend. The ambiguous situation of large numbers of white women left them with much to explain and as yet no categories of explanation. Was it really racist to say "no"? Maybe it was racist to say "yes"? Guilt lurked in all directions and behind that guilt lay anger. But the anger would have to wait until the patterns of sexual exploitation set in the south were transferred to the northern new left. When the same treatment came from white men in a white movement it would eventually prove easier to apply the categories of "sexual exploitation" and "objectification."

Hundreds of young white women from middle- and upper-middle-class backgrounds went south between 1963 and 1965. A few, unable to withstand the pressures of parents, of their own fears, of cultural shock, of black ambivalence and hostility, and of their own contradictory motives, fled immediately. Most, however, fulfilled their commitments and returned to the north seared by an experience that marked a turning point in their lives. Stronger, angrier, more committed, "for a lot of women, it was a coming into their own. . . . It was new turf for the white women . . . the first real break into political activity." Taking themselves seriously, often for the first time, they returned to northern campuses to organize and speak in behalf of the southern movement, to join the growing student movement, and to organize SNCC-style in northern urban centers.[23] The conflicts they experienced as women were an intensified version of contradictions endemic to American society. As yet, few were able to name them or to respond to them directly. But many would be ready to hear and to act when the word was spoken.

4

Black Power— Catalyst for Feminism

It needs to be known that just as Negroes were the crucial factor in the economy of the cotton South, so too in SNCC, women are the crucial factor that keeps the movement running on a day-to-day basis. Yet they are not given equal say-so when it comes to day-to-day decisionmaking. What can be done?
— "SNCC Position Paper (Women in the Movement)," November 1964

Black women struck the first blow for female equality in SNCC. Their half-serious rebellion in the spring of 1964 signaled their rising power within the organization. On the front lines black women received their share of beatings and incarceration, but back at the headquarters—the "freedom house"—they still, along with the white women, did the housework; in the offices they typed, and when the media sought a public spokesperson they took a back seat. Gradually they began to refuse this relegation to traditional sex roles. Ruby Doris Smith Robinson, no longer a daring teenager, was on the way to becoming one of the strongest figures in SNCC. Donna Richards reclaimed her maiden name after marrying Bob Moses, one of the most highly respected and influential men in the organization. Few understood her abrasive rejection of the slightest hint of sex stereotyping, though many remember it.

The patterns set by such women prepared the way for a new generation of black women who joined SNCC in 1964 and 1965 firmly believing that a woman could do anything a man could do. Fay Bellamy, Gwen Patton, Cynthia Washington, Jean Wiley, Muriel Tillinghast, Annie Pearl Avery—according to Gwen Patton they were equal to any man in SNCC. Taking women like Diane Nash and Ruby Doris Smith Robinson as models, they asserted themselves in unmistakable terms. Perhaps at some cost. Gwen Patton felt that they had to be "superwomen" to maintain their standing. Others pointed out that anyone who was effective in SNCC in those days—whether male or female—had to work long hours, take incredible risks, and refuse to be pushed around by anyone.[1] Such toughness in women exacted a personal toll: "Probably if you looked at all our personal lives, we've probably had a very difficult personal life in terms of relations with men. Many of us made decisions not to go with SNCC men, because in some kind of way we didn't need to be fucked . . . it was very confusing." Patton's fumbling effort to explain the dilemma is revealing. She did not mean that women had no sexual needs, though they may have had to set them aside temporarily. The slang usage of "to be fucked" meant to be abused or taken advantage of. Women found it difficult to be tough and vulnerable at the same time.

White women on the SNCC staff shared many of the tensions and ambiguities that affected black women. For a moment it seemed that their perceptions might coincide as the summer of 1964 raised sexual tensions to new heights. During the summer a group of women led by Ruby Doris Smith Robinson, and including Mary King, Casey Hayden, and Mary Varela, sat down to write a paper on the movement's failure to achieve sexual equality. Yet King, Hayden, and Varela lacked the self-assurance of Robinson, and they were "reluctant, and even afraid to sign" their own document.[2] As white women they were in an increasingly ambiguous position in a black-led movement. Compared to the black women's growing power, whites were losing ground. Women like Hayden and King understood that their roles in many ways had to be supportive, that the movement must be led by blacks. Yet they also wanted to be taken seriously and to be appreciated for the contributions they made. To fresh recruits they appeared to be in a powerful position. They had an easy familiarity with the top leadership of SNCC, which bespoke considerable influence, and they could virtually run a freedom registration program; but at the same time they remained outside the basic political decisionmaking process. Staughton Lynd observed the contradiction during the summer of 1964. It was, he said, as if "they had power but they didn't have power." Mary King described herself and Hayden as being in "positions of relative powerlessness." To the extent that they were powerful, it was because they worked very hard. According to King, "if you were a hard worker and you were good, at least before 1965 . . . you could definitely have an influence on policy."

Thus white women, sensing their own precariousness within the movement, held back from a direct engagement on the issue of sex roles and instead raised it anonymously, thereby inadvertently drawing on the growing strength of black women. Racial tension and controversy swirled ominously about the November 1964 SNCC staff retreat at Waveland, Mississippi, where thirty-seven papers were presented on staff relations, SNCC's goals and ideology, organizing, decisionmaking, and race relations among the SNCC staff. On the mimeographed list of paper titles, Number 24 read: "SNCC Position Paper (Women in the Movement)"; the authors' names "withheld by request." Casey Hayden and Mary King had written it in discussion with Mary Varela. They debated whether to sign it, but concluded

that they "wouldn't want it to be known at that point that
[they were] writing such a thing." Thus they invited a fight
but stayed out of the ring.

The paper indicted SNCC in strong, "scrappy" language. "The woman in SNCC," Hayden and King charged,
"is often in the same position as that token Negro hired in a
corporation. The management thinks that it has done its bit.
Yet, every day the Negro bears an atmosphere, attitudes and
actions which are tinged with condescension and paternalism . . ." They used their own anonymity as an example:
"Think about the kinds of things the authors, if made known,
would have to suffer because of raising this kind of discussion.
Nothing so final as . . . outright exclusion, but the kinds of
things which are killing to the insides—insinuations, ridicule,
over-exaggerated compensations."

Evidence of sexual discrimination in SNCC filled the
first of three pages: eleven specific examples of the automatic
relegation of women to clerical work, exclusion of women
from decisionmaking groups and leading positions, the tendency to refer to men as people and to women as "girls."
"Undoubtedly," the argument continued, "this list will seem
strange to some, petty to others, laughable to most. The list
could continue as far as there are women in the movement."
The source of the problem, according to Hayden and King,
lay in the "assumption of male superiority . . . as widespread and deep rooted and every much as crippling to the
woman as the assumptions of white supremacy are to the
Negro." Though such a message would not be well received,
they presented it

> because it needs to be made know[n] that many women
> in the movement are not "happy and contented" with
> their status . . . women are the crucial factor that
> keeps the movement running on a day-to-day basis. Yet
> they are not given equal say-so when it comes to day-to-
> day decisionmaking.

Unhappy and discontented women, however, had already discovered that men in the movement would find such issues too threatening to discuss. Furthermore, they had found that women also remained "unaware and insensitive." The analogy with black oppression worked once again. Women's lack of consciousness paralleled that of blacks, who failed to "understand they are not free or who want to be part of white America. They don't understand that they have to give up their souls and stay in their place to be accepted." The purpose behind the position paper, therefore, was precisely to provoke discussion and recognition among women of the discrimination they suffered. "And maybe sometime in the future," Hayden and King concluded prophetically,

> the whole of the women [*sic*] in this movement will become so alert as to force the rest of the movement to stop the discrimination and start the slow process of changing values and ideas so that all of us gradually come to understand that this is no more a man's world than it is a white world.

Tucked in among dozens of papers at the Waveland conference, the one on women in the movement provided a certain relief as the butt of ridicule and speculation about its authorship, but otherwise went unnoticed. Many in attendance at the conference have no memory of it at all. Others recall sitting out on the dock after a day of acrimony and rocking with laughter at Stokely Carmichael's rebuttal: "The only position for women in SNCC is prone."

But this was the same conference at which Donna Richards reclaimed her maiden name and her husband, Bob Moses, joined her, publicly adopting his mother's maiden name, Parris. The issues asserted themselves in many forms. Speculation about the authorship of the paper on women centered on black women, particularly Ruby Doris Smith Robinson. Soon it was common knowledge among the white women who cared to remember that Robinson had presented the paper herself. This myth has become a staple in accounts of feminism in the civil rights movement. Its pervasiveness recognized an important truth: that black women occupied positions of growing strength and power which challenged sexual discrimination. Their example inspired white women outside SNCC's inner circles, who believed that if anyone could be expected to write such a paper, it would be black women. In particular the myth honored the memory of Robinson, and it took on reality as tales of the memo and of Carmichael's response generated feminist echoes throughout the country.[3]

Carmichael's barb was for most who heard it a movement in-joke. It recalled the sexual activity of the summer before—all those young white women who supposedly had spent the summer "on their backs." The impact of the freedom summer, then, had both raised the issue of sex roles and infused the issue with racial tensions. For a moment black and white women had shared a feminist response to the position of women in SNCC, but objectively black and white women lacked the trust and solidarity to call each other "sister."

Soon after the summer, some black women in SNCC confronted black men with the charge that "they could not develop relationships with the black men because the men didn't have to be responsible to them because they could always hook up with some white woman who had come down." Deeply resentful of the attraction of white women to black men, they began to search for definitions of femininity that included blackness. Robinson herself hated white women for a period of years when she realized that they represented a cultural ideal of beauty and "femininity" which by inference defined black women as ugly and unwomanly.[4]

The black women's angry demand for greater trust and

solidarity with black men constituted one part of an intricate maze of tensions and struggles that were in the process of transforming SNCC and the civil rights movement as a whole. By the winter of 1965 SNCC had grown from a small band of 16 to a swollen staff of 180, of whom 50 percent were white. The earlier dream of a beloved community was dead. The vision of freedom lay crushed under the weight of intransigent racism; of disillusionment with electoral politics, the system, and nonviolence; and of the differences of race, class, and culture within the movement itself. The anger of black women toward white women was only one element in the rising spirit of black nationalism.

As early as 1963 Ella Baker had sought to counteract growing separatist sentiments:

> I can understand that as we grow in our own strength and as we flex our muscles of leadership . . . we can begin to feel that the other fellow should come through *us*. But this is not the way to create a new world. . . . We need to penetrate the mystery of life and perfect the mastery of life, and the latter requires understanding that human beings are human beings.

But such rhetoric of community and brotherhood was a fragile weapon against the realities of racial and class tensions within the movement. Prior to the 1964 summer project, many blacks on the SNCC staff had expressed strong reservations about the impact of large numbers of whites on the movement. They feared that the white college students would try to "take over." Their verbal skills would "put down" local people and impede the development of indigenous leadership.[5]

In specific instances many of these fears were realized. Southern blacks especially distrusted students whom they perceived to be "out for a thrill." Moreover, in many cases the students—sharp, articulate, trained in the verbal skills of the upper middle class—did take over. One volunteer's comments reflected conflicts that were widespread:

> . . . Several times I've had to completely re-do press statements of letters written by one of them. . . . It's one thing to tell people who have come willingly to Freedom School that they needn't feel ashamed of weakness in these areas, but it's quite another to even acknowledge such weaknesses in one's fellow workers. Furthermore, I'm a northerner; I'm white; I'm a woman; I'm a college graduate; I've not "proven" myself yet in jail or in physical danger. Every one of these things is a strike against me as far as they are concerned. I've refused to be ashamed of what I cannot change; I either overlook or purposely and pointedly misinterpret their occasional thrusts of antagonism. . . .

Another white volunteer noted that blacks in SNCC, faced with "this onslaught of insensitive Northern energy," would sullenly fade "into the background." The white volunteers were often in the limelight, their bravery constantly extolled in the press. Yet "implicit in all the songs, tears, speeches, work, laughter was the knowledge secure in both them and us that ultimately we could return to a white refuge."[6]

In addition, the summer that motivated young whites to explore their own potentials for courageous action and to build a new vision of social equality also exposed the weakness of a movement whose impulse was fundamentally moral. As they watched their idealism dashed upon the realities of power in American society, SNCC and CORE workers became bitter and disillusioned. The summer project had been built on the assumption that massive registration of black people in Mississippi, accomplished through publicity and the protection of the federal government against blatant repression, would create real power for black people. It was a naïve if noble attempt to force the political process to live up to the democratic ideals it professed.

Those hopes were crushed repeatedly. The federal government continued its policy of protecting people's rights by writing down whatever happened to them. Again and again the FBI and the Justice Department officials would stand by and take notes while demonstrators were beaten and illegally jailed. Finally, at the Atlantic City Democratic Convention the Mississippi Freedom Democratic Party (MFDP) brought the summer to a climax by offering a delegation to challenge the all-white representatives of the state Democratic machine. Fannie Lou Hamer testified to the Credentials Committee that she had been denied the right to vote, jailed, and beaten. At a rally the next day she repeated her story and pleaded: "We are askin' the American people, 'Is *this* the land of the free and the home of the brave?'"

The "compromise" that Democratic officials offered—to seat the white delegation if they would take a loyalty oath and to give delegate-at-large status to two from the MFDP—seemed to those who had spent the summer in Mississippi unthinkable. That they should be asked to give up so much to white racists after all they had suffered showed them, finally, that those in power could not be compelled by moral considerations. "Atlantic City was a powerful lesson," according to James Forman, "not only for the black people from Mississippi but for all of SNCC. . . . No longer was there any hope . . . that the federal government would change the situation in the Deep South." Others saw the result in racial terms. Stokely Carmichael and Charles Hamilton argued two years afterward:

The lesson, in fact, was clear at Atlantic City. The major moral of that experience was not merely that the national conscience was generally unreliable but that, very specifically, black people in Mississippi and throughout this country could not rely on their so-called allies.[7]

Many movement workers went to Atlantic City with their hope already eroded. Anne Moody, a young black woman from Mississippi, had worked her way through Tougaloo College and in the process become deeply involved in the civil rights movement. By the time she entered a bus to travel to Atlantic City, she had lived through too much to share the movement's optimism:

> I sat there listening to "We Shall Overcome," looking out of the window at the passing Mississippi landscape. Images of all that had happened kept crossing my mind: the Taplin burning, the Birmingham church bombing, Medgar Evers' murder, the blood gushing out of McKinley's head, and all the other murders. I saw the face of Mrs. Chinn as she said, "We ain't big enough to do it by ourselves." C.O.'s face when he gave me that pitiful wave from the chain gang. I could feel the tears welling up in my eyes. . . .
> We shall overcome some day.
> I WONDER. I really WONDER.

The growing bitterness of young blacks in the movement sprang from the depths of their idealism. The commitment they had made—once almost lightly—grew and made new demands daily, even hourly. Danger, fear, monotony, isolation, and loneliness took a heavy toll. A work ethic approaching martyrdom had developed, which made self-denial a condition of participation. Robert Coles described a "syndrome" of weariness, depression, and guilt as a result of "constant exposure to frustrating social struggle. . . ." The symptoms he found occurred almost universally among young people spending significant amounts of time in seriously dangerous situations. The real danger can hardly be overstated. There were murders. Men, women, and children were beaten severely and publicly humiliated. The effect over time was evident in clinical signs of depression:

> Briefly the symptoms reveal fear, anxiety, and anger no longer "controlled" or "managed." Depressions occur, characterized by loss of hope for victory, loss of a sense of purpose, and acceptance of the power of the enemy where before such power was challenged with apparent fearlessness. The youth affected may take to heavy drinking or become silent, sulky and uncooperative. Frequently one sees real gloom, loss of appetite, withdrawal from social contacts as well as from useful daily work in the movement . . . sometimes a precursor of the abandonment of a commitment to nonviolence.[8]

The toll may have been highest on black men in the field. According to Jean Wiley, a woman knew that "the first shot fired wasn't going to be fired at me, it was going to be aimed at a guy. . . ." In addition, men expected more of themselves in terms of courage and audacity and were at the same time less able to express their fears. It was "more legitimate for a woman to say, 'I won't go, I am afraid.' " Women could discuss their feelings with each other and with men, "but whenever men approached the subject they always reduced it to a comic situation."

Yet women too suffered from the constant demands, from reaching beyond themselves day after day. Some just disappeared. "Suddenly they weren't there anymore." Jean Wiley found herself doing the same thing:

> I said I was going one place and I knew I wasn't. And I went to the place where one can get lost quickest, and of course that's New York City. I really haven't put that in

perspective. But I know that something was lack-
ing . . . not that I wasn't free . . . almost that I'd
been too free; that I'd been so emancipated that I
couldn't move personally, couldn't sustain having to relate to everything and practically everybody in terms of
a larger political situation. There was another side of me
that is a very personal side, perhaps a "softer" side that
just had to come out, and it couldn't come out there because I just had to be too many things to too many people. So I got lost in the big city.

In the fall of 1964 tensions within the movement were
massive and still growing, and SNCC's anarchic lack of
structure served only to magnify them. When the staff met in
October, eighty-five new members were voted in, most of
them summer volunteers who had decided to stay on and
work in Mississippi. The meeting was chaotic and alienating.
Many recognized that the power base that had been built in
Mississippi over the summer would soon be lost, because no
one could agree on an internal structure for SNCC, much less
build a unifying mass organization for Mississippi. Swollen in
size, increasingly diverse, SNCC had split into mutually suspicious factions.

The dominant group in the fall meetings came to be
known as the "freedom high" faction. Based largely in Mississippi, it represented a strange amalgam of the oldest and
the newest elements in the southern movement. The position
they represented was an exaggerated version of "Let the
people lead themselves," focusing on individual freedom,
reacting against the least suggestion of authority, and romanticizing the local people. James Forman charges that this faction represented the northern middle-class students, black
and white, who had come south in 1964. The middle-class
idealism and moralism of these youth, added to their own
cultural rebellion against the world their parents repre-

sented, led them to take ideas like "participatory democracy" to logical extremes. They were frequently the people who challenged any decision not made by the whole group or reached by consensus, who were continually suspicious of anyone they perceived as powerful. They prefigured the anarchist factions of SDS and the counterculture's "do your own thing" focus on lifestyle and drug culture. Jack Newfield described them more sympathetically as emerging from the summer of 1964 "in the image of Camus' existential rebel," with a "mystical and transcendental faith in the inherent goodness of the poor, even in their infinite wisdom." This was not simply a set of ideas imported from the north. Rather, it was the final distillation of the "beloved community" in the face of too frequent defeat. The informal leadership of the "freedom high" faction was made up not of northern students but of black and white southerners who had been in the movement from 1960. For them the issues were fundamentally moral, and the validation of the individual's sense of personal worth within the movement was the prerequisite for effective action outside it. Racial hostility and a formal, hierarchical structure within the movement thus represented a betrayal of the beloved community, the vision which now formed a core of their identity. And it came at the moment when the physical and psychological damage they had sustained in three or four years of constant work left them desperately in need of a warm, loving, sustaining community.

The "freedom highs" were opposed by the "structure faction," generally longtime field staff whose growing militance and nationalism was born of a disillusion with whites, the impatience of frustrated anger, and a wish to bring coherence and order to the movement, to shift from moral issues to questions of power. James Forman and Ruby Doris Smith Robinson led the fight against hiring the eighty-five new staff members, arguing that SNCC should be black-dominated and black-led and that SNCC staff should undergo both careful training and security checks before being hired.[9]

The southern black field workers carried with them wounds that refused to heal and that intensified the atmosphere of suspicion and recrimination: bitterness that the press was outraged when whites were murdered and hardly noticed when blacks died in the struggle; awareness that the country reveled in stories of blue-eyed blondes living with poor blacks and ignored blacks who had been working in Mississippi for years:

> Didn't anyone care about Willie Peacock, born and raised on a Mississippi plantation, who couldn't go back to his home town because he was an organizer for SNCC and the white people would kill him if he went to see his mother? Apparently not.

Hostility toward whites in the movement also reflected a rising militance and impatience with nonviolence, magnified by events outside the south. In 1964 there was the Harlem riot; in 1965 Watts erupted. African nations were demanding and winning their independence with slogans about colonialism, pan-Africanism, and African socialism. Malcolm X began to voice anti-white attitudes that American blacks had previously expressed only to each other or had been afraid to acknowledge at all. Many were attracted to his angry words; many more were jolted by his violent death in the spring of 1965. Alienation from the concept of nonviolence and "black and white together" was completed with the Selma campaign that same spring, when the breach between SNCC militants and the more traditional approach of SCLC moderates became unbridgeable. As Julius Lester put it:

> Each organizer had his own little techniques for staying alive. Non-violence might do something to the moral

conscience of a nation, but a bullet didn't have morals, and it was beginning to occur to more and more organizers that white folks had plenty more bullets than they had conscience.

By February 1965, the "structure faction" gathered its forces and prevailed in a "stormy," "traumatic," and "confusing" SNCC staff meeting. The road to "black power" was clear.[10]

When Mary King asserted that "if you were a hard worker and you were good, at least before 1965 . . . you could definitely have an influence on policy," the key phrase in the quote was "at least before 1965." By 1965 the position of whites in SNCC, especially southern whites whose goals had been shaped by the vision of the "beloved community," was in painful decline. Whites were less and less welcome in any part of the civil rights movement. An activist in CORE and COFO described the situation:

> Hostility against white faces was such that even those few white organizers who had earned the respect of their black co-workers found it impossible, and unnecessarily disagreeable, to operate any longer within existing movement organizations. . . . Many had been questioning their own roles for a long time, and . . . their approach had always been that of consciously working toward their own elimination from leadership positions.[11]

Most northerners simply returned home, changed but confused, fearful that in their attempt to do right they had done wrong. The two northern white women in the inner circles of the SNCC staff, Betty Garman and Dottie Miller Zellner, sided with the "structure faction" and finally agreed that they too must go. But for southern white women who had devoted several years of their lives to the vision of a beloved community, the rejection of nonviolence and the shift toward a more ideological, centralized, and black nationalist movement was disillusioning and made them bitter. One southern woman felt that she "could understand [the movement] in Southern Baptist terms like 'beloved community,' but not in Marxist terms—that was someone else's fight and someone else's world." And Mary King recalled:

> It was very sad to see something that was so creative and so dynamic and so strong [disintegrating]. . . . I was terribly disappointed for a long time. . . . I was most affected by the way that the black women turned against me. That hurt more than the guys. But it had been there, you know. You could see it coming. . . .

Many women had simply "burned out" and left the deep south. Jane Stembridge had withdrawn quietly to write. SSOC provided an institutional context within which other whites like Sue Thrasher, Cathy Cade, and Cathy Barrett could continue to function. But for Casey Hayden and Mary King, there was no alternative. Their lives had centered in SNCC for years and they could neither imagine leaving nor give up the moral idealism of the "beloved community"—the south was home. What would they do here without the movement?

In the fall of 1965 King and Hayden spent several days of long discussion in the mountains of Virginia. Both of them were on their way out of the movement, although they were not fully conscious of that fact. Finally they decided to write a "kind of memo" addressed to "a number of other women in the peace and freedom movements." In it they argued that women, like blacks,

> . . . seem to be caught up in a common-law caste system that operates, sometimes subtly, forcing them to

work around or outside hierarchical structures of power which may exclude them. Women seem to be placed in the same position of assumed subordination in personal situations too. It is a caste system which, at its worst, uses and exploits women.

King and Hayden set the precedent of contrasting the movement's egalitarian ideas with the replication of sex roles within it. They noted the ways in which women's positions in society determined such roles in the movement as cleaning house, doing secretarial work, and refraining from active or public leadership. At the same time, they observed,

having learned from the movement to think radically about the personal worth and abilities of people whose role in society had gone unchallenged before, a lot of women in the movement have begun trying to apply those lessons to their own relations with men. Each of us probably has her own story of the various results. . . .

They spoke of the pain of trying to put aside "deeply learned fears, needs, and self-perceptions . . . and . . . to replace them with concepts of people and freedom learned from the movement and organizing." In this process many people in the movement had questioned basic institutions such as marriage and child rearing. Indeed, such issues had been discussed over and over again, but seriously only among women. The usual male response was laughter, and women were left feeling silly. Hayden and King lamented the "lack of community for discussion: Nobody is writing, or organizing or talking publicly about women, in any way that reflects the problems that various women in the movement come across. . . ." Yet despite their feelings of invisibility, their words also demonstrated the ability to take the considerable risks involved in sharp criticisms. Through the movement they had developed too much self-confidence and self-respect to accept subordinate roles passively.

The memo was addressed principally to black women—longtime friends and comrades-in-nonviolent-arms—in the hope that "perhaps we can start to talk with each other more openly than in the past and create a community of support for each other so we can deal with ourselves and others with integrity and can therefore keep working."[12] In some ways it was a parting attempt to halt the metamorphosis in the civil rights movement from nonviolence to nationalism, from beloved community to black power. It expressed Casey Hayden and Mary King's pain and isolation, as white women in the movement. The black women who received it were on a different historic trajectory. They would fight some of the same battles as women, but in a different context and in their own way.

This "kind of memo" represented a flowering of women's consciousness that articulated contradictions felt most acutely by middle-class white women. While black women had been gaining strength and power within the movement, the white women's position—at the nexus of sexual and racial conflicts—had become increasingly precarious. Their feminist response, then, was precipitated by loss in the immediate situation; but it was a sense of loss heightened against the background of the new strength and self-worth the movement had allowed them to develop. Like their foremothers in the nineteenth century they confronted this dilemma with the tools the movement itself had given them: a language to name and describe oppression; a deep belief in freedom, equality, and community—soon to be translated into "sisterhood"; a willingness to question and challenge any social institution that failed to meet human needs; and the ability to organize.

It is not surprising that the issues were defined and confronted first by southern women, whose consciousness developed in a context that inextricably and paradoxically linked the fate of women and black people. These spiritual daughters of Sarah and Angelina Grimke kept their expectations low in November 1965. "Objectively," they said, "the chances seem nil that we could start a movement based on anything as distant to general American thought as a sex-caste system." But change was in the air and youth was on the march. In the north there were hundreds of women who had shared in the southern experience for a week, a month, a year, and thousands more who participated vicariously or worked to extend the struggle for freedom and equality into northern communities. Thus the fullest expressions of conscious feminism within the civil rights movement ricocheted off the fury of black power and landed with explosive force in the northern, white new left. One month later, women who had read the memo staged an angry walkout from a national SDS conference in Champaign-Urbana, Illinois. The only man to defend their action was a black man from SNCC.

5

A Reassertion
of the Personal

We regard *men* as infinitely precious and possessed of unfulfilled
capacities for reason, freedom, and love [no emphasis added].
—SDS "Port Huron Statement,"
1962

The sweeping movement of rural and urban blacks
across the south also helped bring to life a new activism
among northern college students, and the northern ferment
addressed not only civil rights issues but also questions of dis-
armament, student rights, even the meaning of education itself. It was the entire range of social and political activism
between 1960 and 1965 that came to be known as "the movement." Above all the term "movement" was self-descriptive.
There was no way to join; you simply announced or felt
yourself to be a part of the movement—usually through some
act like joining a protest march. Almost a mystical term, "the
movement" implied an experience, a sense of community and
common purpose.

For young blacks it was the civil rights movement in the
south—SNCC, SCLC, CORE, and hundreds of localized
struggles. For whites it was civil rights, the Northern Student
Movement formed in response to SNCC, Students for a Democratic Society, the Student Peace Union, and a number of
other national and localized activist organizations. For some
it was a specific issue, a particular organization, or even a

single demonstration in a particular community at a particular time.

For a number of people "the movement" was all of these. They were primarily whites who became involved in the early sixties before black nationalism and the anti-war movement. They saw work in the south and in the north as parts of the same thing. Mary King remembers thinking of friends in the northern Students for a Democratic Society (SDS) as "our northern counterparts." Danny Schecter, a northern white who worked with the Northern Student Movement (NSM), moved easily and familiarly among the ranks of SNCC and SDS. He saw black power developing first in the NSM before it reached SNCC. Sharon Jeffry engaged in nonviolent direct action in Miami with CORE in the summer of 1960, worked on a National Student Association (NSA) voter registration project in Raleigh, North Carolina, directed by Dorothy Burlage in the summer of 1962, started the SDS chapter at the University of Michigan, spent a summer setting up tutorial projects for the Northern Student Movement, and was on the national board of the Student League for Industrial Democracy from which SDS sprang. At the Port Huron SDS conference Jeffry argued that civil rights issues were related to the economy and to issues of war and peace.

In the south, the northern movement seemed distant and unreal, especially to blacks. In a sense the intensity of their experience led to an almost parochial view—the further anything was from small-town Mississippi, "the people," the less reality it had. They were where the action was and the duty of others was to support their struggles. The strongest sense of national unity was felt by whites in the southern movement with ties to the northern student movement. Two women were married to key SDS leaders, Casey Hayden and Dorothy Burlage, both of whom had also been active in NSA, which was SDS's primary recruiting ground in the early years. Casey Hayden, Mary Varela, Bob Zellner, and Jim Monsonis frequently attended national SDS meetings. Sue Thrasher, as executive secretary of the Southern Student Organizing Committee, looked to SDS for help in learning how to run an organization. Networks of communication multiplied as more and more northern students came to the south for brief periods and returned to work in the Northern Student Movement, SDS, or other "movement" groups.[1]

Thus activist northern students in the early sixties knew a great deal about the south. They could easily identify leaders and important personalities, and discuss recent events reported through the movement grapevine. They defined their work in the north as in many ways a spinoff, an extension of events in the south through supportive picketing, fund raising, and community organizing. They looked to Fannie Lou Hamer, James Forman, and Stokely Carmichael for leadership.

Northern activists also developed more analytical and abstract versions of the southern movement's concepts like racial equality and beloved community, reflecting the different environment of the northern insurgency. For example, in a talk at the University of Michigan Tom Hayden argued in March 1962 that

> . . . the essential challenge is . . . to quit the acquiescence to political fate, cut the confidence in business-as-usual futures, and realize that in a time of mass organization, government by expertise, success through technical specialization, manipulation by the balancing of Official Secrecy with the Soft Sell Technique, incomprehensible destructiveness of the two wars and the third which seems imminent, and the Cold War which has chilled man's relation to man, the time has come for a reassertion of the personal.

Tom Hayden had spent the previous year working jointly with SNCC and SDS in the south. In the spring of 1962 he and his wife, Casey, had moved from Atlanta back to Ann Arbor, Michigan, where Hayden immersed himself in the writings of C. Wright Mills, Camus, Erich Fromm, Michael Harrington, William A. Williams, and other leftist intellectuals in preparation for drafting an SDS manifesto.[2] The emerging ideas expressed in the speech and with greater elaboration and clarity in the manifesto, the Port Huron Statement, represented a fusion of the personal and moral optimism of the southern civil rights movement with the cultural alienation of educated middle-class youth. This "new left" politics nourished the seeds of a new feminism whose central assertion five years later would be, "The personal is political." Yet the intellectual mode that dominated the early years of the new left operated to exclude women as leaders, and only those with roots in an older left tradition ever thought to raise the "women question" before the mid-sixties.

Students for a Democratic Society, the youth organization of the League for Industrial Democracy, was only one of a number of national and local campus organizations between 1960 and 1963 which became vehicles for the new activism. That activism was beginning to emerge from a generation raised in middle-class affluence and the atmosphere of the cold war and then abruptly shocked into the realization that the "good guys" did not seem so good after all. Studies of the family backgrounds of student activists uniformly find them to be from middle- to upper-middle-class families, a high proportion of which were professional and liberal. They had grown up in an era of expanding suburbs and bureaucracies, in the time of the cold war and the feminine mystique. As cold war liberals, they had accepted the view that defined the world as divided between the "free" and democratic nations of the West and the monolithic evils of communism. The rhetoric of the cold war throughout the fifties was that of a moral crusade.

Such students took their inherited values literally. They

believed in freedom, equality, love, and hope. But their world failed to match up. Within the university they eventually came to perceive themselves as cogs in an expanding system geared to train them to join other cogs in corporate and government bureaucracies, in which efficiency, forced cooperation, and mass organization won out over critical thinking and intellectual community. But at first they did not perceive *themselves* to be collectively oppressed. More likely they were disgusted with the wealth and apparent security of their lives. Rather than specific changes in their own situation, they sought a new starting place, they searched for new communities and simultaneously acted to eradicate the most blatant contradictions perceived within their ideals. Thus the moral impulse was first toward the outside world—the existence of evil in American society—and it resulted in anger at the failure of the nation to live up to its own professions.

Whereas the beats had chosen simple withdrawal and a rejection of bourgeois culture, the generation entering the sixties had the opportunity to act on their ideals and beliefs when black students in the south initiated a wave of sit-ins in the spring of 1960. The northern student response was massive, particularly when contrasted with the previous passivity of the "silent generation" of the fifties. One historian has estimated that between 5,000 and 10,000 students actually participated in picketing northern chain stores whose southern branches were targets of the sit-ins. When one takes into account the less active supporters who contributed money, passed petitions, and attended rallies, the numbers swell to between 60,000 and 80,000. In every case student activists came out of discrete and identifiable campus groupings, usually on the fringes of the campus and alienated from the dominant sorority and fraternity campus life, restive about rules and restrictions that hampered personal life, intensely concerned with philosophical issues, and organized primarily around a common interest in folk music. Their meeting places were the coffee houses where music was performed or the off-campus apartments of students who managed to escape dormitory life. While many in this subculture were determinedly apolitical, even they could not avoid having their lives shaped in part by the experiences of those who started "the movement" with this subculture as their home base.[3]

Those who acted welcomed the opportunity to make a moral witness. Sandra Cason (Casey Hayden) spoke from her southern religious background, but she won a standing ovation from the congress of the National Student Association in 1960 with her declaration,

> I cannot say to a person who suffers injustice, "Wait." Perhaps you can. I can't. And having decided that I cannot urge caution I must stand with him. . . . I am thankful for the sit-ins if for no other reason [than] that they provided me with an opportunity for making a decision into an action.

For several years insurgent students tended to mobilize around issues remote from their daily lives—civil rights, nuclear testing, the House Un-American Activities Committee. Not until 1964 at Berkeley did they really bring the movement home to campus. Their leaders were veterans of the Mississippi summer. According to Jack Newfield, the new left was

> . . . at bottom, an ethical revolt against the visible devils of racism, poverty, and war, as well as the less tangible devils of centralized decision making, manipulative, impersonal bureaucracies, and the hypocrisy that divides America's ideals from its actions from Watts to Saigon.[4]

One could guess that such a politics would be doubly attractive to women whose alienation as middle-class students was intensified by their oppression as women. Women, like students, experienced their oppression first as cultural, as qualitative. It had to do with self-definition, the basic premises of human identity, and it was centered in the most private personal arena, the family. In addition, within the traditional culture women had been delegated the guardianship of precisely those concerns that the new left endorsed. In a sense the new left affirmed "feminine" qualities in its assertion of morality and its concern for feelings, community, and process. These constituted the positive side of the bureaucratic values of cooperation and "teamplay." As a moral crusade against the evils of war and racism and anonymity, one might anticipate that the new left, like the nineteenth-century abolition movement, would draw heavily on the talents and leadership of women. In fact, this was not the case prior to 1963–4.

For all its emphasis on personal relationships, on openness, honesty, and participatory democracy, the northern student left was highly male-dominated. Where SNCC had provided an open environment within which women utilized the skills they already had to grow in strength and self-confidence, the northern movement reinforced the traditional roles by building on a competitive intellectual style. According to Betty Garman, an early participant in SDS and later northern coordinator for SNCC, "If I were to compare SDS and SNCC as experiences, as a woman . . . I was allowed to develop and had and was given much more responsibility in SNCC than I ever was in SDS. It would have been tougher for me to develop at all in SDS." Because it was focused on outside causes—the oppression of others—and because of the environment from which it developed, the movement in the north was highly cerebral. Idealism and moral concern expressed themselves in sporadic pickets and marches, but more consistently and continuously in the attempt to develop an ideological critique of American society. As a result the segments of the movement that had the most continuing impact were centers of intellectual ferment. SDS became the dominant institutional expression of the student new left, in part at least because it produced the most far-reaching critique. It is important, then, to focus on SDS both because it represented the essence of the intellectual mode of the early new left and because it subsequently created the conditions for feminist revolt.

From the beginning it was clear in SDS that the intellectual work was primarily a male task. No one said it in so many words, but then no one made a direct challenge to the shared cultural assumptions. And the reality confirmed it. According to Steve Max, the women "were always there and were respected but it was always the guys who did the writing and position formulating."

The competitive intellectual mode of the young men who formed the core of early SDS reflected their training in campus politics and the National Student Association before becoming involved in SDS. Al Haber was a student leader at the University of Michigan; Tom Hayden edited the *Michigan Daily* and founded VOICE political party; Robb Burlage edited the *Daily Texan;* Paul Potter was vice-president of NSA; Todd Gitlin attended the Bronx School of Science and Harvard University and was president of TOCSIN, a campus political group. Many women had also been campus leaders, but, according to Dorothy Burlage, they were "not as stellar."

In many respects the world of student politics mimics the adult world. It serves as a training ground for future lawyers, leading journalists, critics, and politicians. Success as a student leader requires both charm and aggressiveness, self-confidence and tenacity. According to Paul Potter:

As a group the men who were attracted to SDS, particularly early SDS, were highly motivated, success oriented, competitive men. Perhaps one of the reasons some of us got into SDS was because we didn't like the modes of competition that had been set up, thought that they were too destructive, in fact wanted some more fraternal set-up for that to take place in, and also wanted more control than you have if you go to work working your way up somebody else's hierarchy. . . . So it was both fraternal and competitive, but everybody talked about fraternalness, nobody talked about competition.

Kirkpatrick Sale similarly described this early group as

. . . often extremely bright and, more than that, *intellectual*, having gotten good grades in high school, moved on early to the best universities, proved themselves then among the top ranks academically, and many were planning (or engaged in) graduate work and professional careers; they were diligent readers, active thinkers and talkers, and, as the later literature lists of SDS will show, prodigious writers.

Most of his description could apply to the women as well, but the writing for which SDS became known was almost always done by men. SNCC people, who rarely wrote anything, thought of SDS as "those northern intellectuals that sat around and talked about a lot of theory and used big words that nobody could understand and wrote endless papers to each other." The later lists of literature reveal little by women. In October 1963 the SDS *Bulletin* mentioned twenty-seven articles available for circulation. Only one of them was by a woman, Mary Varela's "Catholic Students and Political Involvement."* A month later the titles had been

---

* Perhaps because of the cultural expectation that women should be more religious, the student Christian movements had strong female participation. Mary Varela was one of the most important activists in both her participation in

"updated" to omit women altogether. In the later, longer lists, female works never comprised more than 10 percent of the total, and certain headings such as "Politics" and "Economics" appear to have remained exclusive male preserves.[5] No one was forbidding the women to write. Rather, it was simply the men who carried the internal expectations and self-confidence necessary to do so. In addition they were in a position to define the nature of the movement, and they created one most appropriate to their own needs and skills.

In practice the intellectual mode meant that women in the new left occupied a position much like women in the society as a whole. Frequently they were important but invisible. When Paul Booth was interviewed by Kirkpatrick Sale for a book on SDS, he made the statement that in 1961, "Tom [Hayden] was SDS's project. . . ." When he was interviewed several years later for this study on the roots of feminism, he recalled that during that year, "the only program of the organization was having Tom *and Casey* [my emphasis] run the so-called southern office which was a reporting and journalism operation." While it is true that Tom Hayden did most, though not all, of the writing and reporting, Casey Hayden had developed considerable reputation and organizing skills by that time. Booth recalled, "Casey Hayden was probably the most important woman at Port Huron." In talking with old SDS friends in 1973, Dorothy Burlage was amazed to discover that the male leaders of SDS had "always perceived women as attached to men and as second class citizens, as if they had not played important roles in the movement, which wasn't true." At the time women apparently did not realize they were viewed that way. Such an observation is substan-

---

SDS and later in SNCC. Though religious motivation was far from universal as it was in the south, it remained an important avenue into activism for northern women. Interviews with Steve Max, Pam Parker Allen; interview with Charlotte Bunch, Washington, D.C., June 21, 1973.

tiated by the degree to which women interviewed in this study mentioned couples like Barbara and Al Haber and Tom and Casey Hayden, while the written histories, also based in part on extensive interviews, tend to use Haber and Hayden to refer to the men only. The written sources used in such histories confirm and exaggerate the tendency to make women invisible, since the men were the prolific writers.

Women's invisibility was heightened by the fact that public positions were virtually monopolized by the men. The membership and convention attendance lists generally reflected from 32 to 39 percent women, only slightly lower than the actual percentage of women receiving bachelors degrees. Executive Committee membership among women, however, grew from 14.3 percent in 1961 to 23 percent in 1962 and 26 percent in 1963, only to plunge to 6 percent in 1964. The women's importance in lower-level positions was indicated by the fact that in 1964, while only one of seventeen nationally elected National Council members was a woman, five of the nine chapter delegates were female. Key mailing lists generally had about 25 percent women, though one went as low as 17 percent. Most startling is the fact that until 1966 no major national office was held by a woman. At that time Helen Garvey was elected *assistant* national secretary. Two years later women finally penetrated the top ranks when Jane Adams became national secretary. In effect, while the general membership reflected the ratio of women to men in the student population, the balance became heavily skewed in favor of men as one progressed to higher levels of leadership.[6]

The skills that were most valued in SDS promoted male leadership. Kirkpatrick Sale suggests that in the early years the national office of SDS, supported by the League for Industrial Democracy, tended to push it into a bureaucratic mold that placed a premium on efficiency and manipulation.

Verbal skills, political maneuvering, reliance on proper form and precedent quickly raised young male politicos into prominent positions. Most of the women, by contrast, filled the ranks of implementers and listeners.

At the Port Huron convention, Casey Hayden played a vocal role. A number of women participated in drafting sections of the statement—Judith Cowan on foreign aid and economic development; Theresa del Pazo on economics. Mary Varela joined vigorously in a debate on religion. Sharon Jeffry pushed for broader integration of issues. But when men in attendance are asked to recall women who were there, they have to rack their brains to remember.[7] One may guess that Casey Hayden's "vocal role" was crucial, for she, though not considered a movement intellectual, had shared in the conversations leading up to the conference; she had the gift of being forceful, articulate, and persuasive; and the key concept that emerged in the Port Huron Statement, the notion of "participatory democracy," bore the stamp of SNCC.

Accounts of the Port Huron convention always emphasize the intensely warm sense of community shared by all the participants. It seems clear that women were not conscious of being shunted aside or invisible at the time. Instead, they experienced a taste of what they were writing about: "We seek the establishment of a democracy of individual participation. . . . Human relations should involve fraternity and honesty." If on some level the men thought of the women as secondary, the women were not aware of it then. In general they all felt that they had re-created the "beloved community" in the north. Port Huron was one of the high points of the early "SDS Community" that Paul Potter described, a community both "fraternal and competitive." As SDS grew, community suffered and competition heightened. As a result the unconscious male dominance became increasingly overt.

National meetings frequently witnessed debates between competing factions headed by men. When an intense debate erupted at the December 1963 National Council meeting, Dick Flacks worried that

> . . . strategic questions are being turned into matters of basic moral principle; positions are being asserted as matters of absolute non-negotiable finality; personality clashes are becoming ideological conflicts and vice versa; fairly vituperative labels and stereotypes are coming to replace honest confrontation of opposing views, etc.

A mailed questionnaire on the meeting brought back comments like "thoroughly verbose" (Boston); "too damned much B.S. . . . blathering" (MIT); and

> The NC [National Council] can be partly explained by . . . SDS diseases—male supremacy, agenda debates, jargon—diseases which are carry-overs from bourgeois society. . . . Plenaries are a projection of masculine sublimation as can be seen by examining the roots of the word. (University of Michigan)

On the other hand, two comments from women's colleges indicated that while women may not have played a prominent role in the large debates, some were vicariously stimulated:

> Very, very impressive . . . at times it was exhausting and painfully slow, but such a large group needed to understand itself . . . I also learned many helpful things in informal discussions and the discussion on campus programming with Helen. (Pembroke)

> I can't relate to you how much stimulation and "zeal" I received from the NC. I now feel a part of SDS. (Simmons College)[8]

The problem for women was not necessarily a lack of knowledge or intellectual sophistication. It was more a matter of style. Barbara Easton, a sophomore at Radcliffe who was a sophisticated Marxist and a member of the Communist Party (CP), felt totally "overwhelmed" when she attended an NC meeting in December 1964. "It was all going on in such a high powered sort of level . . . much more than in the Party." With the meeting dominated by Tom Hayden and others, "there was absolutely no possibility that I would get up and say anything." When asked to describe the male leaders, she said they were "fairly competitive and domineering, and rather determined to impress people a lot." Those in the inner circle knew each other well and talked easily; those on the outside like herself saw it as "sort of a spectacle." Similarly, Naomi Weisstein spoke of the fears she felt at large, male-dominated meetings of the New Haven CORE in 1964:

> I was so scared. I was so intimidated . . . also they were coming on very tough and I hadn't learned how to come on very tough yet. I remember saying to a friend of mine at the meeting, I remember punching him on the arm and saying, "Get up and say this, get up and say this," and he said, "You do it," and I said, "I can't," and I couldn't.

When less educated black men in the group formed a democracy faction and argued that everyone had a right to speak, she was very moved to see people who had not developed rhetorical and intellectual skills standing up for themselves, and she felt that they spoke for her as well.

Most campus SDS chapters were not as large or as intense as the civil rights movement in New Haven. Until 1965 they tended to be fairly small; but the manifestations of the intellectual mode were clear everywhere. On coed campuses the leaders tended to reside in a clique together, either in a dormitory or off campus. "Participatory democracy" often led to a lack of structure and clear responsibility, which only intensified the tendency toward informal, male leadership groups. At Harvard this meant that "all of the decisions got made in Adams House, which was where all the men lived. They'd get together at two o'clock in the morning and make decisions and then we'd all read about it the next morning in the *Crimson*."* As a result women were excluded, not necessarily by design, but thoroughly nonetheless.

Although the new left was engaged in a cultural revolt, championing openness and honesty, sexual freedom, and the end of campus regulations *in loco parentis,* it reflected more than it challenged the underlying sexual stereotypes of these early years. While SDS was certainly no worse than the society as a whole, it was only marginally freer for women. A few strong women in the inner circles, frequently married to key men, helped to shape SDS's politics, and chapters on women's campuses were very active. But the new left embodied the heritage of the feminine mystique far more strongly than the older left had. Its obliviousness to the issue of women's oppression was a sign, in fact, of how thoroughly the "new" left represented a break with the "old."

The "woman question" has a prominent, if frequently overlooked, place in Marxist literature. As a result the old left, primarily the American Communist Party, had to pay at least lip service to the struggle against "male supremacy." While the Communist Party has not been known for its feminism, it did emphasize the development of female leadership in local situations. Steve Max, whose father once edited the *Daily Worker,* recalls that in New York in the 1950s the local leadership was predominantly female:

---

* Interview with Barbara Easton. This was a dominant pattern for campus chapters, generally reported by the women I interviewed and also noted in numerous informal conversations.

There was something of a distinction between what men and what women were doing on the left, different kinds of activities. The old left was very conscious of the need to have women leaders, black leaders, working people's leaders. They knew all the categories that the population could be divided into and that there had to be a communist leader for each category. You know, so Elizabeth Gurley Flynn was a women's leader, that kind of thing. . . . Every time you had a committee or an organization . . . there certainly had to be a leading woman, at least one, in the leadership. In fact there really were. They were not merely tokenism. They really ran the American Labor Party clubs and a lot of other activities. The new left had no such notion of the black leader, the women's leader, the trade union leader, and the balanced committee and the balanced ticket. . . . So that when the issue did arise in the new left, it arose in a much more gut level, conscious-y kind of way than it ever did in the old left. . . . In the old left you could be brought up on charges of male [supremacy]. So they were aware of it in an institutional way, which doesn't mean they didn't practice it. But at least there was a recourse if they did.

James Weinstein, a former member of the CP, reported that among young members in the late 1940s and early 1950s the woman question and the problem of male supremacy were taken very seriously, although discussion centered almost exclusively on the personal lives of party members rather than on their organizing and propaganda work. When he joined, in the late forties, there was great concern with both "white chauvinism" and "male supremacy." Young people in the party were very serious about the principle of sexual equality, including sharing housework and ensuring equal opportunity. Sexual divisions of labor were eliminated as much as possible within the party. Yet party politics were such that the ideal could exist within the party culture, but when members did political work in the world of liberal politics, they "had to live like everybody else." He gave the example of a close friend, a woman, who worked in the same factory. Later she married a college friend of his who had also become a party member. As young party members, "we were very militant on the woman question." So when he visited his friend and found her staying home as a housewife while her husband worked at an industrial job, he was "outraged." They in turn were furious about his criticism and announced that they were living the way all workers lived.

Such a dichotomy between the ideological critique and the active capitulation to resurgent traditional roles represented a weak legacy indeed. Nevertheless, those around the new left with a background of experience in old left organizations were sometimes shocked by the crassness of anti-female sentiments which the intellectual mode combined with the lack of emphasis on women encouraged. Weinstein recalled his amazement at an incident he came to see as typical of the new left. He wanted to review a book by an old friend, Aileen Kraditor. Men on the staff of *Studies on the Left*, a major center of new left thought, laughed at the idea; "review a book by a woman!" At first Weinstein considered it "a joke in very bad taste. Then I realized it wasn't a joke."

The differences between the old and new left were articulated sharply by the minuscule number of women who participated simultaneously in both. Barbara Easton did not like the fact that decisions at the Harvard-Radcliffe SDS were made by a tiny clique of men.

> . . . when one of the men doing this was one of my comrades, I got very upset about it. . . . I remember marching over to his room one morning and dragging the club chairman with me. . . . We dragged [him] out of bed and told him he was being a male chauvinist. . . . Well, he

admitted it. That was the way things were in the party, that you could bring up that kind of question and people had to listen to it seriously. I don't remember that things changed much after I said that, but at least it was possible to say. Inside SDS on the other hand, you see, it was laughed at. I tried to bring this up in SDS and it was impossible.

But in the early 1960s no radical group saw the oppression of women as more than a peripheral issue. In addition, the devastation of the McCarthy era meant that the new insurgents built their movement virtually in a vacuum. Far more important than the ideological remnants of the old left in the sixties were the children who had grown up having some contact with the left tradition. A significant proportion of the early new left consisted of "red diaper babies," that is, young people whose parents had been at one time in or near the Communist Party. Several hundred thousand people joined or were close to the party in the 1930s and 1940s.* Together they created a significant subculture, particularly in New York City, and not surprisingly also produced a high proportion of activist children. Within this tradition, the Communist Party was the strikingly dominant element. But there were many others as well, radical groups and traditions that provided similar impetus to their sons and daughters, including socialists of many stripes; labor, religious, and peace activists; and left-wing Zionists. It is a tragedy of the

---

*Sale suggests that 2,000,000 passed through the Communist Party in the 1930s, but the figure seems greatly exaggerated. The Communist Party's membership never rose far above 100,000 members at its greatest strength during World War II. But the membership turnover rate was quite high and many more people were active on the periphery of the party than ever joined. Kirkpatrick Sale, *SDS* (New York: Vintage Books, 1973), p. 89. For more accurate treatment of membership, see Irving Howe and Lewis Coser, *The American Communist Party: A Critical History* (New York: Praeger, 1957), pp. 419–24.

McCarthy era that even two decades later much of this history cannot be discussed openly. Many parents are still terrified of being identified with the left, though their activism may have taken place forty years ago.* Nevertheless, some of their daughters emerged as leading figures in the revival of the "woman question." They had a tradition out of which they could name oppression, and growing up with the role models of politically active mothers, they drew strength from the sense of participating in an activist heritage.

Perhaps most important for their role in responding to the position of women in the new left, daughters of the old left tended to grow up knowing, at least on some level, that women were oppressed. The term "male supremacy" was a staple of the left vocabulary. The contemporary term "male chauvinism" indeed represents an amalgam of "male supremacy" with "white chauvinism," the term used to refer to racist attitudes and actions. It was prompted by women's perceptions in the wake of the civil rights movement that their oppression had many parallels to that of blacks. In the early sixties, the term "male chauvinism" never appeared, but an occasional correspondent to the SDS office complained of "male supremacy."

Whereas southern women had been forced by the civil rights movement to break with their culture, women from old left families were not raised with a reverence for American culture in the first place. One woman pointed out that while she did not remember specific discussions of women in her family, the basic message came through, almost subliminally: "I always knew that women were fucked over. . . . I

---

* These families must therefore remain anonymous, even though for the purposes of this study the specific connections are very important. It is also important to note that in my research I did not seek out "red diaper babies." Rather, I pursued women and men who had participated in specific new left activities and in particular the women who provided the links between the new left and the early leadership of the women's liberation movement. Again and again I was surprised to discover a radical family background.

cannot conceive of a child growing up not being aware of all these things." When she complained about being forced into "the woman's role" in the movement, she was unaware of the fact that most of the women she complained to were not conscious of their situation as something to be changed. Another woman said that she had been mildly aware of the woman question—to the point of reading work by Clara Zetkin. Frequently the message came through that a woman had to be prepared to deal with discrimination. One young woman was "aware of such a thing as discrimination against women. . . . I thought it was a problem I was going to run into someday." Then when she sneaked *The Second Sex* from her mother's bookshelf thinking it might be something like the Kinsey Report, she was shocked into the realization that "I was living it . . . [it] permeated every aspect of my life."

The experience of girls growing up in activist families tended to encourage independence and self-confidence and to place a premium on egalitarian ideals. One woman described how she grew up "with incredible self-confidence." Her family was infused with a great sense of morality and social concern that generated a continuing interest in current events. As a very small child she expected herself to defend anyone who was being mistreated. In the first grade she stepped into a circle of children throwing stones at a black child; in the second grade she intervened to stop an Italian child from being beaten; and in the third grade she defended a student against a teacher who was administering corporal punishment. Such an intense identification with the downtrodden coupled with a strong sense of self led her later to become active in civil rights, SDS, the anti-war movement, and to provide key leadership in the initial phases of the women's liberation movement. Another woman described herself as a tomboy whose parents "taught me to develop my human potential . . . to be independent and self-starting."

Many liberal families, following the guidelines of Dr.

Spock, also encouraged their daughters to "develop their potential." Perhaps more important, such radical families often provided the model of a politically active mother. The model was a complex one, however, for in many instances they were also not immune to the pressures of the feminine mystique. Many mothers modified their activities in order to have families, but few assumed primary identities as housewives. One woman recalled:

I remember one day I said to somebody, "My mother's a housewife." And [my mother] got furious and she said, "I'm a musician!" And I couldn't understand her fury at that time, I just didn't know what it was about. I thought it was so good to be a housewife, that that's what people were supposed to be. At the same time I also thought that I was never going to be a housewife. It was clear to me that I was going to be a doctor. In some senses, it was a confusion of roles because what does every Jewish kid from New York do if they're upwardly mobile? They become doctors. . . . So the idea of marriage and the family never hit me really until I got to college. . . .

These were mothers who directed tenants' councils, organized union drives, pushed for day-care funding, worked for civil rights. Some of them presented overwhelmingly positive models—sure and competent in their work and political activity, pillars of the family. Others were more ambiguous. Many women urged their daughters to read *The Feminine Mystique*, perhaps because Friedan had touched their latent feminism, perhaps because she also had described more of their day-to-day reality than they might have wished. The families who actually functioned in traditional ways despite their egalitarian rhetoric presented their daughters with a double message. As one daughter of a prominent old left family put it:

On the one hand I was being expected to perform equally to men . . . that's the rhetoric, the political belief . . . but that wasn't the model that I saw. . . . At the time all I felt was terribly confused because on the one hand I was supposed to be sweet and docile and subservient and pleasing everybody 'cause that's what my mother did. . . . Basically when you cut away the political stuff . . . my mother was a typical American woman . . . that was my model. My father made the decisions in my family.

None of the women interviewed with activist family backgrounds grew up believing that they would be primarily defined as housewives, even though they lived out their adolescence in the fifties and were aware of that broader cultural message. Nor, on the other hand, was their primary identity always an activist one. Nevertheless, they have little sense of "becoming" a radical. In response to the question, "How did you get involved in the movement?" they replied with statements like, "Actually, my development was kind of a constant stream," or, "I always was political," or, "My parents were radicals . . . I always felt radical," or, "I was brought up being very political, tuned in to things . . . going to May Day parades when I was a kid in New York." There was a sense of strength and self-assurance in this continuity with their past. Most were activists in high school, in the fifties when even college students were "silent." One woman invited Norman Thomas to speak to her school; several joined civil rights pickets; one was the only person in her high school to travel to the anti-bomb march in Washington, D.C., while two others organized busloads from their high schools to attend a march for integrated schools in Washington. Some of these actions flourished in the radical subculture of New York or Berkeley. Others were solitary acts taken either in defiance of one's peers or simply in lonely confusion. In either case, by the time the women reached college, activism was nothing new and they assumed roles as leaders early and easily.

Activists with radical family backgrounds were always in the minority in the new left. They constituted, however, a significant proportion of the early leaders and women with such backgrounds provided much of the key leadership in developing a new feminism. They were not schooled in Marxist analysis. Rather, they simply had learned a willingness to question and a deep sense of social justice. They were not feminists from the start. Like most students of their generation they were generally not focused on issues of sexual equality. Yet somewhere along the way they had heard that there was a "woman question" and that as women they could expect discrimination. Their mothers mixed in varying degrees the contradictory roles of political activist and homemaker. Those who became active in high school entered college with a background of experience that tended to place them squarely in the middle of resurgent activism. And again and again, when a voice was raised within the new left pointing out male domination at Chicago, at Harvard, at Wellesley, at Swarthmore, at Michigan, it came from one of these women—these "red diaper feminists." Like southern women in the southern struggle, they were in a situation that allowed them to name an experience shared by hundreds.*

Nevertheless they, like women in the southern movement, needed a supportive milieu within which to consolidate and develop their strengths and skills. The intellectual

---

* One group that would have been in a structural position to raise or name the issue of women's oppression because of their culturally defined "deviance" would be lesbians. The new left's concern for sexual freedom, however, was generally couched in heterosexual terms, and the bias against homosexuality was only slightly less than in the broader society. If there were lesbians in early SDS, they remained in the closet. None of the women I interviewed became lesbians until *after* the emergence of the women's movement.

mode of the early new left was from the start culturally bi-ased toward men. To be effective, women needed to be able to acquire some of the skills that gave many men confidence and self-assertiveness. The few radical women who could argue against male supremacy also tended at first to be the ones most capable of competing with men.

The ideas for the revolt were there: the importance of the personal; the need to change the quality of human rela-tionships; the belief in participatory democracy and the im-portance of equality. What was still needed was a basis of experience within the new left from which women could ini-tiate a new self-assertion. That basis developed between 1963 and 1965 when SDS moved into community organizing in northern cities, using the model of SNCC.

6

Let the People Decide

Casey Hayden left the south in early 1965 and worked for several months in an SDS community-organizing project in Chicago. Her views in January 1966 represented a synthesis of the SNCC-SDS ideology, framed in terms of SDS experience in the northern urban ghettos:

The first task, I think, is expanding the group of people really committed to democratic change . . . toward the end of creating institutions of power for those who have no power. . . . In trying to build such institutions for the poor I think we've learned a few things about building and sustaining a radical movement: People need institutions that belong to them, that they can experiment with and shape. In that process it's possible to develop new forms for activity which can provide new models for how people can work together so participants can think radically about how society could operate. People stay involved and working when they can see the actual results of their thought and work in the organization, so power must be distributed equally if large numbers are to be organized. . . . It's hard for many of the poor to function in large groups . . . rotating leadership and strengthening of each person's faith in the value of his own opinions can halt leadership sellouts . . . electing administrations and leadership on a rotating basis helps assure democratic control of funds and knowledge. People then tend to resist society's arguments that they be "responsible" (i.e., responsive to those with power) and they then tend to turn to each other for strength. . . .

These things we've learned from work in the movement in turn shape our view of what the world could be like.[1]

By 1963 the intellectual approach that characterized the early days of SDS had grown increasingly inadequate. Radical analysis was hardly enough when churches were bombed and demonstrators attacked with dogs and water hoses in Birmingham. Schoolwork seemed dry and mechanical, and graduate school pointless. Students could not sit around and talk about it any more, nor fulfill their need to act through an occasional supportive event. They had to do something more. Through 1962–3 campus groups languished except where there was a civil rights movement nearby. No one conceived of an offensive against the university itself. Since the only compelling activist model was SNCC, SDS sought new ways to apply the experience of the southern movement to northern communities.

The push toward community organizing and away from campus was more than a simple wish to get in on the "action." It was also an expression of the cultural alienation that undergirded the new left. How better to express one's disgust with American commercial materialism than to identify with those who are most totally excluded from it? As Tom Hayden put it, "Students and poor people make each other feel real." And one leader of the movement into the ghetto, Todd Gitlin, elaborated in retrospect:

The ERAP [Economic Research and Action Projects] organizers, in wading into the ghettos of the poor, were in some part of themselves trying to forge an alliance of the useless: the post-scarcity "middle class dropouts," convinced that the society offered no useful work, with the poor, who knew that the society had defined *them* as useless. This alliance . . . was also knit in the organizers'

sense that the culturally separate poor (the blacks and
Appalachian whites) were insulated involuntarily from
the treadmill consumerism of the middle classes from
which the organizers had come. . . . Many organizers
were tempted to romanticize the poor, to imagine them
Noble Savages.[2]

Such subjective needs coincided with a widely held economic analysis that reinforced the focus on the very poor.
Since Michael Harrington's *The Other America* had called
public attention to the existence of extreme poverty in the
heart of American affluence, a number of economists had
proposed that an impending economic crisis would increase
the ranks of the impoverished. They argued that growing cy-
bernation, decreased defense spending, and heightening economic competition threatened to create depression levels of
unemployment, particularly among marginal and unskilled
workers. With the postwar boom about to end, a vast constituency of discontented, and therefore potentially radical, unemployed was thought to be forming in the northern urban
ghettos.*

Thus, SDS set out to create "an interracial movement of
the poor," arguing that "a movement can be developed
among persons whose economic role in the society is marginal or insecure. . . . Our immediate identification is with
the Negro movement and the problems of the unorganized
poor."[3] The idea was to develop community organizations in
the northern slums that could win concrete economic re-

---

*Michael Harrington, *The Other America* (New York: Macmillan, 1962). In
light of the economic troubles of the seventies this analysis no longer seems as
ludicrous as it did only two years after it was presented. At the time, economists
could not have predicted the escalation of the war in Vietnam, and they seriously
overestimated the immediate impact of technology in destroying jobs. See Ray
Brown, "Our Crisis Economy: The End of the Boom" (New York: Students for a
Democratic Society, 1963); W. H. Ferry et al., "The Triple Revolution," *Liberation*, IX, no. 2 (1964), 9–15.

forms, especially jobs, and could undertake struggles for community control. Such organizations would in the process begin to realize the goals of the Port Huron Statement:

. . . [the] search for truly democratic alternatives to the present, and a commitment to social experimentation with them. We seek the establishment of a democracy of individual participation governed by two central aims: that the individual share in those social decisions determining the quality and direction of his life; that society be organized to encourage independence in men and provide the media for their common participation.

So the evolution of the SDS community-organization effort—known as the Economic Research and Action Projects (ERAP)—from 1963 to 1965 was the most important attempt to build in the north the sense of engagement, community, and identity with the very poor that SNCC had achieved in the south. It represented as well a specific response to the expressed wishes of black civil rights leaders that white radicals create allies for the civil rights struggle within the poor white community.[4]

In August 1963 SDS received a $5,000 grant from the United Auto Workers to set up ERAP. At the December 1963 National Council meeting the community-organizing forces led by Tom Hayden won an overwhelming victory in the decision to establish ERAP projects in northern communities by the following summer. The new direction infused the entire organization with a sense of excitement. As Paul Booth described the new mood, "By that time we were *it*. We were the wave of the future." Rennie Davis became director of the ERAP office in Ann Arbor. Through the spring he raised $20,-000 with considerable liberal support, and by the summer of 1964, SDS had established ten ERAP projects with over 100 student volunteers.[5]

As SDS moved off the campus into the ghetto it was

transformed in a way that was similar to SNCC when it
moved into the rural south. After visiting several SDS projects in the spring of 1965, Andrew Kopkind wrote:

> To visit with the SDS projects for a week is a wrenching
> experience. . . . Hardly anyone on the "outside" can
> imagine the completeness of their transformation, or the
> depth of their commitment. They are not down here for
> a visit in the slums. They are part of the slums, a kind of
> lay-brotherhood, or worker-priests, except that they
> have no dogma to sell. They get no salary; they live on a
> subsistence allowance that the project as a whole uses
> for rent and food. . . . Most of them have committed
> their lives to "the movement" no matter if in a few years
> they change their minds. It is important that they now
> have the expectation of remaining. . . . In some in-
> stances they are more proletarian than the proletariat:
> they eat a spartan diet of one-and-a-half meals a day,
> consisting mainly of powdered milk and large quantities
> of peanut butter and jelly, which seems to be the SDS
> staple.
>   Most of them come from middle-class and profes-
> sional-class families; many of their parents do not
> approve.[6]

Community organizing in the north was not the terrifying ordeal of civil rights work in the deep south, but there
were risks—some endemic, some self-imposed. All ERAP-ers
romanticized poverty. In the beginning the projects were almost ascetic, with a self-imposed discipline of poverty and
hard work. Mimi Feingold, after several summers working
for CORE in Louisiana, felt that the poverty of the Cleveland
ERAP project was even more depressing than what she had
lived with in the south. "Rural poverty," she said, "had it all
over urban poverty."

One of the keys to SDS's success was its ability to realize, however ambiguously, the wish of northern white students to join the action by moving to organize in the poorest northern ghettos. While ERAP never generated an "interracial movement of the poor," which was its goal, it did provide formative radicalizing experiences for hundreds of students and ex-students. Nanci Hollander wrote:

> [The] organizer's job is not complete by the mere creation of a neighborhood organization. . . . Behind the formation of the groups and throughout their progress must be a basic challenge to the whole system of a welfare state.

Their experiences paralleled those of SNCC. The system did not give, did not respond to the existence of suffering within it. "We are now enemies of welfare state capitalism," wrote Richard Rothstein,

> with little faith or desire that the liberal-labor forces within this system be strengthened vis-à-vis their corporatist and reactionary allies. We view those forces— and the social "reforms" they espouse—as being incompatible with a noninterventionist world policy and as no more than a manipulative fraud perpetrated upon the dignity and humanity of the American people.
> We owe these conclusions in large measure to four years of ERAP experience. In a healthy pragmatic style we tested an optimistic hypothesis about the limits of American pluralism.[7]

ERAP also infused the northern new left with a kind of antileadership, anarchic democracy such as had characterized SNCC. The slogan on the buttons of the Newark, New Jersey, ERAP project became the touchstone of the student movement as a whole: "Let the People Decide."

Few students in SDS were prepared for the realities of day-to-day organizing. They had chosen a constituency, the urban lumpen proletariat, which in comparison to southern blacks showed no signs of self-organization or collective consciousness. As a result, the style of organizing that SDS adopted became tedious, frustrating, and anxiety-ridden. It consisted of going into a neighborhood and knocking on door after door hoping that whoever was inside would be willing to talk to a stranger. The next step was talking and listening, sometimes for hours, trying to learn what the problems were, looking for targets for collective action, providing personal support, earning trust. "The organizer spends hours and hours in the community, listening to people, drawing out their ideas, rejecting their tendency to depend on him for solutions," said Tom Hayden in describing the experience.

It was hard to be an organizer when you had no clear plan about what you were organizing for; yet to have a clear plan was considered manipulative and not in the spirit of participatory democracy. Moreover poor people, unused to meetings, did not necessarily like them. Over and over again meetings were held at which the only people to show up were the organizers themselves. Sharon Jeffry wrote to a friend, "Recruitment is a drag, man." She contacted women who never came to meetings or who seemed really interested but could rarely come because of the very problems the meetings were intended to address—health, children, physical surroundings. One project put their frustrations to song, to the tune of "Penny's Farm":

Oh, well, you go to your block and you work all day;
Till way after dark but you get no pay;
You talk about the meeting, the people say they know;
You come to the meeting and three or four show;
It's a hard time in the North, working for the SDS.

You go back to the block and you talk some more;
You're knocking on a door, it's on the second floor
Lady says who's there and who you looking for;
I ain't got time, slip it under the door;
It's a hard time in the North, working for the SDS.[8]

As the organizers trudged from door to door, they aimed
to convince people not only to come to one meeting but to
stay involved. Here lay a major difference with the southern
civil rights movement. In the south the door-to-door work
was generally voter registration. Some of the problems were
similar—apathy, fear, lack of trust. But the goal was far more
clearly defined: you wanted the recruit to do one specific
thing, register; and the enemy was clearly visible. Direct action movements in the south had specific targets, moreover—a restaurant, a bus station, a swimming pool—and
they could win concrete victories. Those who put their
bodies on the line enjoyed the support of a movement that
seemed to engulf the entire community. Mass meetings and
mass marches were led by community leaders, and even those
who did not participate knew friends and relatives who did.
In the north not only were meetings and marches likely to be
small, but they seemed further diminished by the vast urban
environment and the distant, multiple targets. Visible op-
pressors in the south—the Klan, White Citizens Councils,
George Wallace—shaded into invisible and impersonal enemies in northern ghettos: an absentee landlord, the city
council, the welfare or recreation department, town
bureaucrats.

In the south, where the targets were segregation and
overt racial discrimination, one could presume a consciousness of collective oppression and had only to generate the
will to act. In the north, organizing began a step back. People
first had to understand that their problems were social and

not personal in nature and that only collective action could solve them. Thus SDS evolved an essentially intellectual notion of the process of radicalization, an idea perhaps more applicable to college students than to the urban poor and one that eventually achieved spectacular success in the women's movement, where it was named consciousness-raising. People change, it was believed, through a process of talking together, discovering common problems, and thereby understanding the need for collective action. Once people could "get together" they would see what to do:

> Once you start talking to people and bring them together you can start moving to do something for your neighborhood. . . .We called a meeting with the people and discussed our problems. We found that most all of us had the same problems. We decided to go on a rent strike.

Sometimes there was the hope of radical results:

> . . . [welfare mothers] understand when you say, if we could get a whole lot of women to stand together, maybe it would not be that you would just help each other out in emergencies, perhaps we could change things so that these emergencies don't happen.

And sometimes ERAP organizers would get people together with very concrete goals in mind:

> The experience of meeting and talking with other poor people from different cities could demonstrate better than any amount of discussion back home the similarity of the problems that poor people face everywhere, and the necessity of a national movement of poor people. So the Community People's Conference was conceived at

an ERAP staff meeting, and Cleveland chosen as the most convenient location. [Once there] people were able to feel the idea of an interracial movement of the poor as an emotional reality.[9]

After a year of community-organizing experiences, SDS had come to express its goals for the future most clearly in terms of the internal working of the movement itself. A vision of "participatory democracy" was the key, "a kind of democracy in which those who are affected by decisions make those decisions, whether the institutions in question be the welfare department, the university, the factory, the farm, the neighborhood, the country." As an ideology undergirding the organizing work, participatory democracy constituted both goal and method—people getting together, acting together, and eventually winning some power over their lives.

While they urged poor people to stand up together in the name of future change, SDS youth turned more and more to expect that the movement itself should embody the kind of future they were working for. The term "beloved community" was not used in the north, since by this time it was out of vogue in the south. But the meaning was there.

One thing that has happened is that we have begun to see JOIN [Jobs Or Income Now] as the focus for building . . . a movement around a community. . . . We don't want to lose perspective and begin to see JOIN as a charity organization, but we are beginning to become less defensive and see that those kinds of activities (hairdressing and legal advice) are ways of building a community around JOIN. Of tying people together, making JOIN a place where people come for various parts of their lives, various normal life activities, which are movement activities as well. To build an alternative community, around a political movement.

Most often this sense of community developed within the
staff and the few neighborhood people who became intimately involved in a project. In close cramped living quar-
ters, in the poverty of peanut butter and the frustration of
daily organizing work, participatory democracy came to
mean all-night staff sessions "that sounded like group
therapy."[10]

The emphasis on democracy led, as in SNCC, to an anarchic ethic that rejected hierarchies of any kind. An ERAP
worker from the local community in Newark explained:

> We don't believe in leadership. We believe in one man,
> one vote. We have a program committee meeting once a
> week. All our blocks that we have organized come to-
> gether at the program committee meeting. We discuss
> each problem that occurs on our blocks and let the peo-
> ple decide what kind of action they want to take to solve
> the problem. . . . We have rotating chairmen who
> serve four weeks and then are replaced by the program
> committee. We in NCUP [Newark Community Union
> Project] do not believe in leadership because so many
> organizations have been sold out by leaders. That is why
> we demand one man, one vote.

The concept was to talk to people without imposing any pre-
conceived ideas and to follow their lead in developing the
issues and organizations. "We just talked with the women.
They decided they wanted to do something. We said we'd
help them do whatever they wanted," according to a staff
member in Cleveland. But when the welfare mothers' organization was set up, SDS-ers advised them to avoid a fixed
structure, the tendency to bureaucracy, and specific leaders
by using a system of rotating chairmanships and volunteering
for tasks. Andrew Kopkind observed the results: "The anar-
chy, which is so characteristic of the SNCC-SDS movement,

was a bit much for the older women of CUFAW [Citizens United for Adequate Welfare]."[11]

Ultimately the notion of a "leaderless movement" held serious contradictions for those who called themselves "organizers." In an agonizing meeting in January 1965, the national ERAP staff wrestled with the ethical problems—Do we have any right to be telling people what to do? Isn't organizing inherently manipulative? Can we have a national strategy without imposing it unfairly on local groups? SNCC organizers at the meeting painted in glowing terms images of an "organizer who never organized, who by his simple presence was the mystical medium for the spontaneous expression of 'the people.' " The result of this logic came the next summer when the ERAP staff decided to "decentralize" in order to avoid having an office or a single leader. Those who had worked in the ERAP office in Ann Arbor moved en masse to the JOIN project in Chicago, and ERAP no longer existed as a national movement. The most extreme local example was the Hoboken nonproject in which SDS students simply entered the community and looked for ordinary jobs, with no plans for organizing.[12]

The parallels are striking between the fused ideology and practice of SNCC and SDS-ERAP on the one hand and the women's movement that emerged several years later on the other: the anti-leadership bias and emphasis on internal process in ERAP found counterparts in the women's movement's experiments with rotating chairs, long, intensely personal meetings, and distrust of public spokeswomen; the theory of radicalization through discussions that revealed the social origins of personal problems took shape in the feminist practice of consciousness-raising; the belief in participatory democracy and the idea that "in unity there is strength" helped feed the new ideas about sisterhood and the power of women united. What was required to produce a movement was only for women to apply the new ideas directly to their own situation, to make the connections between "the people" whom they sought to aid and themselves as women. For a period such realizations were submerged beneath the sense of mission, visionary expectation, and middle-class guilt that animated the organizing efforts. But simultaneously women in ERAP, like their immediate predecessors in civil rights, were discovering in the concrete realities of day-to-day work a newfound strength and sense of self that would make sexual oppression seem more and more burdensome and unacceptable.

"Almost all the leadership-type women who were around the organization [SDS] in sixty-three went into ERAP . . . Nanci Hollander, Sharon Jeffry, Carol McEldowney, Jill Hamburg," according to Steve Max. For them the initial decision to join ERAP represented a deepened commitment to social change, often an expression of a feeling that the "movement" was a lifetime commitment. A number of newer recruits also often chose ERAP as a substitute for going south. Leni Zeiger, isolated in the art department at Bennington, thought of the southern movement as "a whole world out there [where] things are happening." Unsure about what organizations there were in the south, she happened upon a list of ERAP projects and "decided to go to work for this thing, this organization." Beth Reisen "ached" to be in Mississippi through the summer of 1964. Then she met some ERAP people at an Amherst conference on civil rights. The next summer she went to work in the Newark project. Marya Levenson graduated from Brandeis in 1964 and worked in a summer stock company in Illinois. She had been slightly active in anti-war work with TOCSIN at Harvard and knew several people who were in Mississippi that summer. When three volunteers disappeared she felt trapped in Goldwater territory, overwhelmed by anger, helplessness, and isolation.

Returning to Cambridge in the fall she determined to do something, though she was not sure what. She joined an organizing project that soon became affiliated with ERAP.

Many women worked in ERAP projects for brief periods of time, a summer, six months. Their motives ranged from changing the world to being with a boyfriend. For those who stayed with it, however, the ideas and the reality of community organizing shaped a new sense of identity—a vocation as an "organizer." Participation in any substantive sense brought risk and, for most people, a sense of achievement and growth.

Distrust and hostility from the local people were hard to take. Leni Zeiger "felt like this [Chicago ERAP] was even rougher than the south. In the south your enemy wasn't hard to find." In Chicago she experienced the enemy as "the whole ghetto around." Only nineteen years old, she found herself in the middle of a northern Appalachian ghetto. "I hadn't even gone to school with black people." The summer was difficult. Street gangs threatened the staff. Two "huge guys," one of whom later went to jail for a number of years, were "after my ass." Though she never heard anyone talk about being afraid, she thinks in retrospect that they all were. Especially for women, "it was really, really hard."

Several projects were red-baited. In Philadelphia, Connie Brown and Sandy Warren had just walked through a housing project when "a group of young Negroes and two old, white guys called out—'There go the Commies.' The girls stopped to talk to them for awhile" and apparently succeeded in defusing the situation. In Cleveland, SDS organizers developed a tenants' council around the need for recreation facilities in a housing project. Their activities provoked an investigation by the city "Red Squad," a kind of miniature FBI. The investigators persuaded several older tenants that the students were Communists, and enough pressure developed so that SDS finally withdrew.[13] There were also more militant actions modeled on the civil rights movement—rent strikes, sit-ins at welfare offices, and marches. Under such conditions, even if a woman joined ERAP for superficial reasons, the decision to stay and the commitment to work required a level of courage and autonomy beyond the normal cultural expectation, all of this further heightened by the realities of organizing itself. A few men in ERAP were good organizers, but most of the good organizers were women. In general women were better trained in the interpersonal skills that good organizing required—empathy, listening, warmth, and noncompetitiveness in personal relationships.

The original analysis on which ERAP was based specified that the key strategic population would be the unemployed, probably youths. Implicit in this calculation was the assumption that unemployed people are male. A mother on welfare is not considered, and does not consider herself, unemployed. So in the beginning project members passed out leaflets at unemployment centers and went door to door looking for unemployed men. But the analysis proved wrong. The Vietnam War intervened to heat up the economy, and the unemployment rate fell instead of rising. The only unemployed men left to organize were the very unstable and unskilled, winos and street youth.

As a result reality soon forced all of the ERAP projects that survived for any time to focus on the more mundane concerns of community life among the very poor—recreation, day care, schools, street lights, housing, and welfare. The shift in emphasis was briefly posed as a conflict between the strategic concept of JOIN (jobs or income now—the demand of the unemployed) and GROIN (garbage removal or income now— the "nitty-gritty" issues of daily life in the ghetto). In cultural terms the GROIN approach built on "women's issues," that is, issues that sprang from the woman's sphere of home and community life. It is a general rule, but one to which ERAP was blind, that women provide the backbone of most community-organizing attempts, though not necessarily the publicly known leadership. Not only do community issues touch women more directly, but also women are more likely to be at home during the day when the organizer comes around to talk.[14]

Women were often aware of their effectiveness as organizers in ERAP. For the first time within SDS women had an independent ground from which to draw their self-respect and to command the respect of others. SDS was never able fully to face this reality, but it nevertheless created unwittingly the practical basis for female revolt: an arena in which women could start with the skills they already had and build from there a new sense of potential and self-respect. Moreover, although ERAP failed in its attempt to organize an "interracial movement of the poor," its most important immediate legacy may have been the groundwork it helped lay for a national welfare rights movement. While the men futilely tried to organize unemployed men, street youth, and winos, women quietly set about creating stable organizations of welfare mothers.

Two of the most successful projects were dominated by women and focused almost exclusively on welfare. In Cleveland, Sharon Jeffry and Carol McEldowney along with Cathy Boudin and Charlotte Fein started a project together in what Sharon Jeffry thinks in retrospect was an attempt to avoid working with the "intellectual heavies" like Tom Hayden, Richie Rothstein, and Rennie Davis. The only male "heavy" who went with them was Paul Potter, probably the least dominating male leader in early SDS. Potter himself recalls that he liked the project because the style was "much less macho. . . . I felt like the style was much too competitive in, say, Newark or Chicago. . . . I didn't want to be in one of those places with all the other heavy men." Potter retained his role as analyst, but the leading women, Sharon Jeffry and Carol McEldowney in particular, were by far the best organizers. And out of that success, confidence grew in their own ideas. More and more they found themselves able to hold their own intellectually as well.

According to Paul Booth, "Cleveland was the first place to discover that the political analysis didn't fit reality." It became the center of the drive to substitute "Let the people decide" populism for the original strategy. Sharon Jeffry, sent down to start the project by herself, had decided that the monthly lines at the food stamp redemption center might prove more fruitful than the short ones at the unemployment center. Passing out leaflets, Jeffry and McEldowney soon had revived a dormant organization of welfare mothers, Citizens United for Adequate Welfare (CUFAW). Subsequently CUFAW won from the city a free lunch program in the public schools for children of welfare recipients, one of the two concessions ERAP "gained from the power structure," according to Richie Rothstein.

Long after ERAP had died and SDS had turned its attention to campus revolt, Sharon Jeffry and Carol McEldowney continued to work with welfare mothers in Cleveland.[15] When they chose to, they could command respect and stature within SDS as a whole. By 1965 Carol McEldowney may have become the most powerful woman in the organization. She wrote to the national office frequently and with great authority, and her comments appear to have been taken very seriously by the leadership.* When the woman question first came up in SDS, Carol McEldowney and Sharon Jeffry assumed a leading role.

----

* This conclusion is based on a reading of the office correspondence in the SDS collection at Wisconsin. There were very few female correspondents, and of those Carol McEldowney was the only one whose letters had the same frequency and tone as those of the male leadership. See, for instance, a letter criticizing the worklist mailings printed in SDS *Worklist Mailing*, II, no. 13 (1965).

The Boston project began in 1965 after an earlier effort had failed. Marya Levenson and Pat Hansen led the project, which joined ERAP. "We didn't have any great theory, didn't have it all worked out," according to Marya Levenson, but they organized around playgrounds and street lights and other day-to-day issues. Their most effective campaign brought food stamps into Boston and took them into welfare organizing, which was

> . . . definitely women's organizing, and women were the only ones who felt comfortable doing that. . . . It had to do with our strategy. We were organizing people at home. People who were unemployed. We wanted to get something for them. The welfare department was extremely open to pressure. You could find so many things in the bureaucracy that weren't being done. . . . You could win. . . . Also, it was only among welfare mothers that we were effective doing the interracial organizing.

Mothers for Adequate Welfare (MAW) developed five chapters in two years, and when the National Welfare Rights Organization began in 1967, members of MAW joined as veterans.[16]

Another project in Boston organized around community schools. "Both those issues, welfare and schools, are women's issues, basically," according to Marya Levenson. The effect of this situation on the women who worked with it was the development of personal strength:

> What happened in Boston was that a group of us who were women became much stronger. We learned how to deal with a lot of situations. We learned how to fight. We went in there and fought welfare battles. We went in there and really pushed other people to take a lot of initiative. And so when it came to appearing in SDS national things, I had no question I could talk. I was a little

intimidated, but I wasn't very worried about it. . . . I really believed the rhetoric that there were no leaders and that the most important thing was to decentralize power. So I went in and out of those national ERAP [and] SDS conventions not at all dealing with the reality that there was a great deal of centralized power . . . [but as a result] I don't have the bitterness a lot of women have who had to struggle with strong men. They were irrelevant to me.*

The two most famous projects, which like Cleveland and Boston lasted for several years beyond the dissolution of national ERAP, were in Newark and Chicago. In each case they were dominated by well-known men—Tom Hayden in Newark, Richie Rothstein and Rennie Davis in Chicago. But women's roles, though less visible, remained crucial to the projects' successes.

In Chicago a long period of trying to organize unemployed men preceded the shift toward welfare and housing. With the shift, women became more prominent in the project. In retrospect Richie Rothstein conceded that "our two main constituencies were women and unstable men." In the summer of 1965 Harriet Stulman, who had been an important leader in Newark, came to Chicago with the Ann Arbor ERAP staff, and Casey Hayden, looking for ways to work with whites and with women, came up from the south. Together they started to organize welfare recipients. According to Leni (Zeiger) Wildflower, it was Casey Hayden who conceived the strategy of organizing a union of welfare recipients. Richie Rothstein recalled that she arrived "saying that . . . first of all we needed more women organizers and that was one reason she came, and second . . . that women

---

* Other early feminists who worked briefly with the Boston project included Sarah Eisenstein and Jean Tepperman. Interview with Barbara Easton.

organizers like herself should organize women. And that struck us all as being a very novel idea." People remember her sensitivity to women's problems with husbands and children and to their need for support from other women. Whereas organizing was an anxious process for young new recruits, Casey Hayden was an old hand:

> . . . I just picked a block and went into what looked like the worst building. The first door I knocked on, I asked the lady about JOIN, and asked her if she knew any people who were having trouble with Welfare. She said the lady across the hall was trying to get on. So I met the lady across the hall who turned out to be a very strong person—well known in the building and in the two block area which is about the worst in the neighborhood. Through her I met a lot of other people in the building. . . . I have never liked the idea of going into a building cold. I try now to never go into a building without someone else from the building with me when I start knocking on doors.[17]

While Richie Rothstein and Rennie Davis, both talented organizers in their own right, pushed and pulled over the major direction of the project, women proceeded to do most of the long-term organizing. Many in the project remember Harriet Stulman, who was in charge of welfare organizing after Casey Hayden left at the end of the summer, as the most experienced and respected woman. Rothstein commented that "most of the best long-term organizers were women." Other strong women included Fran Ainsley, "an extremely good organizer. . . [who had] good honest relationships with people, which wasn't something which was emphasized by the style of the project," and Jean Tepperman, who "also had more honest relationships with people than a lot of others." Vivian Leburg developed a project with teen-age girls through the local poverty program. She persevered even though one of the men on the staff asked why she thought "that teen-age girls had anything to do with the revolution." As it turned out, they developed a screening project for children with lead poisoning by working through the mothers of children the teenagers babysat for. The logical conclusion of the lead poisoning project was to do "something about the landlords, because the hospitals won't release the children until the apartments are fixed up. We didn't believe that the parents should fix up the apartments. So we ended up picketing the landlords." They pursued this strategy for a year and a half.

In Newark, too, there were several women who were central to the project. Tom Hayden clearly dominated the scheme but his involvement was sporadic. Carol Glassman awed newcomer Beth Reisen by her capacity for work. When others were too frustrated, anxious, or caught up in personal tensions to be effective, she plugged ahead, organizing her block and working patiently with one fourteen-year-old girl. Welfare rights organizing developed from her work on that block. Others remember Connie Brown and Corinna Fales as also filling the second rank of leadership with Glassman. Moreover, other shorter lived projects appear to have followed similar patterns. In Hoboken, "Helen Garvey was the only one who did any real organizing," and she, too, worked with welfare mothers, according to Mimi Feingold. In Philadelphia, as Paul Booth recalled, "Cathy Wilkerson was just the best block organizer." In each case some women, at least, proved their competence to themselves and to others in the daily work of organizing.*

---

* There were also those, both female and male, who never felt like "good organizers" at all. Beth Reisen left Newark with the feeling she had been a "drag on the project," while others were competent.

Like the young women in the south, as they organized poor women they also learned from them, developing in the process new role models. Some of the women they met impressed upon them the strength necessary simply for survival. Vivian Leburg called this new awareness the "JOIN experience." "I don't think that we could ever forget about poverty. . . . It was just so profound compared to our upbringing. . . . I never learned as much since then, about people." Other women overcame a deeply entrenched sense of fear and passivity in order to stand up for themselves against landlords and welfare bureaucrats. Judi Bernstein asserted that the experiences in Chicago that encouraged her the most were observing "the woman who never before thought she would be able to deal with the bureaucracy of the welfare system [and] all of a sudden understands that it can be done. The woman who is forced to learn all the rules of the welfare system because she now knows that they can be changed." In every city there were some of the "incredibly strong women" that Sharon Jeffry remembered in Cleveland. In Newark Mrs. Ira Brown joined a rent strike protesting over 100 building code violations. When others in her building became frightened and began to pay their rent, Mrs. Brown carried on a solitary strike for five months.[18]

Since virtually all of the local leaders in most projects were women, they provided the most positive images available to the young organizers. Equally important, however, was the pervasive model of the southern civil rights movement. Most ERAP organizers had worked in civil rights at some time and felt deeply identified with SNCC. When they held a "Conference of the Poor" in Cleveland in February 1965, ERAP organizers gathered constituents of ERAP projects in Baltimore, Boston, Newark, Chester (Pennsylvania), Hazard (Kentucky), Chicago, and Detroit. They also invited a number of blacks from the Mississippi freedom movement, including Fannie Lou Hamer and Mrs. Unita Blackwell. Connie Brown of the Newark project wrote:

> Four Negroes from rural Mississippi were at the conference. Perhaps because of the extreme youth of the Northern organizations, the personal strength of these Mississippi Negroes, their experiences in organizing, their dramatic tales of oppression and brutality in many ways dominated the conference.

She admired the way that the "people from Mississippi were able to cut through again and again" to the contradictions behind making adjustments to "the system."[19]

Thus community organizing in the north offered young women new models who could reinforce the experiences in the south. There was the image of a woman who recognizes and names her own oppression and then learns to stand up for herself, breaking through patterns of passivity and learning new self-respect in the process. It was also true that the powerful image of the southern "mamas" penetrated the northern movement as well. Inevitably these models carried with them important lessons, which were bound to be absorbed in some measure by young women who spent weeks and months going from door to door exhorting people to stand up for themselves. Casey Hayden, when she worked with JOIN in 1965, was five to eight years older than many of the other women in the project and had behind her many years of experience in the civil rights movement. What was elementary for her was still vague and unrealized for most of them. Her sensitivity to the degree to which poor women's problems related to the dual fact that they were both poor and female was both interesting and puzzling to others. Younger women did not have the experience to empathize with family-related problems—fights with husbands, hassles with children. But they soon would. For many there would be the stress of personally oppressive relationships within the movement. For all there was the contradiction of doing most of the concrete long-range organizing work and remaining largely invisible. Women were effective, but men were the stars.

While the leading women in SDS all went into ERAP in 1963 and became stronger, the leading men in SDS also went into ERAP and maintained their intellectual hegemony. Most projects were known by the men who "led" them: Tom Hayden, Richie Rothstein, Rennie Davis, Carl Wittman. If the women took the strong neighborhood women as models, some of the men, even more overtly, adopted the manners of the less stable, culturally macho street corner youth. Steve Max described the difference:

> When it actually came out to relating to people in the community, particularly because so many of the early ERAP activities were regarding welfare mothers, it was the women who were able to relate to the community people and the ideological men were always kind of hanging back, you know, trying to develop southern accents [like the Appalachian whites in JOIN's target constituency].

In the beginning of ERAP the theoretical focus on unemployed men obscured the existence and importance of women staffers in organizing projects. An early pamphlet from the Chicago project called *What Is JOIN?* asserted that "JOIN is an organization of employed and unemployed *men* who are demanding government policies which guarantee everyone a decent job or income" (my emphasis). When the first year's work had produced mainly female leaders, a long and tense debate began over the problem of developing stable male leadership and it lasted throughout the life of the project. The problem was twofold. Without stable male leadership from the community, male organizers had no clear constituency, and at the same time they were unable then to accept or respect female leadership. Richie Rothstein felt that "not just men but women as well did not take our project as seriously if it was just led by women." Yet no one saw such an attitude, in themselves or in the local constituents, as something that should itself be challenged or changed.[20]

In several projects male organizers began to hang out in the bars and on street corners, the places where men could be found in the community. Where this was elevated to the highest form of "organizing," women were by definition virtually excluded. With no criticism to guide them, men were often drawn into romanticizing and emulating the exaggerated macho subculture. For example, Rennie Davis described his process of working with unemployed high school dropouts in these terms:

> There was an informal gang structure on the corner where we began our office. It was possible to get to know them by going out of your way and I went out of my way the first week—I was virtually drunk all week—the fellows drink all day on that corner. My feeling is that they are the potential revolutionary force in Uptown Chicago, if there can be said to be such a force. They are the force that is least afraid of the police, do have some sense of justice—and are willing to act on that sense. . . . [When] you're OK with the guys . . . you can talk about how poor people get screwed, and how people who back each other up can stop that from happening. . . . Complications are very great. One is that to work with them really requires that you live their way . . . that you run, and fight and drink and do the things they do, and still have the capacity to direct it towards something. It means you have to have some sort of separation from the other community

people you are trying to organize; welfare people and older people, because those older people consider the kids Hillbilly punks. . . .

Davis referred several times in the interview to the "tradition of violence in their families," and asserted that to gain their respect, "you have to be ready to fight. . . . I haven't had to, but on one occasion I stood up in a bar and said I would whip every mean son of a bitch in there—or something—and they pulled me back down."[21]

Such views, held by the charismatic male leaders in Chicago, meant that organizers in the Cleveland project, where the main work was with welfare recipients, felt constantly criticized. And in Chicago, work with groups who were not considered "tough," like teen-age girls or welfare mothers, was not accorded the same status. A participant observer on the JOIN staff noted: "It is my impression that for a considerable period of time women on staff viewed themselves as inferiors." He offered the example of two women who were "impressed to the point of intimidation by the articulate male leadership at JOIN. They tended to refrain from speaking at meetings even though they had a better touch for the community than most other staff members." Work that men did was considered "exciting" and "daring," while women were assigned the more routine door-to-door work. Men worked on rent strikes, while "women's work at JOIN" was welfare organizing. The official leadership of ERAP was almost exclusively male. In 1964 the director of each of the ten projects was a man, and from 1963 to 1965 Sharon Jeffry was the only woman on the ERAP Executive Committee.[22]

ERAP's male leaders, like those in early SDS, brought to the movement the aggressiveness and competitiveness they might have been expected to exercise as successful professionals. They struggled among themselves for leadership, dominated meetings with their verbal abilities, actively sought positions of authority, and in addition adopted the aggressive characteristics of those they sought to organize. Yet their commitment to the movement and their identification with the very poor required a break with the traditional avenues of success—money, prestigious jobs, respectability. In a sense the only avenues left for proving their "manhood" were those that community organizing offered. And a major arena for male self-assertion proved again to be sexual conquest.

In the first summer of 1964 ERAP projects were known for their asceticism and hard work—no sex, no drugs, no alcohol. By the next summer that had changed radically, and the sexual revolution which was taking place in the civil rights movement and the new left subculture intensified, if anything, in ERAP projects. One woman who arrived in Chicago in August 1965 was appalled to realize that "everyone was sleeping around with each other." Some of the men were known for bringing one girlfriend after another into the projects. Women were aware that when they became involved with a man in the inner circles, they were privy to many conversations and decisions central to the project's development. Thus at times a woman's status could rise or fall according to the changes in her sex life.

Some of the women refused to play, either by avoiding relationships within the project altogether or by developing a single, primary, monogamous relationship, sometimes even a marriage. Others enjoyed their new "freedom." But many women were caught somewhere in the painful middle. They rejected many social norms concerning sexual relationships, but they were confused about what should replace them. People talked about openness, honesty, and democracy in relationships, but few felt sure how such values might be achieved. In the absence of any clear understanding of the ways sex roles continued to shape behavior, the double standard collapsed into a void. Men believed that women would simply adopt their own more promiscuous standards. But what then should women do with the needs already socialized into them for security, stability, and dependability in relationships? One woman spoke of her struggle over several years to be "independent" although she was deeply in love with one of the male leaders. Within ERAP she sensed that there were unspoken codes of behavior. The dominant ideas specified that people should be independent and autonomous in their work and their decisions. "Love," she believed, "was having a relationship with a person that you met, where two people were independent, where they functioned independently. Dependence was really up the wall. Dirty. Ugly. It was the women who tended to slip into that most often." Hence it was unseemly to make a decision about where to work on the basis of whom you wanted to work with. So she spent several years making "autonomous" decisions to be anywhere but where she really wanted to be, which was with the leader she loved. "It was highly romanticized. . . . It was a group of loving people who were going to change the world. It's wrong to say that's not how life is. It's more accurate to say it wasn't very fulfilling. . . . I don't think it took into account people's needs."

Throughout the interviews conducted for this study with women active in ERAP, the reality of painful personal relationships appeared as a contrapuntal theme to that of personal growth and self-confidence. One woman explained the origins of women's vulnerability in the projects: "We were all super-intense, super-sincere in everything we did, everything, you know, one hundred percent. And, as women, you know, none of us were very sophisticated sexually." Sometimes women were recruited into the movement through sex-

ual liaisons with project members and then suddenly expected to be completely independent. Women were also sexually exploited by men in the neighborhood when they had
neither the theoretical basis—an analysis that named sexual
aggression as sexist—nor the experience or personal support
to resist without at least feeling very guilty. Some women
gained guilty pleasure from being suddenly in the inner circles; others became hysterical when treated simply as the ap-
pendage of an "important man." It was awkward and
mystifying, but to talk about the feelings would be seen as
selfish and weak.

The oppressive style of many ERAP and SDS leaders affected not only women. Men suffered as well, and even the
men who assumed these roles, though they could not have
admitted it at the time, felt inadequate and "put-down" at
times. Todd Gitlin wrote in 1970 that the movement was
flawed by

> . . . arrogance, elitism, competitiveness, machismo,
> ruthlessness, guilt—replication of patterns of domina-
> tion and mystification as we have been taught since the
> cradle. . . . What movement men had done to move-
> ment women we have also done, perhaps more subtly, to
> movement men. Women have been oppressed as a caste;
> we have all been oppressed, damaged, twisted, ne-
> glected by each other. [23]

Feminism was nurtured in the contradiction that the in-
tensification of sexual oppression occurred in the same places
where women found new strength, new potential, and new
self-confidence, where they learned to respect the rebellion
of strong women. The ERAP projects created an environment far more conducive to female leadership than the
highly intellectual campus movement. Community organizing in the north, like that in the south, allowed women to de-

velop a strong sense of their own capabilities. ERAP represented the "SNCC-izing" of the northern movement. One of the hitherto unrecognized elements of this process has been the key role of women. These women, utilizing the ideology of participatory democracy that was imbedded in SNCC and ERAP, led the critique of women's position in the new left that was the beginning of "women's liberation."*

By the spring of 1965 ERAP women were talking among themselves about the "woman question." Their conversations merged with similar ones in SNCC when Casey Hayden came to spend the summer working in Chicago. In the fall, when Casey Hayden and Mary King wrote their "kind of memo," it went not only to women within SNCC but also to a number of ERAP women—Harriet Stulman, Sharon Jeffry, Carol McEldowney, Connie Brown. In response to the memo several women planned a discussion of the issue for the December 1965 SDS conference. What happened there was both the climax of the early new left feminism and the embryo of a new movement that would not fully emerge for another year and a half.

---

* Women provided at least half and perhaps more of the connecting links between SNCC and ERAP, and only women made the transition from leadership in one to the other, e.g., Betty Garman, Jane Adams, Mary Varela.

7

The Failure of Success—
Women in the Movement

BE IT RESOLVED, baby: that the NC suggests to all SDS organizers (potentially the entire membership) that they encourage
the formation of women's liberation workshops and projects.
—*New Left Notes*,
October 23, 1967

Heather Tobis sat alone in the cafeteria on the University of Illinois campus. Hundreds of other SDS-ers ate, talked,
and milled around during a break at the SDS "rethinking
conference" of December 1965, but she did not know any of
them. The meetings that weekend were very different from
the close, tight communities of SNCC and early SDS—these
new ones seemed confusing and acrimonious, and no one
bothered to talk to her. She did not join in until the part of
the conference she had come for, a workshop on women in
the movement. While the rest of the conference dissolved
into shambles, small groups—most composed only of women
but a few including men—engaged in an exciting, searching,
angry, and enlightening conversation that continued on into
the night and through the next day. Older ERAP women led
the workshop, which culminated in their expressed concern
about their position in the movement. Simultaneously they
laid the foundation for a younger generation of activist
women, people like Heather Tobis, Vivian Leburg, and
Cathy Barrett, whose experiences in the south or in community or anti-war organizing were more recent, to pursue the
issue of women's role both in the movement and in society.

Thus the workshop constituted the real embryo of the new feminist revolt. But the changes in the movement's setting surrounding the women's discussion—the new tones of stridency and feelings of anomie that accompanied SDS's chaotic growth—meant that the impact of the new insurgency would be delayed for nearly two years. And the changed character of the movement also meant that when the feminist revolt reappeared, it would do so with an explosive and bitter force.

The "rethinking conference" was a kind of agonizing last stand for those who had led SDS through the early years and the ERAP phase. Within the space of a year the movement had metamorphosed into a new thing, with roots in the old phase but noticeably different. Much of the original leadership had become isolated from campuses in the northern ghettos. And another student generation, symbolized by the Berkeley Free Speech Movement (FSM), began to reshape the campus movement.

Berkeley brought radical activity back to the campus and demonstrated that students could act in their own self-interest, not only in behalf of others. As whites were pushed out of the black movement they began to apply their experiences there, and the radical visions shaped by those experiences, to their own environment. Mario Savio had been a Mississippi summer volunteer in 1964; John Lewis of SNCC came to Berkeley to speak at Sproul Hall. Most of the FSM leadership were veterans of CORE demonstrations in Oakland.[1]

Other campuses erupted in the winter and spring of 1965—Yale, Ohio State, Kansas University, Brooklyn College, Michigan State, and St. John's University. Every uprising offered wider numbers of young women the chance to be involved. In some cases campus activism constituted a first step that led back to the southern movement or to ERAP-type community organizing. Vivian Leburg demonstrated with CORE in Oakland and San Francisco her freshman year at Berkeley. She turned eighteen in April and was arrested exactly three weeks later with 700 other people. The next fall she joined the Free Speech Movement, and by late spring, "tired of being just a participant who had to take orders from the leadership without any say in decisions," she determined to go to work in Mississippi. Jo Freeman, a member of the FSM steering committee, had spent the previous summer desperately wanting to be in Mississippi. In August, she had hitchhiked across the country alone to attend the Atlantic City Democratic Convention. The summer after FSM she joined the staff of SCLC and spent a year working in the deep south.

The student movement grew most spectacularly, however, in reaction to the Vietnam War. One observer had noted an anti-war poster on the wall of the COFO headquarters in Jackson, Mississippi, in the summer of 1964. The war was not a significant issue for young activists, however, until President Johnson unleashed American bombers on North Vietnam in February 1965 and simultaneously began to draft men of their generation in large numbers to fight. Campuses suddenly ignited with protest. The "teach-in" constituted an academic equivalent of its southern model, the sit-in. Thousands of students sat through all-night marathons learning the history of Vietnam, of Asia, of American intervention, and debating the morality of American foreign policy.

By a fortuitous coincidence the SDS National Council in December 1964 had called for a national demonstration protesting the Vietnam War on April 17, 1965. As originally conceived, they would have been delighted to have a crowd of 2,000. Caught on the crest of rising campus activism, however, coupled with the bombing of North Vietnam, the SDS march brought over 20,000 protestors to Washington, winning the ambivalent support of a wide array of adult peace groups. Suddenly SDS catapulted into the leadership of a burgeoning anti-war movement.

Money, letters, and volunteers poured into the SDS office. By the end of the spring there were 40 new chapters and 2,000 paid members, a trend that accelerated when school reconvened in the fall. The new influx was more heterogeneous than the original SDS-ers, as much from the midwest and southwest as from the Berkeley-Boston-New York axis. Shaped by the civil rights movement—many were veterans of a summer in the south or of local civil rights movements and community-organizing attempts—they were less likely to come from radical families. Fresher, more individualistic, they took to the ERAP anti-leadership ethic while rejecting the old-guard ERAP leaders.[2]

As the movement grew and changed, the question of women's roles had simultaneously begun to surface. Carol McEldowney outlined her ideas for the 1965 ERAP institute, planned to precede the summer convention, and included two questions about women for discussion:

> What is the role of women in the organization and in the movement and how would that relate to our concerns about democracy? . . . Why is there a tendency to think about women as filling certain "slots" in the movement and why do many men deny that that problem exists in ERAP?

At about the same time, Harriet Stulman wrote in a letter to the office concerning the convention: "Include role of women . . . really important. Too many people are talking about it for it to go undiscussed. Don't think it's totally a paper tiger or tigress!"[3]

There is no evidence that the role of women was discussed at either meeting. But an undercurrent of tension ran through the convention. About 600 student radicals convened at Kewadin, Michigan, in June. Throughout the undisciplined and confusing meeting only a few people at the top understood what was taking place. A new spirit prevailed as

newcomers resisted leadership from the original élite. They
insisted that local chapters were all that mattered and that a
national staff or national program were secondary at best and
probably unwise. It was an early glimmer of the "do your
own thing" counterculture, which would be in full bloom by
the summer of 1967 when a whole generation, it seemed, was
headed for San Francisco's Haight Ashbury.[4]

Superficially, it seemed that women had never been
more invisible. All of the working papers and documents for
the conference were prepared by men. Hardly a woman
spoke in plenaries and only a tiny number in workshops.
Liora Proctor chaired one tumultuous session, and as she attempted to gain control she was booed and hissed. Carol
McEldowney leaped to her defense, but the meeting did not
take the charge of "male supremacy" very seriously. Later,
when McEldowney became annoyed that there were no
women nominated for office and threatened to organize a
protest, the leadership "bought her off by giving her a place
on the National Council," according to James Weinstein. An
older radical told Anne Froines that the lack of female participation was incredible to him and would never have been tolerated in the old left. James Weinstein had been aware of
women's subordinate roles in previous conventions, but he
was amazed at the further deterioration by 1965:
" . . . women made peanut butter, waited on tables,
cleaned up, got laid. That was their role." Here and there a
few people, from the old left or from ERAP, noted the dis-
crepancies, but the issue of women's participation was never
raised publicly. The new male recruits were too busy asserting themselves; the old male leadership was too busy defend-
ing itself; and female partisans on both sides were too
wrapped up in the issues at hand to join together as women.
That would take some time, and an added shove from the
south—the memo from Casey Hayden and Mary King.[5]

Throughout the rest of that summer and fall, the SDS office could not handle the vast quantities of mail, literature orders, and inquiries about membership that continued to pour in. Wherever students were moved to protest the war, campus restrictions, or civil rights, they were likely to form an SDS chapter in the process. Over the next few years there were many chapters that the national office did not register until months after their formation, if at all.[6]

The old guard had hoped that the "rethinking conference" in December could be a kind of second Port Huron, where SDS would be able to "get it together" again ideologically. It had been very hard for the original leaders to witness the dissolution of the early sense of community when a massive influx changed the organization, and on top of such wrenching changes, it was traumatic to witness "their organization" being taken over by these new "outsiders." In addition, many of the early relationships and marriages were reaching a breaking point, a factor that added to the sense of personal chaos, gave impetus to discussions among women, and perhaps also made such discussions anxiety-producing.[7] At any rate, the "woman question" could no longer be contained or avoided. Casey Hayden and Mary King's memo on women in the movement provided the final impetus to plan a discussion for the "rethinking conference."

The memo was printed up along with the other conference papers. Though the workshop on women did not appear on the official agenda, such a meeting was a foregone conclusion. The conference failed to live up to the old guard's expectations.* SDS had grown too large and too diverse to re-create the earlier sense of unity and community. Its un-

------

* Sale quotes Todd Gitlin as saying that everyone there considered the conference a "disaster." Heather Booth and Vivian Leburg Rothstein emphasized in interviews the jargon and intimidation of the conference.

wieldy size and ideological conflicts intensified the attributes
that had always made national meetings difficult for women:
jargon, verbal competitiveness, wrangling, and posturing.[8]

When the women's workshop convened it included both
men and women, but it gradually broke down into three or
more subgroups. One group of women soon split off and went
down to the Student Union cafeteria. Some accounts imply
an angry walkout; others say that Harriet Stulman simply announced she was going down for coffee and several women
followed. The men and women remaining in the lounge of
the Student Union began to argue about whether there was
an actual "problem." Some women took the position that
men held a set of attitudes toward women, analogous in
thrust and content to those of racists. Both men and women
disagreed, some on a theoretical level and others more personally: "Not me," "I'm not a problem." For a number of the
women it seemed clear that the discussion they wanted to
have could not happen in a context where they had to debate
the need to talk at all. Others argued that discussion was fu-
tile unless it included both men and women. Soon there was a
mixed group at one end of the lounge and an all-female group
at the other. Some of the men, left alone, fumbled about for
something to say for the first time in the conference.[9]

The various discussions quickly became the most ab-
sorbing and serious aspect of the conference. They also provoked conflict. Some of the men followed the women who
separated off, demanding to be allowed to participate. On
one occasion two black women were the only ones with the
courage to tell the men to leave. On another occasion Jimmy
Garrett, the black SNCC organizer from Los Angeles, nearly
got into a fight with some of the SDS men who asserted their
right to be included in all discussions on the ground of "participatory democracy." Garrett insisted on the women's right
to meet alone and rather sarcastically pointed out that "I

myself had not tried to get in, so what is *your* problem?"
Others' memories of Garrett were not so positive. As a member of SNCC who had come to talk about the growing sentiment on the west coast for self-defense (violence), he was not terribly interested in the issue and tended to speak with condescending sarcasm about the uselessness of all this conversation.*

Heather Tobis had come committed to talking with both women and men, but when she felt it was impossible, she left with a group that included Sarah Murphy, New York regional coordinator, and Nanci Hollander Gitlin.

> What we did there was trace back our own roots, and figure out what made us as we are, and then what are the forms of the ways we are not allowed to fulfill what we could be. A specific focus on SDS, but also the movement in general. It was much broader.

They discovered that most of them had had supportive families, so they had been raised to be strong. They felt consistent with their pasts—mothers with considerable self-respect, families that tended to be politically active and radical. Then they shared stories about the opposition they had met in school or SNCC or SDS, the feelings and the experience of not being respected or allowed to participate in decisions:

> . . . it was really inquisitive . . . trying to find out [each one's feelings] and comparing notes. . . . For many women it was the first break of caring for other

---

* On the incident with Garrett, Leni Wildflower's account was positive; Heather Booth, Vivian Rothstein, Paul Booth, and Steve Max remember him as obnoxious. Garrett himself says he was not very interested but was generally sympathetic to talking about the issue. His account matches that of Leni Wildflower. He seems to have rather enjoyed seeing SDS men so threatened about an issue "that could be talked about in SNCC but not in SDS."

women . . . the feeling that women should organize women and that situations had to be developed so women could support other women.

In another group women from ERAP projects talked for the first time as women about the "women's problems in the communities that we worked in." They discussed the fact that most of the community leaders were women, as were a majority of the ERAP organizers assigned to local communities. In all the projects there were touchy problems between student organizers and neighborhood men. Vivian Leburg Rothstein recalled

. . . feeling a little bit defensive about it [the discussion] and not being sure it was totally legitimate. But part of it was, if I remember correctly, that we were organizing a lot of women. . . . We ran into a lot of women's problems in the communities that we worked in. It was the first time we'd ever talked about that as women. . . . One of the things about JOIN was that almost all the leadership was female . . . the majority of organizers were female. The relationships between the sexes were a very touchy thing on all the projects and . . . we weren't able to develop any male leadership from the community, because the male organizers competed with them. And people knew that. The only people we could attract were quite incompetent men who were willing to be bossed around. That was a real issue, and I think we talked about stuff like that.

Following the conference Sharon Jeffry and Carol McEldowney mailed out the notes from their workshop. Exactly who was in that group remains unclear; there may have been some overlap with the groups described above. The incomplete notes outlined a wide-ranging discussion of women and society that posed most of the problems "consciousness-raising" groups would face in the future: How are women different from men? Why are women different? Why are the qualities and actions defined as feminine looked down upon? They expressed a fear that their notes would fail to convey "the excitement and emotion, and real seriousness with which these questions were persued [*sic*]," but the breadth of their questions did convey an excitement even through the medium of dry, somewhat ungrammatical notes. Such ideas, almost commonplace after nearly a decade of the women's movement, must have appeared novel, difficult, even shocking and unsettling to many in 1965.

First they focused on the question of woman's identity. Some argued that women's role was determined by biology, but arguments about the power of culture and socialization were apparently more convincing:

> Women are reared with expectations of family and motherhood being the most important goal, or important with a career. Men are more geared to success in something professional, political, laboring, etc. The childrearing patterns in this country, the way the male and female roles are defined at an early age, have a big influence on this. The kind of toys boys are given and the kind of toys girls are given.

An examination of the degree to which adult female behavior hinged on the need for male approval and for status reinforced such insights:

> Men get defined or are given status according to their job level and amount of income. The women then share this status. She is seldom able to establish an identity separate from that of her husband.

Seeking for ways for women to establish their own identities, the group proposed two possibilities: "accepting herself"

("one of the biggest problems to deal with is teaching women
to accept ourselves, to accept our limitations, abilities and
needs, as WE define them, and not as men define them") and
"work" ("something which you create, that comes from you,
that is more than being just docile or emotional"). Their definition of work reflected a radical rejection of the careerist solution advocated by Betty Friedan, and forced a questioning
of socially valued understandings of "work": "What happens
when a woman does do something which gives her definition,
but which is not respected or regarded as very high cal-
iber . . . by the society or men?" The questions circled back
to the issue of "femininity" and whether there could be any
inherently female quality.

The group criticized SDS for its tendency to encourage
uniformity, and deplored

> . . . those people who hold the very same values and
> ideas about politics, who use a certain kind of language
> to explain, who have learned to think and conceptualize
> in similar ways. If you don't think [in] these ways then
> you don't fit; you don't belong whether you are [a] man
> or [a] woman, but it is especially a problem for women.

Their criticism of the emphasis on ideas and conceptualiza-
tion stemmed from the generally oppressive use of intellectual and verbal skills by men in SDS. Many of the more
confident women in the group, however, experienced another problem. When they demonstrated their competence,
men treated them as threats and they found themselves becoming overly conscious of such male reactions. The group
wondered whether women attracted to SDS were more likely
to be already somewhat liberated, and attracted partly by
"the expectations that a revolutionary organization has revolutionary forms of relationships." Then they considered the
other side—do women join the movement for emotional rea-

sons? Do they come in simply as a side effect of having relationships with men in SDS?

The latter question led logically into a discussion of sex, a topic they agreed most people in the movement were reluctant to discuss. The central issue involved the tension between wanting to be accepted as sexual persons but finding themselves treated frequently as sexual objects. "Why are many young attractive girls in the movement exploited sexually? How does one deal with the race problem and the general guy-girl problems?" Someone countered the criticisms of sexually exploitative men with an argument that women also used men sexually, manipulating them while "bitching" about not being treated as persons.

Only one idea for change was explored in the notes, a suggestion apparently made by Nanci Gitlin. If men and women shared equally in the tasks of rearing children, that might lead to changes in the kinds of careers both sexes would consider appropriate, as well as to redefinitions of work to include such possibilities as job sharing.[10] Throughout the workshops tension existed not only between men and women but among the women themselves. For some of the younger women the issues raised were more immediately sensitive. Discussions validated and provided a vent for feelings of hurt and anger. One woman remembered being very impressed with an angry, outspoken southern white woman from SSOC (possibly Cathy Barrett). Several women who were in the younger generation of activists at the conference mentioned in interviews the defensiveness of older and married women. It seems possible that some people who were crucial in raising the issue of women's roles in the movement found it difficult, once the issue was raised, to identify with the depths of anger in those who had never felt as accepted or as respected, as heard, as they had been.

One of the women's groups, probably the one quoted above, produced a statement that was submitted to and endorsed by the National Council. Recognizing that the SDS style constituted a norm that made it hard for many people, including women, to participate fully, the statement asserted that SDS should encourage individuality rather than uniformity in style in order to promote "participatory democracy":

> Men must learn and understand the problem of free independent women and encourage full participation by each woman as she defines herself, as should be the case with any individual. We realize that matters of attitude cannot be legislated, but SDS as an organization must recognize that the problem does exist, that many women are neither able to nor encouraged to become participatory democrats in the organization.

The statement stressed that SDS must promote "honest and open discussion" as a "necessary first step," and encourage women to assume such responsibilities as writing and speaking. Men as well as women had to confront the problem directly. While women sought moral support from one another, men "must also begin to understand themselves and their own reactions to the raising of the 'woman question'; they must be willing to engage in introspection."[11]

Thus the problem was posed primarily as an internal issue. A post-conference analysis summarized the conclusions of many participants:

> For the first time at an SDS conference women came together to talk about problems of women in the movement or women as an oppressed class. Movement men unaware of the problems of women should reflect that in most ERAP projects, in many "radical" marriages, and in the National Office, women frequently get relegated to "female" types of work—dish washing, cooking, cleaning, clerical work, etc. At national conferences, conventions, or council meetings, the problems of

women become part of the general problems of prestige within the organization. Leaders with established reputations for cogent thinking are listened to with much more attention than people with equally good ideas who are less skillful (i.e., less experienced) in presenting their ideas. In an atmosphere where men are competing for prestige, women are easily dismissed, and women, accustomed to being dismissed, come to believe their ideas aren't worth taking the time of the conferences; in short, they accept the definitions men impose on them and go silent. These are problems for the whole organization which deserve further attention.[12]

Changes in the movement, however, diluted or postponed that "further attention" for the next year and a half. The ERAP women who originally raised the issue of sex roles existed within a tight network of people built up over the years. SDS was growing so fast, however, that it was no longer capable of careful introspection, and it was so diverse that thoughtful conversations tended to deteriorate rather quickly into acrimonious debate. Old-guard men in SDS were no less threatened by the issue of sex roles than younger men, but they knew, respected, and frequently were married to the women who confronted them. If such a confrontation had taken place simply within that network, they might not have liked it but they would have had to listen. The result might have been some amelioration of sexism within the movement and a much slower development of women's liberation as a social movement and a broad political issue. But in the developing organization women had less and less place, and the questions raised in 1965 faded into the background until women finally decided that they needed a movement of their own.

Kirkpatrick Sale has described the period from 1965 to 1968 in SDS as one of growing resistance. In response to the war in Vietnam, black power, ghetto uprisings, and another generation of alienated youth on campuses, students increasingly saw themselves in opposition to the "system." They described their own oppression as students, generating the demand for student power. They saw themselves as potential cannon fodder, and initiated massive draft resistance. As both the symptom and the vehicle of the new mood, SDS grew significantly and initiated more and more militant campus actions. Tactics from the civil rights movement were adapted to new issues. Sit-ins now occurred when recruiters from Dow Chemical, the Navy, or the CIA appeared, or when universities refused to respond to demands concerning selective service ranking, tuition increases, *in loco parentis*, wages for university workers, or curriculum reform.

For the new generation of students, black power ensured that the south and the ghetto had ceased to provide outlets for the activist impulse. The essential roots of student protest remained: cultural alienation, the passion to act meaningfully and, above all, morally. However, students were no longer simply making the world better for others. To do that they now felt they had to start with themselves. Woven into the texture of this radicalization were the more personal, more apolitical expressions of alienation: the changes in dress, hair style, and lifestyle associated with the "counterculture." One version of "look to your own oppression" became "do your own thing."[13]

For women the movement became more alienating, more massive, competitive, and sexually exploitative. At the same time it also opened up the process of radicalization to thousands and sharpened the ideology women eventually would use to describe their own oppression. In an important way these years produced a mass constituency for the women's liberation movement. By 1967–8 hundreds of thousands of young women had been to a march, a meeting, a sit-in, a rally. When a few women with longer movement histories broke away to concentrate on women's issues, this was the first constituency to which they turned.

The new campus militancy offered innumerable new opportunities for activism that were not as drastic, initially, as leaving to work in the south or in a ghetto. Betty Chewning had been aware during her freshman year at the University of Chicago that many students had gone to Mississippi and she even flirted very briefly with the idea of going herself at Christmas. She knew the traumas people went through with parents, conflicts "almost more important than the actual act itself. . . . It was that first striking out into a movement activity without parental support or anything else, [that constituted] a new definition of self." But while she observed others rebelling, she was much too frightened to go all the way that first year. Over the next two years she befriended many activists, attended a few SDS meetings, and grew very concerned about the Vietnam War. When SDS led a student sit-in in the administration building in May 1966, to protest academic ranking for the selective service, Betty Chewning was one of the 400 who joined. She had never participated in civil disobedience before, but "I felt really good about the sit-in. I was surprised that I was there. . . . It felt really good to be with so many people who were unified. . . ." Her sense of clarity and commitment grew:

I remember some friends who thought we were being used at the time, [and] cautioned me against allowing my name to be used in participating in the whole sit-in thing. I remember getting really upset about that . . . trying to convince people that it was an all right thing. That was really the first time that I started publicly [to discuss political issues]. . . . I started to defend my act of being there . . . coming up with these very moral arguments.

While Betty Chewning defended her beliefs for the first time in personal conversations, Naomi Weisstein began to discover her own capacities for public leadership at the same Chicago sit-in. She had been peripherally active in CORE in New Haven where large, male-controlled meetings intimidated her into silence. However, it was the period in Chicago between 1964 and 1966 that she remembered as "those ecstatic years. . . . We really were being driven by a kind of moral force . . . and vision of what the world could be like. We believed very strongly that people could change and change fast." The 1966 sit-in constituted an emotional high point, reminiscent of the civil rights movement:

> . . . we had such feelings of ecstasy, such feelings of being able to make the new world right there; this was our building, we were setting up the institutions governing this building, they were going to be fair and just and generous and democratic, and all this was going on while the sexism was going on. That schizophrenia of not being able to talk, of being terrified to talk . . . and yet feeling the ecstasy.

During this period Naomi Weisstein began to speak up in large groups, "which [for me] was just terror and throwing up and all sorts of stuff and I made myself do that." Despite her fear, she became a popular and respected leader and an important example to younger women in the movement. Already she was known for being outspoken in behalf of women, and she and her husband, Jesse Lemisch, gave talks on their conception of equality in marriage. During these same years she had suffered continual isolation and humiliation as an academic whose demonstrated brilliance as the first in her class at Harvard never mitigated the refusal of male colleagues to support her research. Yet neither she nor anyone around her connected the blatant sexual discrimination that had marred her academic career with the concerns of the movement. Once the women's liberation movement made that connection it would unleash Weisstein's considerable analytical and oratorical powers.[14]

On different levels, then, events like the Chicago ranking sit-in provided opportunities for women to move beyond the limits of their fears and expectations and to begin to speak for themselves with increased confidence. Campus organizing for SDS offered another opportunity for women to develop their skill as travelers or workers in both regional and national offices. Generally, however, the campus environment was neither as supportive of nor as conducive to female leadership as community organizing was. Men monopolized the organizing, the constituency was more than 50 percent male, and it was lonely work. But in the south Lyn Wells became a legend in her travels for SDS's southern counterpart, the Southern Student Organizing Committee (SSOC). Having dropped out of high school to work with SNCC in Washington, she was younger than most college students. When she arrived on a small or large southern campus, she would walk around the Wesley Foundation or the Student Union until she found students interested in what she had to say. By the time she left, there would be an embryonic SSOC chapter and several additions to her list of southern student movement contacts.[15] Within SDS Jane Adams, Marge Piercy, Sarah Murphy, and Carolyn Craven among others developed considerable campus-organizing skills.

On the whole, however, the ideological development of the new left after 1965 overshadowed the rare opportunities for female leadership as a basis for the development of women's liberation. Following the suggestion of black power advocates, who stated that each oppressed group should organize itself first and flatly rejected as paternalistic racism any wish of young whites to engage in civil rights work, the leaders of the new left turned more and more to themselves and to their own environment, the university. There they found much to protest: the community of scholars meshed in a thousand ways with corporate America, providing weapons research, training corporate managers, producing knowledge and technology according to corporate need, aiding the selective service, spying on its own students, acting as over-zealous parent, continuing racial stratification through restrictive admissions policies, and exploiting the surrounding communities. Any of these issues could incite moral outrage, but in addition students not only saw their environment as corrupt, they saw themselves as oppressed. The theory of the "new working class" made explicit the subjective experience. Briefly, the theory argued that the key element in the modern working class in a highly technological society was the group consisting of educated clerical, service, and professional workers. Students at universities, being trained and socialized to fill these slots, were in consequence a pivotal group to organize. Greg Calvert, national secretary of SDS, argued in the spring of 1967:

> Students are the "trainees" for the new working class and the factory-like multiversities are the institutions which prepare them for their slots in the bureaucratic machinery of corporate capitalism. We must stop apologizing for being students or for organizing students. . . . We can see that it was a mistake to assume that the only radical role which students could play would be as organizers of other classes.[16]

Kathie Amatniek recalled that during these years she was not active in any organization but was in and out of movement circles thinking more and more about women's liberation. A friend suggested that the most radical thing to do was to fight against your own oppression. To her, that was the final theoretical link needed to become a full-blown, single-minded radical feminist.

Students were becoming more introspective in general. The fringe subculture of folk music lovers that had nurtured the early new left had blossomed into a self-identified counterculture greatly concerned with personal life and lifestyle. Self-consciously alienated and political in varying degrees, these "hippies," as they came to be called, declared themselves with long hair, beards, sandals, and jeans. They glorified gentleness, love, community, and cooperation, and spurned competitiveness, polished professionalism in work, and materialism. Later on their trademarks became events like "be-ins," "love-ins," and phrases like "getting your head together" and "do your own thing." Crucial ingredients for the future of women's liberation lay in this counterculture's rejection of middle-class standards and lifestyles and its focus on personal issues. It called into question basic defining institutions for women like marriage and the family, asserting in fact that communal living was superior. And it pushed into reality the potential sexual freedom inherent in the pill.

Out of the new themes and the focus on organizing students there emerged a highly personalized technique, which again presaged the consciousness-raising of the feminist movement. Dubbed the "Guatemala Guerrilla approach," the method required an SDS campus organizer to begin any meeting with local members or potential members by talking about himself or herself, his or her background, and the process of his or her radicalization. Then the organizer would encourage the others to do the same. According to SDS vice-president Carl Davidson:

You'd be astonished at the reception this gets, when people realize that they aren't alone, that the failures and the problems they ascribed to themselves stem in large part from the society in which they live and the images of themselves they accepted from society.[17]

At the same time other countercurrents made it more and more necessary for women to step out on their own. As the student movement and its counterculture swelled after 1965, the spaces that had nurtured women's strength and self-assertion contracted. The size of the movement rendered women invisible. Meetings of hundreds, rallies of thousands, marches of hundreds of thousands, did not constitute arenas conducive to female leadership, except for those already exceptionally strong and self-confident. Now there were movement "groupies," both male and female, who hung around to be near the action, vicariously involved and anonymous. Stardom was increasingly defined by glamour and rhetorical verbal skills, and the talents that could prove effective in small groups or in community organizing had little place in the broader movement. A Bettina Aptheker here, a Jane Adams there, stood out as highly unusual anomalies to the general pattern of male leadership.

In Berkeley all the tendencies of the movement became exaggerated. Vivian Leburg finally went to Mississippi in 1965 after two years of participation in the massive Oakland civil rights movement because she wanted more control over her activity. As time went on, many others may have felt the same but there were no longer other options. Campus SDS chapters became exaggerated versions of the male clique-dominated chapter at Harvard described earlier by Barbara Easton. Betty Chewning attended only a few meetings at the University of Chicago. She found them so alienating that she came away feeling that while she would participate in marches, she would avoid any further involvement in such organizations:

> It made me feel like other people were making decisions for me and were making assumptions about me, as to who I was and what my political views were. And some

of those assumptions were right, but, the fact that the group was moving without my [input] really bothered me a lot. . . . In some instances I felt used . . . [because of] the kinds of things which I had to do in the organization, which included mimeoing, typing, secretarial types of things, but when it came to making real decisions about marches, when and where, what would be the content of speeches . . . the decisions were already reached by the time I was involved in it.

In such experiences lay the roots of the fury and pain articulated by Marge Piercy in 1970:

If the rewards are concentrated at the top, the shitwork is concentrated at the bottom. The real basis is the largely unpaid, largely female labor force that does the daily work. Reflecting the values of the larger capitalist society, there is no prestige whatsoever attached to actually working. Workers are invisible. It is writers and talkers and the actors of dramatic roles who are visible and respected. The production of abstract analysis about what should be done and the production of technical jargon are far more admired than what is called by everybody shitwork. . . .[18]

The counterculture that existed in and around the new left added new forms of sexual exploitation. For some women it meant a new freedom to accept themselves as sexual beings; the double standard had been abolished. In practice, however, men frequently demanded that women accept sex with anyone, any time, or admit that they were "uptight" and "unliberated." Some SDS chapters struggled over the relative political importance of the counterculture's focus on sex and drugs. When the Seattle *Barb* published a series of articles by Jim Brown, e.g., "To Fornicate Is Divine," the University of Washington chapter split down the middle.

Karen Manarolla argued that those who believe "that all the good things of life are liquor, drugs, sex, marijuana, and LSD" were escapists. Others said that the *Barb* was making a serious effort "to link sex and drugs to politics and therefore to life." John Veneziale, the chapter correspondent, concluded his report on the situation sarcastically: "It looks as if raising the banner of 'free love' and 'free sex' is a dangerous thing even in SDS."

At the University of Texas the connections were more subtle. The SDS chapter sponsored a "Gentle Thursday," recommending that people engage in warm and playful activities such as wading in fountains, floating balloons, flying kites, reading poetry, singing songs, drawing on sidewalks with chalk, and talking with strangers. But the most concrete example offered on the leaflet constituted a directive to women to make overtures to men and was framed in terms of male fantasies: "SDS chicks should hug fraternity guys and sorority chicks should take emaciated beatniks out to lunch."[19]

Perhaps the most acute stress came when women and men alike made a "revolutionary duty" out of developing these new forms of relationships. In a movement that had not seriously confronted sexual roles and oppression, this simply created another area of male dominance:

> Fucking a staff into existence is only the extreme form of what passes for common practice in many places. A man can bring a woman into an organization by sleeping with her and remove her by ceasing to do so. A man can purge a woman for no other reason than that he has tired of her, knocked her up, or is after someone else; and that purge is accepted without a ripple. . . .

One woman recalled that in the Resistance, an anti-draft movement on the west coast, there was

. . . a real concentration on life styles and new sexual forms, all these supposedly revolutionary ways of living that weren't tied down to the old modes. . . . These terrible communes. Nobody knew what they were doing. These gross situations of people trying to sleep around. . . . Instead of becoming more human it became more and more inhuman. Nobody cared about anybody else, what they were feeling, what they were going through, this gross kind of individualism. You just go ahead and do what you want.

When women's liberation came along, the men who were not hostile tended to think it would be a good thing because it would help their girlfriends get over being so uptight about their sleeping with other women.[20]

Even those who were married ran into the same problems. One couple, veterans of civil rights, ERAP, and the draft resistance movement, married with the notion "from the very beginning, at least in theory, that we were going to be some kind of model of a liberated marriage." They never discussed whether that meant sharing housework; rather, they focused on the importance of not "owning" each other. In theory, they could each have affairs without feeling tied to or responsible for the other. In practice, he had other relationships and she did not. "I was perfectly 'free' to," she explained, "but I didn't want to. The problem was, deep down in my heart of hearts and gut of guts I didn't want him to either, but I couldn't say that."

In addition to becoming lost in the crowd and suffering sexual humiliations, women after 1966 found that they were auxiliaries to the central issue of the movement—the draft. Men were drafted, women were not. Men could resist the draft; they burned draft cards; they risked jail. And women's role was to support them. "Girls Say Yes to Guys Who Say No!" was a widespread slogan of the movement.

The draft resistance movement began in the summer of 1966 when a group of Mississippi veterans met and decided that in light of SDS's failure to evolve a clear program, "people who really knew where it was at like those who had been under fire in Mississippi should create a moral equivalent of Mississippi for the anti-war movement." But this time the only people really under fire would be men.* Many women shared the personal agony of male friends who faced wrenching choices between jail, Canada, conscientious objection, and student deferments. The pain was real, and few men of that generation escaped it altogether. By late 1966 the anti-war movement focused increasingly on draft resistance as the primary mode of opposing the war. Men signed "we won't go" statements, refused induction, mailed in their draft cards or burned them publicly. These were dangerous acts. Many of them carried heavy penalties. Whereas the civil rights movement made fear and danger everyone's fate, within the draft resistance movement heroism was reserved for men. Only men could completely experience the "brotherhood" of common struggle and suffering. Greg Calvert, reporting on the adoption of an anti-draft program at the December 1967 National Council meeting, waxed lyrical with no apparent sense that the specific act that inspired him, draft resistance, could apply only to men:

> . . . the only thing that has given life and creativity to "the movement" [is the struggle] . . . which engages and claims the lives of those involved . . . which has the power to transform, to revolutionize human lives whether or not it can revolutionize the societal condi-

---

* Interview with Staughton Lynd and Alice Lynd, Chicago, November 4, 1972. According to the Lynds, organizers of the Resistance outside the west coast were more conscious than SDS of the problem of a movement in which women were auxiliary by definition.

tions of human existence. It is the struggle which has offered imprisonment and even death as a way of being free—which says that "this is what a human being must do, no matter what the consequences, because this is what it means to be a human being." . . . This is the first act of freedom.

Once women were excluded, as in the Ithaca draft resistance union, "participatory democracy" might take on new meaning:

The draft as an organizing issue lends itself well to the formation of groups where each person has equal participation and influence. Each person has his own experience with the Selective Service, and each person's position can be respected and discussed by the whole group—no one has the special "authority" or the greatest "experience."[21]

Some draft resistance projects, modeled on new left concepts of community organizing, offered more positive work for women, like counseling, writing and distributing leaflets, and other useful jobs; but they were never able to overcome satisfactorily the sexual division of labor. In fact, many attempts to include women only reinforced the secondary nature of their participation:

We now allow women and men who are not of draft age to have equal status and power in our group providing that they sign a public statement advocating draft resistance, which is a violation of the Selective Service Act.

And elsewhere:

. . . draft resistance is the existential stance described by *the man* who would rather die than be forced to kill. It is the action and awareness of a *mother* or *young lover* who hides or otherwise protects her man from the draft. It is that enthralling moment when groups of Americans stand together and express their deepest love for one another by shouting NOT WITH OUR LIVES YOU DON'T [my emphases].[22]

Barrie Thorne demonstrated clearly that the mystique of resistance served as an ideology of "courage, strength, and audacity," in contrast to the stereotypic cowardly "draft-evader" and "minimize[d] the passive ('feminine') connotations of nonviolence."[23] On the west coast especially the idealism of the Resistance was permeated with machismo. As Linda Dauscher, a female participant, put it:

> . . . the resistance was so idealistic, romantic. . . . The main thing that dominated [it was] the whole thing of going to jail. [It] really scared men and at the same time put them on some kind of pedestal . . . you know, like you're really going to give your all. And it complicated that whole men and women issue . . . women had no way, if that's the way to oppose the war, you know.

Mimi Feingold, who shared a house with several Resistance leaders, worked briefly with the movement

> . . . and became immediately turned off to the role that women were playing in the Resistance, because it finally . . . dawned on me that here was a movement where women were playing this most unbelievably subservient role, because that was the only role the women could play, because women couldn't burn draft cards and couldn't go to jail so all they could do was to relate through their men and that seemed to me the most really demeaning kind of thing.

As the draft, the counterculture, and the sheer size of the movement pushed women more and more into the background, it seemed for a time that little would come of the discussion on women at Champaign-Urbana. Cathy Barrett of SSOC had returned to New Orleans eager to pursue the issue of women's role in society and in the movement. Along with Cathy Cade and Peggy Dobbins she initiated a course on the sociology of women as part of the New Orleans Free School in the summer of 1966. As sociology graduate students they planned a heavily academic agenda and even so found themselves a center of controversy. Among themselves they could never decide whether their goals were academic, political, or personal, and in the middle of their confusion several men showed up to laugh at their effort. In response to harassment they grew angrier and more assertive. Cathy Cade argued with Fred Lacy of the Progressive Labor Party, a Maoist sect, that sexual oppression was as important as that of class. Though they imagined that the course should be academic— hence "serious"—"it kept getting personal. . . . We liked that, we knew we liked that." Yet there was little discussion of problems connected with relationships with men because, according to Cathy Barrett, "all of us were active organizers or women with fairly independent lives." In a different context this group would have persisted, but there was not yet a movement to identify with or an ideology to encourage personal conversation. Alone, it floundered. The next year Peggy Dobbins led in founding WITCH (Women's International Conspiracy from Hell), a militantly activist branch of the women's liberation movement.

Heather Tobis helped to organize a "women's workshop" at the "We Won't Go" conference at the University of Chicago one year after the Champaign-Urbana conference:

It was designed as a women's workshop (not for the exclusion of men but directed to the role of women in the movement of draft resisters) in order to focus on two specific problems. First, women are socially trained to accept the role of the nonpolitical; therefore they may generally lack confidence, experience and specific knowledge to act effectively politically. Second, the specific issue of the draft has been structured by men for only male action (at least at Chicago).

She felt that women needed to develop "self-consciousness as women" in order to participate effectively in movement activities.[24] Many women at the workshop, however, did not share her views. They wanted to suggest new tasks for women in the anti-war movement but felt that discussion of women's position was secondary and self-indulgent. Naomi Weisstein supported the idea but recalled that the conversation often deteriorated to "I'm not oppressed, are you oppressed?" Alice Lynd argued that "our duty was to support our men," a view that Naomi Weisstein thought was "a really reactionary position on women." Lynd, for her part, was "thoroughly disgusted" by the workshop.

Most women at the conference avoided the workshop altogether, feeling that it was beside the point. Betty Chewning attended the conference with a friend who was facing the draft. The long personal conversations in which men explored the options of jail and exile moved her because "I was with a man and I was relating to his pain of trying to decide what to do and I had a sense of torture about it." By comparison, then, the women's workshop did not seem particularly important. "It didn't seem . . . as legitimate a concern in a way, as the war. . . ." In retrospect she also recognized that "part of it had to do with my being in a relationship with a man at the time and feeling pretty threatened by women's things."*

---

* Florence Howe, future feminist leader and founder of the Feminist Press, wrote up the conference for *New Left Notes* and gave the women's workshop one

Betty Chewning probably represented the majority of women at the conference. Caught up in outrage about the war and empathizing with their male friends, they perceived "women's issues" as secondary, selfish, divisive, and threatening. Nevertheless the problems of women in the anti-draft movement were so obvious that they continued to provoke comment. In March 1967 Francine Silbar wrote an angry analysis of the role of women in draft resistance for *New Left Notes*. Furious at their secondary roles, Silbar suggested that women should organize separately from men to reach both women and men outside the "We Won't Go" groups. She rejected the two alternatives of forming auxiliaries to do clerical work or "women's Kamikaze groups to show commitment and daring equal to that of the men" by engaging in civil disobedience and risking arrest in anti-draft demonstrations. Instead, she pointed out:

> Our most obvious tool for getting a foot inside the door is to talk about us. All women have misdirected antagonisms to our role or lack of one in this "fucked out" society. . . . Let's define our own roles; we don't have to be secretaries to be useful. What's the matter with men's hands anyway?

Yet Francine Silbar did not advocate that women organize in their own behalf. Rather, she was looking for ways to organize women to be useful around the issue of the draft outside the limitations of demeaning work. She suggested, for instance, talking to women attending ROTC balls on campus.[25]

There were other signs of feminism on the rise but none of them yet fully self-conscious. Naomi Weisstein taught a

---

line: "A group of women, mainly U. of C. students, met to discuss how they could work as an effective, independent group and at the same time support a draft resistance movement" ("We Won't Go Conference," *New Left Notes*, December 9, 1966).

course on women in 1966 at the University of Chicago, and undergraduate women in SDS began coming to talk to her and attending her classes in great numbers. "Everybody knew I was mouthing off about women all the time." Yet there still was no one to talk to about her own personal experiences of humiliation and struggle:

> In those days I was doing personally abusive things to fight sexism. SDS kids would come to our house and ask, "Is there any water?" and I'd say, "Is there any water? You'll have to check if there's any water, maybe the kitchen would be a good place to start." And yet defining myself as a legitimate political issue was something I could not do until the women's movement, until a real social movement started. Though I was talking it, I was teaching it, I was writing it. We were still not legitimate.

At national SDS meetings the "woman question" stimulated an occasional small workshop. The Chapter Skills Workshop prior to the spring 1966 National Council meeting held an informal evening discussion on "the woman question." The issue apparently did not come up in an organized way at the National Council, however, where women constituted only 22 percent of the delegates.* Neither were sex roles a prominent issue at the 1966 National Convention in Clear Lake, Iowa. For the first time, however, the conference plans included child-care provisions. "Hopefully this will work to resolve the age-old debate about who should stay home. Equal amounts of time will be spent [in child care] by both parents." Nominations for the National Interim Committee at the Clear Lake Convention revealed that the

---

* Among the women present were Carol McEldowney, Helen Garvey, Susan Eisenstein, Jean Tepperman, and Kathy McAfee.

women leaders within SDS tended to come from those with experience in SNCC or ERAP. Of the seven women nominated, four had worked in ERAP, three extensively, and one had been on the SNCC staff in Mississippi. A sixth woman, Dana Clamage, had worked in the anti-war movement and served as an editor of the national SDS Vietnam *Newsletter*.[26] The importance of ERAP as a training ground and perhaps the main outlet for female leadership was further indicated by the plans for the December 1966 National Council. Out of four workshop divisions (Labor Movement, Developing a Third Party, Campus Organizing, and Community Organizing) female speakers were suggested only for the last. In that case, of ten suggested speakers, three were women: Casey Hayden, Ida Casido, and Carol McEldowney. Community Organizing was apparently the only arena in which women were recognized to have any expertise.

In January 1967 Jane Adams, a former SNCC staffer in Mississippi and an SDS regional traveler in the midwest, raised the issue of women's equality again in the pages of *New Left Notes*. Her roundabout and abstract analysis reflected the low level of legitimacy accorded the issue within the organization. She defined the problem as the need to understand "the institutional necessity, the class necessity if you will," of female submissiveness. She prefaced her analysis of women with a long peroration on the belief that people could be free but that in contemporary society they were not, and then concluded briefly that patterns of inequality based in social institutions "carry over into . . . personal life." For Adams herself, personal life as such was not an issue, but she urged that women in the movement demand equality and refuse "to be intimidated by the male chauvinism which does exist, even within the movement."[27]

By the April 1967 National Council meeting, the "woman question" had gained the stature of an official work-

shop. Articles by Jane Adams, Heather Tobis, Francine Silbar, and others through the spring indicated that women
would have a more central role in the upcoming convention
than they had ever had before. Not only was the draft movement—with its implicit emphasis on the resistance of men—
forcing women publicly to raise the issue of women's roles,
but also the new left's growing contacts with revolutionary
movements in the third world, particularly Vietnam, brought
it back into contact with a tradition that took the issue of
women's place and status seriously. When delegations from
the United States met with the Vietnamese, female delegates
would be invited to meet separately with the Vietnamese
women. Vivian Leburg Rothstein reported that at a conference in Vladislove, Czechoslovakia, the American women resisted the idea of a separate meeting. The Vietnamese women
insisted that women had important matters to discuss, and
then proceeded with a moving presentation of atrocities
committed against women and children—torture, rape, and
prostitution. When someone mentioned the absence of a
prominent woman delegate, the Vietnamese replied, "Well,
she's a very famous journalist, and she's accepted as a journalist. She doesn't feel the need to meet with women." While
saving face for the journalist, they gently pointed out the
source of her lack of awareness of the problem.

Later Vivian Rothstein was selected to join a delegation
to North Vietnam only because the Vietnamese had insisted
that women should be included—"That was my most clearly
women's liberation experience." In Vietnam the Vietnamese
elevated the status of women delegates further by always re-
questing that they speak first, stressing their importance in
view of the fact that there were many barriers to women becoming active, and pointing out the accomplishments of the
Vietnamese women in surmounting them.

Thus diverse forces flowed together in the summer of

1967: strong women in a movement that was increasingly alienating for women, the draft, black power, the model of the Vietnamese, and the flowering of the counterculture's emphasis on personal life and qualitatively transformed relationships. Separatism was in the cards logically, for the new left was focused on the need for all oppressed groups to organize themselves. But it would be hard for many to "liberate themselves" separately from men, exploring, in Susan Sontag's words, "the grounds of enmity, unsweetened for the moment by the dream of reconciliation."* Marge Piercy described the forces that led her to become a "house nigger" in the movement:

> Two inhibitions have acted on me constantly. One inhibition occurred in relationships where work and sexual involvements overlapped. . . .
>
> The other, stronger inhibition comes from having shared the same radical tradition, rhetoric, heroes, dates, the whole bloody history of class war. It is pitifully easy for radical women to accept their own exploitation in the name of some larger justice (which excludes half the world) because we are taught from childhood to immolate ourselves to the male and the family.[28]

Thus while logic and events pushed them toward a separate movement, women in the new left also resisted. They kept trying to find a way to be equal within the very insurgency that had built the foundation for their growing self-consciousness.

Smiling down from the cover of the convention issue of *New Left Notes* in June 1967 was a young woman with a

---

* Marge Piercy argues that there was a kind of openness in the movement about this time, a genuine interest in developing new relationships. Piercy, "Grand Coolie Damn," pp. 421–2. Susan Sontag, "The Third World of Women," *Partisan Review*, XL, no. 2 (1973), p. 185.

rifle—"The New American Woman." Inside, the schedule listed a strategy panel on the "woman question" for Tuesday morning, June 27. What actually developed was a "Women's Liberation Workshop," which hammered out an analysis and a set of demands to bring to the floor of the entire convention. There, they offered a 1967 version of the analogy between women and blacks that Casey Hayden and Mary King had explored in 1965:

> As we analyze the position of women in capitalist society and especially in the United States we find that women are in a colonial relationship to men and we recognize ourselves as part of the Third World.

The evident inadequacies of this analysis made it a shortlived one. In the context of the new left at that time, however, it served several purposes. Any activist knew that third world peoples—the Vietnamese, blacks in Africa and in the United States, Chicanos, American Indians—were oppressed. Their struggles constituted guideposts for the movement and front-page news to the entire nation. In a sense, therefore, the women were saying to SDS in the strongest language they could find, "We are oppressed as women, and our oppression is as real, as legitimate, as necessary to fight against as that of blacks, Chicanos, or the Vietnamese." They then could leap immediately to the central point of the statement:

> Women, because of their colonial relationship to men, have to fight for their own independence. This fight for our own independence will lead to the growth and development of the revolutionary movement in this country. Only the independent woman can be truly effective in the larger revolutionary struggle.

Consequently they demanded that men in the movement deal with their male chauvinism "in their personal, social, and political relationships." They called upon women to demand full participation in the movement, noting, "It is obvious from this convention that full advantage is not taken of the abilities and potential contributions of movement women," and urging the development of programs to free women from their traditional roles in the family: communal child-care centers, help with birth control and abortion, and equal sharing of housework. Finally, they recommended that an educational campaign should be conducted through articles in *New Left Notes*, bibliographies, and pamphlets, and that a committee should be established to develop an analysis of women under capitalism and to report to the December National Council with a proposed program. The statement concluded on a consoling, even defensive note:

> We seek the liberation of all human beings. The struggle for liberation of women must be part of the larger fight for human freedom. We recognize the difficulty our brothers will have in dealing with male chauvinism and we will assume our full responsibility in helping to resolve the contradiction. freedom now! we love you![29]

When the representative of the Women's Liberation Workshop concluded her reading of the statement, a man jumped up to propose that the analysis and the resolutions be separated for purposes of debate and voting. The chair calmly declared that the analysis was not open to debate or to a vote. The meeting hall erupted. Men were yelling, arguing, cursing, objecting all over the floor. But the women were adamant—or at least acting as if they were—and united. Some who had stayed out of the workshop feeling that the issue was not very important found themselves responding angrily to the derision it provoked. When someone proposed that all discussion on the issue involve only women there was applause. Some men were furious. They thought the analysis was stupid. They wanted to debate it in fine new left style and then vote it down. Finally, the meeting dissolved into a Committee of the Whole in which discussion would be allowed but no voting. Most of the men who spoke accepted the notion of a sexual caste system, but they argued strenuously against the third world analogy. The women had hit a nerve. They were on the verge of declaring independence, and men were not willing to grant that they had rights to self-determination analogous to those the movement accorded blacks. More important than their words, perhaps, was the tone of the meeting. Apparently the discussion was a hard one for men even to listen to, and they retaliated by creating a "constant hubbub" of noise interspersed with derisive hoots and catcalls.[30]

Finally the session reconvened and passed the programmatic section. It all duly appeared in *New Left Notes* alongside a cartoon of a girl—with earrings, polkadot minidress, and matching visible panties—holding a sign: "We Want Our Rights and We Want Them Now." SDS had blown its last chance.

8

The Dam Breaks

Realizing that this is a social problem of national significance not at all confined to our struggle for personal liberation within the Movement, we must approach it in a political manner. Therefore it is incumbent on us, as women, to organize a movement for women's liberation.

—"To the Women of the Left," Chicago, 1967

By 1967 a generation of women in the new left had built on the precedents of people like Casey Hayden and Carol McEldowney and begun to assert their own leadership abilities. In the south, in ERAP, and in personal struggles for self-definition, they had gained a new maturity and self-confidence as they broke through the boundaries of traditional womanhood. Yet as they did so they simultaneously experienced the increased male domination of the left and felt for the first time the full force of accepted adult sex roles.

As young women just reaching adulthood in their early twenties, their relationships with men and entries into the world of work brought them face to face with expectations that may have previously been obscured. A striking number of early leaders in the women's liberation movement that emerged in the winter of 1967 had recently married—many within the previous year.* Most of these marriages were seri-

---

* For example, Heather Tobis had married Paul Booth, former national secretary of SDS and organizer of the National Conference for New Politics; Marilyn

ous attempts to form "democratic" relationships and several have lasted more than a decade. But marriage, however democratically inclined the partners might be, brought with it the cultural burden of certain expectations for both "wives" and "husbands." To discard such roles, it turned out, was no mere act of will or ideological adjustment. Indeed, such changes required a final confrontation with that part of one's identity that was labeled "housewife," and then further called for the strength to deal with the subtle expectations of one's well-intentioned but nonetheless well-socialized mate. Moreover, a high proportion of these early leaders, including most of the single women, had left the illusory equality of the undergraduate world to discover that "economic independence" for a woman often meant demeaning low-paid work. And those who had ambitiously embarked upon careers soon understood that they had to be "twice as good" to be taken seriously.*

These, then, were the women ready to take up the banner of women's liberation when, once again, the new left seemed to be disintegrating in counterpoint to the theme of black power. In sharp contrast to Casey Hayden's and Mary King's goals in 1965, the initial leaders of women's liberation groups were not interested primarily in repairing the fissures within the new left. Armed with a political rationale and the

---

Salzman had married Lee Webb, an early SDS leader and director of the Vietnam Summer Project; Vivian Leburg had married Richie Rothstein, one of the key leaders in SDS-ERAP; Anne Weills had married Robert Scheer, editor of *Ramparts;* Charlotte Bunch had married Jim Weeks when they were both students at the Institute for Policy Studies; and Pam Parker had married Robert Allen, a noted black intellectual who soon became editor of *Black Scholar.*

* For example, Jo Freeman was attempting to work as a professional photographer; Naomi Weisstein's brilliant career continued to be obstructed at the University of Chicago; Kathie Amatniek was beginning a career as a film editor in New York; Shulamith Firestone had recently entered art school; Charlotte Bunch and Marilyn Salzman were encountering galling condescension at the "leftist" Institute for Policy Studies; and Sue Munaker was facing many frustrations in student activities work at the University of Chicago.

knowledge that many women within the left were raising the issue of women's roles, they set out to create something of their own.

"The movement" in 1967 was increasingly fragmented. No single organization, region, constituency, or analysis defined or contained it any longer. The Black Panthers and the Revolutionary League of Black Workers vied with SNCC for leadership of the left wing of the black movement. The anti-war movement, having no center, spun off organizations like the National Mobilization Against the War in Vietnam, whose sole purpose was to organize demonstrations. And it spawned decentralized activities like the draft resistance and the "coffee house movement" to organize GIs. Graduates of SDS in 1967 created the Vietnam Summer Project, held a Radicals in the Professions Conference, set up a Center for Radical Research in Chicago, and continued to pour out analytical pamphlets for the Radical Education Project in Ann Arbor, Michigan. In these multiplying enclaves, female veterans of SNCC, ERAP, and the anti-war movement continued the conversations sparked by two years of sporadic debate on women within SDS. Marilyn Salzman and Sue Thrasher discussed women's roles while working in the office of the Vietnam Summer Project. Naomi Weisstein and Heather Tobis Booth led a course on women at the Center for Radical Research in Chicago during the summer of 1967. Jane Adams called a meeting of women at the SDS national office. Jo Freeman called another meeting in Chicago to plan for women's full participation at the National Conference for New Politics (NCNP).*

---

* The tensions around sex roles generated by the activism of the sixties also surfaced in many other parts of the splintered left during 1967. In the Communist Party youth camp that summer, women from the Bay Area in California (where the CP was sharply influenced by new left style) made heated criticisms of male supremacy within the party and called a separate women's caucus meet-

The NCNP, held late in August 1967, was a parting attempt by early new left leaders to pull together a "movement" out of the new left's increasingly diversified strands—black and white, adult and student, anti-war and anti-poverty. Two thousand activists from 200 organizations—most of them young veterans of civil rights and anti-war activities—converged in Chicago over Labor Day weekend in 1967. The purpose of the conference was to develop a unified left program and to nominate for the 1968 elections a presidential ticket headed by Martin Luther King and Benjamin Spock. It was a faint hope. While the activist base of the various movements may have wished for unity, the leader-

---

ing. In Seattle, a Trotskyist group that had split from the Socialist Workers Party in 1965, criticizing the SWP's failure to place a priority on "the struggle for women's emancipation," formed an organization called Radical Women that soon joined the emerging women's liberation network. And within the black movement a number of women responded with increasing concern to the anti-woman implications of arguments about the "black matriarchy" and the duty of black women not to use birth control. Fay Bellamy wrote reassuringly to Gwen Patton in August 1967:

No revolution, I don't give a shit where it is being fought, can be fought between men alone or by men alone. The women will play a great part in it. African women proved it. . . . We proved it in the civil rights movement. There are legends around persons such as yourself, Annie Pearl, Ruby Doris, Diane Nash, Mildred Forman and others who were always on the front lines. . . . I knew of you before we had ever met. [Letter in Patton's files.]

In Harlem, Black Women Enraged (BWE), organized first to aid the wife and children of assassinated leader Malcolm X, turned to anti-war organizing despite the opposition of men around them. Patricia Robinson, one of the organizers of BWE, provided counsel and support to a number of New York feminists in 1967–8 as women's liberation groups began to form.

Interviews with Barbara Easton, Mike Zagarell, Joan Jordan, Gwen Patton, Patricia Robinson, and Fay Bellamy. On Seattle Radical Women see also Richard Kirk et al., "Why We Left the Socialist Workers Party," 1965, Xerox excerpts; Melba Windoffer to Sisters [Cell 16], December 22, 1970; and Jill Severan (on behalf of Radical Women), "Women and Draft Resistance: Revolution in the Revolution," Seattle, April 1968, Schlesinger Library, Cambridge, Women's Liberation File.

ship had lost all sense of community and mutual trust. The movement had become many "movements." The center of the black struggle in the north had imbibed the bitterness and hostility of the urban ghetto. Stung by defeat and repression, blacks were ready to lash out at whites wherever they could be found. Many black leaders recognized that they needed white allies, but they were determined that this time around they—not whites—would dictate the terms. In a further ironic twist of the intertwined fate of blacks and women, the NCNP provided the final precipitant to an independent women's movement when white men, engaged in a wave of guilty liberal capitulation to black demands, patronized and ridiculed women making similar demands.

Black power was at its zenith. Separatism had meant for whites that they could only admire and emulate from a distance the black movement, which remained the touchstone of "true radicalism." When whites met with blacks again at the NCNP they seemed desperate to receive validation from them. Black delegates in turn needed to unleash their fury at American racism on the whites at the conference. For both, these pressing emotional needs proved far stronger than the desire for a strategic alliance. The politics of moralism reached new heights as the moralism of middle-class guilt clashed head on with the morality of righteous anger. Black delegates shouted: "Kill Whitey!" as they repeatedly insisted that they should cast 50 percent of the conference vote and occupy half of the committee slots though they constituted about one-sixth of the convention. In addition they demanded from this audience full of Jewish radicals a resolution condemning Zionist imperialism. Each time the conference capitulated to black demands, the majority of whites applauded enthusiastically in apparent approval of their own denunciation.[1]

While most of the conference was caught in the vortex

of emotion surrounding the black demands, a women's caucus met, chaired by Madlyn Murray O'Hare, famous for her role in banning prayer from the public schools. A radical minority led by Jo Freeman and Shulamith Firestone found the caucus still more concerned with how women could work against the war than with how they could win equality for themselves and broke off to write a militant resolution on women. Drawing on the logic of the black caucus demands, they devised a resolution requiring that women, who represent 51 percent of the population, receive 51 percent of the convention votes and committee representation. Unlike most of the people at the conference, they were not caught up in self-denial. They had learned a lesson from black power and were demanding their rights without apology. They failed, however, to perceive the dynamic of white guilt, for within the context of racial turmoil their resolution was greeted with ridicule and dismay. When the resolutions committee refused to introduce their statement, they threatened to block the microphones and finally were told that they could present their resolution after the ten resolutions that had already been agreed upon. As one of the women explained a year later:

> So there we were at the end of the Convention waiting for our resolution and they introduced Madlyn Murray's. There we were standing at the microphones, hands stretched up. [The chairman] rams [Murray's] resolution through; refuses to call on us; as soon as the whole thing is over this little kid, smaller than I am, rushes in front of me to the microphone, raises his hand, is recognized and the first thing he says is "ladies and gentlemen, I'd like to speak to you today about the most oppressed group in America, the American Indian." Shulie Firestone and about 3 or 4 other people . . . were ready to pull the place apart. Then William Pepper patted Shulie on the

head and said, "Move on little girl; we have more important issues to talk about here than women's liberation." That was the genesis. We had a meeting the next week with women in Chicago.

The women who gathered in Chicago wrote a hopeful manifesto at their first meeting: "We hope our words and actions will help make women more aware and organized in their own movement through which a concept of free womanhood will emerge." Taking literally the admonition to "look to your own oppression," they concluded that women should organize themselves. As graduates of civil rights and SDS they had little stake in any specific left organization, and, as they saw it, there should be plenty of room within the amorphous new left for a movement of women.[2]

These were women trained as organizers whose experiences of sex role ambiguity were matched by a perception that they had a potential base of support waiting to be built upon. Casey Hayden and Mary King had sent out a memo and then retreated from the movement. Cathy Cade, Cathy Barrett, and Peggy Dobbins had organized a study group but could not see the next step. Now the cumulative impact of two years of discussion removed all hesitation. The women in Chicago instinctively reached out to the female constituency generated by women's experiences in organizing, marches, demonstrations, and campus groups. These would be, they knew, the basis for the new movement they hoped to create.

In typical new left style their first impulse was to get the word out, expose the situation—women's oppression—and call on women to mobilize. They drafted a paper addressed "To the Women of the Left" for mass circulation in new left media in addition to circulation among friends in mimeograph form. In this document they traced their awareness of women's oppression to the attempt to apply the values of "justice, equality, mutual respect and dignity" in their personal lives. At that point, they found themselves up against "the solid wall of male chauvinism." Like Hayden and King, they understood that this lesson indicated something about society as a whole as well as about the movement. Unlike Hayden and King, they were able to take the next step and "approach it in a political manner" because they knew they had an audience. Modeling themselves deliberately on black power, they cautioned new left women to avoid the mistakes of the early civil rights movement: "Women must not make the same mistake the blacks did at first of allowing others (whites in their case, men in ours) to define our issues, methods and goals. Only we can and must define the terms of our struggle." As a result, they argued, " . . . it is incumbent on us, as women, to organize a movement for women's liberation."*

The background to their appeal was a new left that seemed increasingly out of control. As it spiraled into a crescendo of desperation and self-destruction—"attacking the Pentagon" in October 1967; "taking over" campuses and buildings; employing the rhetoric of "revolution" and "guerrilla warfare"—hundreds and then thousands of women flocked to the new women's groups that began appearing everywhere. The new left had begun by raising the "feminine" values of cooperation, equality, community, and love, but as the war escalated, FBI harassment increased, and ghettos exploded, the new left turned more and more to a kind of macho stridency and militarist fantasy. In such a con-

---

* "To the Women of the Left," mimeo, Chicago, n.d., Jo Freeman's files. It was reprinted as "Chicago Women Form Liberation Group," *New Left Notes,* November 13, 1967. By this time, the "left" that Chicago women addressed was almost exclusively white. In 1968, when the women's liberation movement was off and running, SNCC created a Women's Liberation Committee. See Francis Beale, "Double Jeopardy," in *Sisterhood Is Powerful,* ed. by Robin Morgan, pp. 340–52; interviews with Fay Bellamy and Gwen Patton.

similarity. In all parts of the country, women experiencing ambiguity and strain in their roles—whether as housewives, in jobs, or in the movement—and sharing a new left history suddenly discovered each other. The private experience of oppression and the intellectual perception of sexual inequality merged in the emotional realization: "I'm not alone."

Pam Parker Allen provides an exceptional case of isolation transformed into energetic leadership of the women's liberation movement, but her story contains many elements common to other women's experiences. When Pam Parker returned from her year at Spelman and a summer in Mississippi in 1964, she was full of initiative and ideas. She spent her senior year speaking in behalf of SNCC, organizing and agitating on campus at Carleton College. When she married a black activist, Robert Allen, in 1965, she was so well known for her activism that her new husband joked about being "Mr. Pam Parker." At that point, however, she lost her sense of place within the movement. Alienated by the racism of white students, sidelined in the anti-war movement by the male-focused draft issue, and tolerated in the black movement only because of her marriage, she withdrew into the roles of housewife and New York social worker. In the meantime her husband achieved such prominence as a leader of the black draft resistance movement that in the fall of 1967 he was invited to visit North Vietnam. When he left, her sense of isolation—from a movement of her own, from other women, from the awareness of worth and sense of importance civil rights had once generated in her—weighed crushingly. She gratefully accepted an invitation to visit Chicago and there met with Staughton and Alice Lynd. A few days later she was standing in the basement of Chapel House at the University of Chicago when Sue Munaker ran up to Staughton Lynd exclaiming, "We had our first women's meeting." Pam Allen's whole body responded, instantly alert. Swallowed up in her personal identity crisis—as a housewife, as a woman, as an activist—she had not imagined there would be other women willing to talk about similar problems. She turned to Sue Munaker to say, "I'm interested," and when it emerged that these women not only were talking about similar problems but also wanted to create a social movement, Pam Allen offered to organize in New York.

The early meetings Pam Allen and Shulamith Firestone set up sparked a chain reaction of excited commitment. Kathie Amatniek had spent two years in New York after leaving the south extremely alienated from the white left. She had begun a career in film editing and occasionally produced filmstrips for the anti-war movement, but she really came alive again when the women's meetings began:

> Well, when those meetings began, I felt like it was almost being back in the south. . . . I was very conscious that this was a grass roots movement again, and, you know, that these were real people, really seriously going to do something about their lives . . . that could affect people in a mass way, but the feeling was that feeling, you know: people standing up and saying, "I was shot into this movement and they're going to have to shoot me to get me out of it." Well, no one was saying quite that, but it was the same feeling.

Soon she adopted the feminist surname Sarachild, child of Sara. Rosalyn Baxandall, a long-time participant on the fringes of the New York left subculture—organizing welfare rights, planning anti-war marches—and mother of an infant son, read about the new group and searched until she found it. She offered her house as a meeting place, "and it was instantaneous love and I never missed a meeting for two years after that. . . . I'd never talked to people at that level and it just seemed incredible . . . suddenly it was a whole world of people opened up."

The excitement deepened as women began to share

their personal lives. In sharp contrast to the new left ideological debates from which they had been excluded, women found, for the first time, that they could legitimately talk about themselves, their relationships, their hopes and angers. One participant, pointing out the difference between women's liberation and other movements, noted that women "are thrilled, literally, by the certain knowledge that for once, this is their battle in which they can organize and fight without the constant struggle of being an outsider, playing a dual role."[4] Whether their secondary roles had been in civil rights or draft resistance, the responses were the same. In San Francisco, Mimi Feingold—veteran of freedom rides, CORE, and ERAP, and very much involved in the draft resistance movement—organized women in and around the Resistance. The first meeting revealed to them all that their concerns were broader than simply the role of women in the Resistance. "It was something that we had all been waiting for, for a long time. It was a really liberating experience for all of us. . . . This was finally permission to look at our own lives and talk about how unhappy we were."

In New Orleans women who had been active primarily in SNCC and SSOC were more reluctant at first. They wondered aloud whether they were really oppressed when compared to black oppression, "which we knew only too well and vividly." At the same time they began tentatively to explore personal problems with marriage and with children and decided that, though they were not sure women needed a movement, at least they should meet one more time. As the meeting formally ended, Cathy Cade mentioned casually that her boyfriend had made fun of her for going to a "women's meeting." Suddenly everyone had a story about the negative response of the man she lived with. Some had been gently teased, others harshly ridiculed, but each felt that she had had to take a strong stand simply in order to come. At that point they realized that they did indeed have a struggle to wage. Their new collective consciousness transformed the group. Cathy Cade, who had felt frustrated and fumbling in her earlier attempt to organize a women's study group, described the new meetings as a "life release":

> . . . I had been ready to move ahead and then I could. One thing became clear: that in the black movement I had been fighting for someone else's oppression and now there was a way that I could fight for my own freedom and I was going to be much stronger than I ever was. . . .

A similar process occurred among women in Boston engaged in a variety of forms of organizing—community, draft, welfare, hospital, school. Nancy Hawley explained that "though many of us were working harder than the men, we realized we were not listened to and often ignored." After several tentative conversations, she invited some friends over on a night when her husband was away. Over a bountiful dinner they began to talk.

> The flood broke loose gradually and then more swiftly. We talked about our families, our mothers, our fathers, our siblings; we talked about our men; we talked about school; we talked about "the movement" (which meant new left men). For hours we talked and unburdened our souls and left feeling high and planning to meet again the following week.*

The vitality of these exchanges and the growing sense of collective power—the knowledge that there was a *movement*

---

* Nancy Hawley was an early SDS activist, married, recently a mother, and later one of the prime movers of the women's health collective, which wrote *Our Bodies, Ourselves;* Nancy Hawley, mimeo letter to "Dear Sisters," on the origins of Boston women's liberation, October 8, 1970, pp. 1–2.

to back you up—allowed many women to claim for the first time the capacities for leadership that they had already developed. Naomi Weisstein had raised the issue of women's oppression for years, led classes at the Center for Radical Research and at the University of Chicago, but remained terrified of speaking at mass gatherings. As it gradually dawned on her that a social movement of women was emerging, she felt herself transformed. No longer afraid, because she was no longer alone, she soon became one of the most effective orators of the women's liberation movement:

> The women's movement really gave me my voice. Before I was never very good, but with the women's movement I [was] really thunderingly effective, sometimes five minute standing ovations. Very interesting that at the Jeanette Rankin Brigade where I got up and did all the wrong things and got booed, it didn't crush me at all, because I had a movement and the movement was behind me.

On the other hand, the vitality itself could be frightening. This was a movement without barriers. The young women had not begun with a legalistic definition of "women's rights." They were radicals, used to taking on issues and getting down to their roots whatever the cost. And they began with a high level of shared cultural alienation. Personal life had already been politicized in the rebellions against parents, in the emergence of new, alternate lifestyles, in life-shattering decisions about resisting the draft, leaving school, going to jail. "Freedom" and "liberation" were absolutes—to be fought for and won. But whom would they fight? Men? Their husbands and boyfriends? The rest of the left? The consumer society? Maybe even themselves as well. While some women claimed their new strength joyfully, others cringed inwardly, wanting independence but insecure about their capacity to sustain it, fearful that no one could love an independent woman, afraid to test their conviction against male ridicule and rage. As Carol Hanish, a southern woman who had worked with SCEF in the south, described her experience in the New York group in a memo to SCEF (Southern Conference Educational Fund) women:

> . . . I want to say this whole movement is the most exhilarating thing of my life. The last eight months have been a personal revolution. Nonetheless, I recognize there is dynamite in this and I'm scared shitless.

To many women the sudden development of women's liberation groups appeared to be spontaneous and random. In fact, most of the groups were the conscious creation of friendships and contacts made through the movement and internal media. Such networks provided a larger context for each small group and thus permitted the mobilization of a social movement.[5]

In Chicago the first group consisted of long-time activists and organizers whose roots were primarily in the civil rights movement and ERAP. Within six months they had organized four additional groups in the Chicago area. New York women's liberation formed when Shulamith Firestone joined Pam Allen in New York City. Their first recruits came from an SDS women's caucus, an SDS regional meeting at Princeton, and an article in the *National Guardian*.* Other

---

* The four groups included a women's caucus of the University of Chicago SDS chapter, which later became the Women's Radical Action Project, famous for its defense of Marlene Dixon; staff in the Citizens for Independent Political Action (CIPA) and wives of organizers in CIPA; a group of married women in Hyde Park, many of whom had been to the south or had been active in early SDS; and a women's caucus of the New University Conference (NUC). Early members of women's liberation in Chicago included Jo Freeman (FSM, SCLC); Naomi Weisstein (CORE, SDS); Heather Tobis Booth (SNCC, COFO, SDS); Vivian Leburg Rothstein (SNCC, COFO, FSM, JOIN); Amy Kesselman (civil rights,

collectives soon appeared as the word spread through the media and as the original group split and subdivided.

In Canada a women's liberation group similar to the caucuses in SDS developed in September 1967, at the founding meeting of the New Left Committee, successor to the Student Union for Peace Action (SUPA). That collective included Kathy McAfee, with a background in SDS; Myrna Wood, from SNCC; and Judi Bernstein, who had worked in JOIN. During the fall Judi Bernstein visited the Chicago group, where papers were exchanged, and the New Left Committee's *Bulletin* printed the Chicago paper "To the Women of the Left." *

A number of groups formed following the Jeanette Ran-

---

peace, CIPA); Fran Rominsky (CIPA); Sara Evans Boyte (SDS, civil rights, Vietnam Summer); Susan Munaker (World University Service, SDS, civil rights); Laya Firestone; and Linda Freeman (SDS).

The New York group included Shulamith Firestone (NCNP); Pam Parker Allen (SNCC); Kathie Sarachild (TOCIN at Harvard, SNCC); Rosalyn Fraad Baxandall (welfare rights organizing, anti-war, SDS); Cathy Barrett (SSOC, SDS, New Orleans women's course); Peggy Dobbins (SSOC, SDS); Beverly Grant (SDS); Anne Koedt (SDS); and Carol Hanish (SCEF). Robin Morgan joined within a few months.

* The Canadian women presented a paper to the founding convention of the New Left Committee that illustrated the closely parallel developments in Canada and the United States:

> The myth of participatory democracy is just that if one looks at the participation of women in SUPA . . . one sometimes gets the feeling that we are like a civil rights organization with a leadership of southern racists.
>   Sister, do these words reflect any of the thoughts you have secretly had? . . . The time has come to let them out. Such flowers of wisdom are blooming all over among the fairer sex. An important part of the Goderich Conference and the forming of the New Left Committee was the articulation, for the first time, of the feelings of frustration and exploitation of the women in the movement. We had finally come to the point where we could say, all right, if we are really serious about changing our role, then we better start doing it—no one is going to do it for us. (It would hurt his ego too much) (*New Left Committee Bulletin* [October 1967], p. 6).

See also *New Left Committee Bulletin* (November 1967) for a reprint of the Chicago paper. Women in both countries felt that the movements were closely tied together.

kin Brigade, an anti-war demonstration organized by a coalition of old-line women's peace organizations on January 15, 1968. On January 14 and again on the day of the demonstration, new left women from all over the country met to talk about organizing women's groups. Women came from New York and Chicago to proselytize their new movement. They met with fifty women from fourteen cities and shared their experiences. Immediately afterwards collectives formed in Washington, D.C., Berkeley, California, and several other cities.*

Shortly after that the "word" came to Boston from two directions. Kathie Sarachild of New York had visited in late 1967 and talked to an old high school friend, Nancy Hawley, and to Marya Levenson, both of whom were actively involved in community and anti-war organizing. Later, they were invited by Sarachild and friends from ERAP to attend some of the early national meetings of women's liberation. In addition, Roxanne Dunbar, who had been active in the new left on the west coast, moved to Boston in the summer of 1968 and started Cell 16 by placing an ad in an underground newspaper. The group that convened in response ranged from welfare mothers to daughters of the upper class, and it expressed a radical militance that influenced many other groups. They read, as their first order of business, Valerie Solanis's "SCUM Manifesto."†

---

*The Washington group formed around the Institute for Policy Studies. Marilyn Salzman Webb provided the initial push—she had visited Chicago several times and was close to Sue Munaker and Heather Booth. The group also included Sue Orin (WUS) and Charlotte Bunch (civil rights, UCM). The Berkeley group was initiated by Anne Weills Scheer and Eda Hallinan, and included Anne Bernstein, Liz Bunding, Elaine Greenberg, Sydney Halpern, Zoe Isonn, Susan Lyndon, Lisa Mandel, Connie Miller, and Suzy Nelson.

† Cell 16 included Roxanne Dunbar, Jeanne Lafferty, Dana Densmore (daughter of longtime activist Donna Allen, a founder of Women's Strike for Peace), Lisa Leghorn, Abby Rockefeller, Betsy Warrior, and Jayne West. The group published an influential early journal, *No More Fun and Games.*

Women in San Francisco were hardly affected at all by the organization in Berkeley. Rather, they mobilized when Mimi Feingold distributed copies of Sue Munaker's paper, "A Call for Women's Liberation," written for *The Resistance*, January 1968, and when Pam Allen moved there from New York in the summer of 1968. They adopted the nonsense name of Sudsofloppen.* Other groups in California developed out of media contacts. Mary Lou Greenberg organized one group within the Resistance at Palo Alto. An apparently spontaneous meeting at San Francisco State turned out to have been inspired from Chicago as well. Marilyn Webb wrote to Heather Booth:

> I just spoke to Anne Scheer and she told me something you might be interested in. A girl named Sharon Gold started a large, really growing women's thing at San Francisco State. Anne thought it came out of nowhere . . . but remember all the time you spent talking with her last year? It really changed her around. . . . By the way, that happened with me, too, after talking with you then. . . . Thanks, kiddo.[6]

Finally, in the south long-time activists in CORE and SDS in Gainesville, Florida, read the *New Left Notes* accounts of the women's caucus at the 1967 SDS Convention and of the subsequent formation of women's liberation groups. Judith Brown and Beverly Jones wrote a paper in response to the SDS women, arguing strongly for an independent movement for female liberation. Their collective did not begin, however, until Judith Brown had attended a meeting of feminists at Sandy Springs, Maryland, where she immediately formed close bonds with two New York

---

*Early members of Sudsofloppen included Pat Hansen (SDS, ERAP, civil rights) and Anne Farrar (Naomi Weisstein's former roommate at Wellesley).

women—Kathie Sarachild and Carol Hanish. She returned to Gainesville and organized a women's caucus out of the SDS chapter.[7] And another southern group began when two women from Chicago moved to Durham, North Carolina, in the summer of 1968.

Thus the proliferation of women's groups that had begun in the fall of 1967 continued throughout the year and into 1968 at an astounding rate. One participant recalled, "I had never known anything as easy as organizing women's groups—as easy and as exciting and as dramatic."[8] As the groups began to form, differences in style and ideology also quickly emerged. It could hardly have been otherwise; the left as a whole was moving into a period of fragmentation, suspicions, and mutual recrimination. The new movement of women reflected both the weaknesses and the strengths of the background from which it came. Yet for all its problems, the women's liberation movement was infused with a vitality that was rapidly ebbing in other parts of the left. The tide was at flood.

9

Personal Politics

[T]here is no private domain of a person's life that is not political and there is no political issue that is not ultimately personal. The old barriers have fallen.
                        —Charlotte Bunch, "A Broom of One's Own:
                        Notes on Women's Liberation Program
                        Since the *motive* Magazine Issue"

By the late 1960s it was dramatically apparent that most American women's lives bore no relation to the happy housewife image of the 1950s. And like the proverbial child who pointed out that the emperor had no clothes, it was America's youth who first heralded the discrepancy between myth and reality. Young women from the new left had torn away with intrepid zeal and directness the shrouds of ambiguity and mystification surrounding women's roles. Kathie Sarachild compared their new examination of personal experience with the seventeenth-century struggle against the scholastics and dogmatists who clung to ancient texts on anatomy despite the very different facts revealed by dissection: "So they'd deny what they saw in front of their eyes, because Galen didn't say it was there." Thus the women's liberation movement was initiated by women in the civil rights movement and the new left who dared to test the old assumptions and myths about female nature against their own experience and discovered that something was drastically wrong. And they dared because within these movements they had learned to respect themselves and to know their own strength. They could do so because the new left provided an egalitarian ideology, which stressed the personal nature of political action, the importance of community and cooperation, and the necessity to struggle for freedom for the oppressed. They had to dare because within the same movement that gave them so much they were simultaneously thrust into subservient roles—as secretary, sex object, housekeeper, "dumb chick."

The feminine mystique of the 1950s had blinded American women to the realities of their experience. It had depicted happiness where there was frustration. It projected the idea of pleasant housework where that often meant the additional burden of another full-time job. The mystique drew on centuries of tradition and specifically on the separation between the home and work spheres in the modern economy. Yet industrial capitalism, which once had pushed women to the periphery of the paid economy and remodeled the family into a private enclave, now drew women back into the labor force.[1] While the expansion of government and the service sector of the economy pulled women into jobs outside the home, such workers still found themselves performing subservient tasks. And they received in the public sphere, as they had in the private, a low evaluation of their work and worth—this time expressed in the form of low pay and job discrimination. As the public and private spheres interpenetrated, the inherited roles proved less and less adequate as sources of identity and self-esteem. Traditional definitions could not encompass, explain, or help women to cope with the new realities of their lives. Thus, only a movement that simultaneously challenged their roles in both the home and the outside workplace could have tapped the pain and anger of most women and moved them to action.

The new feminist movement made its explosive debut in

the Miss America demonstration of August 1968. With a
sharp eye for flamboyant guerrilla theater, young women
crowned a live sheep to symbolize the beauty pageant's objectification of female bodies, and filled a "freedom trashcan"
with objects of female torture—girdles, bras, curlers, issues of
Ladies' Home Journal. Peggy Dobbins, dressed as a stockbro-
ker, auctioned off an effigy of Miss America: "Gentlemen, I
offer you the 1969 model. She's better every year. She walks.
She talks. She smiles on cue. *And* she does housework." Even
though the coverage of such events was likely to be deroga-
tory—in reports of the Miss America demonstration the
media coined the term "bra-burner"—the dramatic rise in
media coverage in 1969 and 1970 provoked a massive influx
of new members into all branches of the feminist movement.[2]

The experiences of the first few women's liberation
groups were repeated hundreds of times over. Young
women's instinctive sharing of their personal experiences
soon became a political instrument called "consciousness-
raising." The models for consciousness-raising ranged from
the earliest SNCC meetings, to SDS's "Guatemala Guerrilla"
organizing approach, to the practice of "speaking bitterness"
in the Chinese revolution. It evolved into a kind of phe-
nomenological approach to women's liberation. Kathie Sarachild advocated that women should junk all the old theories
and start from scratch, relying on their own experience: "In
our groups, let's share our feelings and pool them. Let's let
ourselves go and see where our feelings lead us. Our feelings
will lead us to ideas and then to actions." Thus consciousness-raising became both a method for developing theory and
a strategy for building up the new movement.[3]

Consciousness-raising exemplified both the frontal assault on sex roles and the personalized approach to politics
that soon became hallmarks of the proliferating new feminist
groups. The radical democracy of the new left carried over

into an unequivocal assertion of sexual equality and an impatience with any belief that women should be treated or expected to act differently from men. The notion that women were different but equal, argued by biological determinists, sounded to the new movement like the "separate but equal" rhetoric of southern segregationists. And their demands led beyond equal *rights*, in formal terms, to a demand for equality of power. Thus they inspired a thorough critique of personal life and of the subtleties of an oppression that was at once internal and external.

The focus on the personal experience of oppression, moreover, led to the creation of small groups within which women could share with mutual trust the intimate details of their lives. Formed almost instinctively at first as radical women gathered in each others' living rooms to discuss their needs, these small groups quickly became the primary structure of the women's revolt. They provided a place, a "free space," in which women could examine the nature of their own oppression and share the growing knowledge that they were not alone.[4] The qualities of intimacy, support, and virtual structurelessness made the small group a brilliant tool for spreading the movement. Anyone could form a group anywhere: an SDS women's caucus, a secretarial pool, a friendship circle, a college dorm, a coffee klatsch.

Each small group—and soon there were thousands—created a widening impact among the families, friends, and co-workers of its members. Soon the radical ideas and cooperative forms of the women's movement were reshaping the more conservative, tightly structured "women's rights" branch of the movement. Within a few years NOW had strengthened its positions on issues like abortion and lesbianism and had considerably changed its style. In several cities NOW became the chief instigator of new consciousness-raising groups. Individual leaders responded as well, for the new movement awakened them to the broader aspects of their feminism. For instance, theologian Mary Daly advocated "women's rights" in the Church when she wrote *The Church and the Second Sex* in 1968. Several years later she had become a leading exponent of a feminist theology that challenged patriarchal images of God.[5]

As feminist ideas and rebellions spread into mainstream institutions—business offices, churches, and the mass media —the advertising and publishing industries, quick to perceive a shift in public mood, tried to make the best of it. By the mid-seventies advertisers had added new appeals to their repertory; in addition to the old standbys about women as sex objects and the glories of housework, they sought to capitalize upon the frustrations of the housewife who feels harried and unappreciated ("You deserve a break today") and even upon the anxieties of the husband who must prepare dinner when his wife is late from work. A spate of books and novels after 1969 by and about women signaled the publishing industry's assessment of the importance of women's liberation. Textbooks were revised to eliminate blatant sexual and racial stereotypes. New words appeared in print: "Ms.," "chairperson," "congressperson." Editors thought twice about using some of the old ones, like "mankind." Liberation, it seemed, was becoming big business.[6]

The combined impact of women's liberation and the women's rights branches of the new feminism rocked institutions of higher education. Women in the New University Conference, a new left group, joined with a large constituency of professional women, many already active in NOW, to form women's caucuses within academic professions. Normally staid professional meetings began to ring with acrimony as women cried "foul" about hiring, admissions, and promotion practices. Then exercising the intellectual tools of their disciplines on the substance of the disciplines themselves, they criticized the male biases involved in the treatment of women and sex roles. Thus armed with new questions and mutually supportive organizations, women generated an outpouring of scholarly studies on the sociology of family and sex roles, female psychology, women's history, and literature by and about women. Women's studies programs encouraged interdisciplinary cross-fertilization and provided points of intersection with the women's movement itself.

The dramatic growth of feminism—a term that itself signaled the blurring lines between women's liberation and women's rights—affected political institutions as well. The women's rights movement had first coalesced around support for the Equal Rights Amendment and Title VII of the Civil Rights Act. Younger radical women pushed hardest for the issues that they felt struck closer to women's fundamental oppression—abortion and child care. As imaginative public presentations, mass demonstrations, and widespread publicity reinforced their lobbying, liberal politicians leaped on the bandwagon and for a moment all the bulwarks seemed to be crumbling. In 1972, after more than fifty years of sporadic debate, Congress passed the Equal Rights Amendment and sent it to the states for ratification. The EEOC and HEW stopped treating discrimination against women as a joke. The Supreme Court ruled that abortion in the first three months of pregnancy was a medical problem to be settled privately between patient and doctor. A bill for massive federal funding of child care found heretofore unheard of support in Congress. For a time it seemed that the power of an aroused, united mass movement of women was irresistible.

Within a few years the women's liberation movement had spread through many layers of American society. Where the public ideology of groups like NOW had originally focused on legal inequities and formal rights, the newer revolt made a critique of family and personal life the very cornerstone of its existence. Without such a critique there would likely have been a strong feminist lobby, for the severe pressures on professional women ensured that they would participate in the reform impetus of the sixties. But there would have been no mass insurgency. For most American women only a movement that addressed the oppression at the core of their identity could have generated the massive response that in fact occurred. Women from the new left had been able to penetrate to the essence of their roles because of their specific experiences in the 1960s, which facilitated the emergence of an insurgent group consciousness.

The issue of consciousness-formation has been posed most often by theoreticians writing from a Marxist perspective. Marxists have distinguished between the concept of a class in itself (one that exists according to objective criteria) and a class for itself (one with a self-conscious collective identity, able to act on its own behalf). Yet despite the Marxist concern with class, the question of how class consciousness develops remains virtually unexamined.* The sociologist Neil Smelser posits the growth of a "generalized belief" which ex-

---

* For example, Karl Marx himself suggested only the most simplistic of causal links between circumstance and the formation of group consciousness, like the immiseration of the proletariat. Bertell Ollman discusses the inadequacy of traditional Marxist approaches at length in "Toward Class Consciousness Next Time: Marx and the Working Class," *Politics and Society*, 3, no.1 (1972), 1–24. See also Ralf Dahrendorf, *Class and Class Conflict in Industrial Society* (Stanford: Stanford University Press, 1959), pp. 3–156, for an extended discussion and criticism of Marx's theory of the formation of class consciousness. One important exception was the study of the growth of class consciousness among English workers in the early nineteenth century by E. P. Thompson, *The Making of the English Working Class* (New York: Vintage Books, 1963). Thompson's description of the semi-autonomous working-class structures in which workers could experiment with new ideas and form a new sense of themselves is an especially provocative and innovative treatment. According to Thompson: "The countryside was ruled by the gentry, the towns by corrupt corporations, the nation by the corruptest corporation of all; but the chapel, the tavern, and the home were their own. In the 'unsteepled' places of worship there was room for a free intellectual life and democratic experiments" (pp. 51–2). Similarly, Harry Chatten Boyte in "The Textile Industry: Keel of Southern Industrialization," *Radical*

plains a collective situation and points to a solution. His theory applies most clearly, however, to crowd and panic forms of collective behavior. When used to explain social movements, the theory implies that social protest is based on an inherently irrational leap from a generalized questioning of values or norms to specific sources of social strain. I have not concerned myself with the development of such a "generalized belief." Rather, I have presumed the existence of an objectively defined collectivity—women—and looked for the roots of the feminist consciousness that developed in the late 1960s, a consciousness analogous to that of Marx's "class for itself" in that it included an awareness of group oppression, an analysis of the sources of that oppression, and a willingness to take collective action. Karl Mannheim's assertion that the self-discovery of groups "begins with groups attempting to take stock of their position in a new situation" goes further than Smelser in explaining the emergence of contemporary feminism, but it remains tantalizing in its abstraction.[7] Examining the social roots of feminism in the fifties and sixties, I would suggest that the essential preconditions for an insurgent collective identity include:

(1) social spaces within which members of an oppressed group can develop an independent sense of worth in contrast to their received definitions as second-class or inferior citizens;

(2) role models of people breaking out of patterns of passivity;

America, March-April 1972, 4–50, develops the concept by arguing that the low level of class consciousness among southern textile workers—a group which conventional theoretical interpretations would predict should have high class consciousness—resulted precisely from the fact that they lacked such autonomous social spaces—"unsteepled places of worship"—since all institutions were dominated by mill management in the mill villages. To my knowledge, these treatments are the first to explore the concept of such "free institutional space" as playing a central role in emerging group consciousness among oppressed groups.

(3) an ideology that can explain the sources of oppression, justify revolt, and provide a vision of a qualitatively different future;

(4) a threat to the newfound sense of self that forces a confrontation with the inherited cultural definitions—in other words, it becomes impossible for the individual to "make it on her own" and escape the boundaries of the oppressed group; and finally

(5) a communication or friendship network through which a new interpretation can spread, activating the insurgent consciousness into a social movement.*

These preconditions evolved as young women participated in the southern civil rights movement, particularly SNCC, and in the northern new left, particularly ERAP.

Women from the new left explained the sources of their new awareness by pointing to the discrepancy between the movement's egalitarian ideology and the oppression they continued to experience within it. What they failed to perceive, however, was the fact that the new left did more than simply perpetuate the oppression of women. Even more importantly, it created new arenas—social space—within which women could develop a new sense of self-worth and independence; it provided new role models in the courage and capability of southern black women and female community leaders; and having heightened women's self-respect, it also allowed them to claim the movement's ideology for themselves. The point at which they did so came when the movement that had opened for them a new sense of their own potential simultaneously thrust them into menial do-

---

* Freeman, *Politics of Women's Liberation*, pp. 44–70, describes the importance of the communication network from the new left to the emergence of the women's movement. I hope that other studies will test the applicability of the specific preconditions for group consciousness proposed above.

mestic roles. Feminism was born in that contradiction—the threatened loss of new possibility.*

Moreover, as conditions within the new left permitted young women to reexamine and reinterpret their own experiences, their situation also proved parallel to that of millions of American women far beyond the enclaves of the left. Indeed, it represented in microcosm the dilemma of most American women, trapped in an obsolete domestic role while new realities generated an unarticulated sense of greater potential. Although women's liberation was shocking and alienating to many, especially as seen through the magnifying lens of a hostile media, the reactions to the outcry on behalf of women's equality indicated that feminism had tapped a vein of enormous frustration and anger. The Harris Survey found in 1971 that 62 percent of American women believed that women had to "speak up" in order to accomplish anything, although most of them disapproved the tactics of picketing and protest and did not support "efforts to strengthen and change women's status in society." Nearly five years later, after the intervening upsurge of activism, 65 percent endorsed such efforts. Previously, ambivalence and fear of change had made women even less likely than men to advocate greater sexual equality. But by 1975 a new sense of rights and possibilities had led women to assert their belief in equal rights and opportunities for females in greater numbers

---

* Alice Rossi, ed., *The Feminist Papers: From Adams to de Beauvoir* (New York: Columbia University Press, 1973), pp. 241–81, describes the social roots of the first American feminist movement. Rossi argues that "[it] was in the abolition movement of the 1830s . . . that American women first showed some corporate expression of their political will, and it was from this movement that the women's-rights leaders acquired the ideas about political organization which they applied to their own cause in the late 1840s." See also Carroll Smith-Rosenberg, "Beauty, the Beast and the Militant Woman: A Case Study in Sex Roles and Social Stress in Jacksonian America," *American Quarterly*, 23, no. 4 (1971), 562–84, for an interpretation that stresses the conflict between the cult of "true womanhood" and the actual life of the homemaker.

and with greater intensity than men. Similarly, on specific issues such as abortion, child care, and the Equal Rights Amendment, opinion polls recorded a steady shift in public opinion toward the endorsement of feminist programs. By the bicentennial year, 1976, the *Reader's Digest* conceded: "Women's Liberation has changed the lives of many Americans and the way they look at family, job and sexual equality." Nearly a decade after the women's movement began, the confused response of most American women would be: "I'm not a women's libber, but . . . I believe women ought to be equal."[8]

Within the context of such massive shifts of opinion, as millions of women readjusted their view of themselves and of the world, many thousands also moved to activism and into the burgeoning women's liberation movement. But success was not without its problems: neither the leaders nor the organizational structures could maintain a unified movement. And at the same time that the issue of sexual equality had become a subject of dinner conversation in households across the nation, the new revolt suffered from internal weaknesses inherited from the new left.

Radical women had used their organizing skills to set up literally thousands of small groups within which hundreds of thousands of women transformed their perceptions of personal inadequacy into a political analysis of women's oppression. They created dozens of journals and newspapers through which they could share and develop these new ideas and actions. The dynamic excitement of such groups sprang in part from their infusion with the anarchist democracy and spirit of radical egalitarianism characteristic of the early new left. Yet the anti-leadership consensus proved inadequate as a basis for organization. A preoccupation with internal process—the effort to live out the revolutionary values of egalitarianism and cooperation within the movement itself—

took precedence over program or effectiveness. As a result, women's groups tended to oscillate between total formlessness at one extreme or a kind of collective authoritarianism on the other. To avoid hierarchies, some groups invented systems of lots for selecting who would be on committees or write or type a press release, even who would speak in meetings. A former member of the Feminists in New York City described how "they made the lot system into a religion, lotting each other to death. The principle of equality was distorted into an anti-individualist mania."[9] Keen insights into the way in which women had been repressed by hierarchical structures thus developed into moral imperatives that were out of touch with the necessary tension between means and ends. Women who developed an ability for public leadership within the insurgency received harsh criticism for being "stars." On the one hand, if they shared the movement's anti-authoritarianism, they quickly withdrew, stung by the criticism. Naomi Weisstein, for instance, felt that the women's movement had given her a voice and then taken it away again; as a result, the women's revolt wasted the very talents it needed most. And on the other hand, women who refused to withdraw from public view operated as spokeswomen for women's liberation when in fact there was no structural means of holding them responsible for what they said and did. Thus, Roxanne Dunbar, brilliant, charismatic, and authoritarian, traveled the country representing only a small group of followers, but to the media she became an important symbol of the new feminism.

The lack of structure and of responsible leadership led, inevitably, to a loss of internal coherence as the women's liberation movement expanded. This fragmentation was intensified by the obstacles and defeats that the women's movement encountered, analogous to those of the civil rights movement and the anti-war protest. New left women,

emerging from a movement high on visions of immediate revolution, failed to perceive initially that the profound changes
they desired would arouse intense opposition and that the
process of change itself would of necessity be long and la-
borious. As a result, they often deprecated their achievements and failed to claim the concrete victories that were
won.

In the beginning, radical women believed that if they
pointed out the inequities in women's position, at the very
least their comrades on the left would understand. And with
a united, egalitarian movement, they would quickly be able
to revolutionize society. They rapidly met the full force of
social tradition on the one hand, however, and the realities of
the left culture on the other. After a child-care bill had sailed
through Congress, Richard Nixon explained his ringing veto
by saying that the family must be protected and women
should stay at home with their children. And on the left,
while a few men responded openly and honestly, others paid
guilty lip service and many were obscenely hostile. "Take her
off the stage and fuck her," shouted members of the audience
as Marilyn Salzman Webb spoke to an anti-war rally in January 1969. Thus, young women in their small groups found
themselves floundering in a morass of left-wing hostility and
establishment derision. As both left and right labeled them
"man-haters" when they demanded equality, they became
acutely sensitized to the way in which it seemed that the
whole culture was biased against women. One new recruit
described her change in consciousness: "I couldn't walk
down the street, read advertisements, watch TV, without
being incensed . . . at the way women are treated." Robin
Morgan's anger grew in the year that she edited *Sisterhood Is
Powerful,* an anger that came "from deep down and way
back, something like a five-thousand-year buried anger." She
continued, "It makes you very sensitive—raw, even, this
consciousness."[10]

The rage, the sensitivity, and the overwhelming, omnipresent nature of "the enemy" drove parts of the women's movement into ideological rigidities, and the movement splintered as it grew.[11] Who could say what was *the* central issue: equal pay? abortion? the nuclear family? lesbianism? welfare policies? capitalism? Groups formed around particular issues, constituencies, and political styles, many sure that they had found the key to women's liberation. After 1970, women's liberation groups in all parts of the country suffered painful splits variously defined as politico/feminist, gay/straight, anti-imperialist/radical feminist.

Yet while some became disillusioned at the fragmentation, the movement continued to spread. Certain more radical branches mellowed and grew critical of their own purism. They recognized that consciousness-raising, as an essentially intellectual mode of radicalization, could not address the daily needs for health care, child care, equal pay, and decent housing of minority and working-class women. At the same time former conservatives were radicalized. The National Organization for Women gradually assumed primary responsibility for creating new consciousness-raising groups and absorbed much of the new left heritage with its slogan: "Out of the mainstream—and into the revolution." But no single organization was able to capture the energy and enthusiasm aroused by the women's revolt and convert it into a sustained power base from which women could demand political and social change.

The difficulties of achieving change grew further as the spread of feminist ideas provoked opposition. Predictably, the traditionalists organized a reaction to turn back the Equal Rights Amendment, proscribe abortion, punish homosexuality, and in general return women to a subservient domesticity.[12] But for all their vehemence and occasional victories, their arguments drew on visions of a mythic past in which women and men knew their places and the patriarchal family served as the stable foundation of a static social order. Although there was reaction, there could be no return.

By the late seventies the realities, both economic and cultural, were far different from those of the 1950s. Not only did 46 percent of American women work outside the home, but just over 50 percent of those with school-age children and no preschoolers had joined the labor force. The decline of women in the professions—relative to men it was a persistent decline after 1920—reversed dramatically in the late 1960s. No longer did most women marry at an early age with the expectation of a lifetime career as a housewife. In contrast to the baby boom of the 1950s, the birthrate fell to a simple population replacement level in the 1970s. Young women anticipated smaller families. Fewer in 1974 expected to have four or more children than did women during the depths of depression in the thirties. Thus among the majority of American women who received wages for their work, or attended college, or entered professional fields, the myth that all women were or ought to be at home was fading fast. By 1975 a scant majority of 51 percent believed that "taking care of a home and raising children is more rewarding for women than having a job." And that number was 20 percentage points lower than the number in 1970. When the Harris Survey questioned women in December 1975 about the reasons they worked outside the home, they expressed a strong desire for financial independence and more than ever before defined their work as economically necessary for themselves and their families.[13]

As the women's movement dispersed, splintered, formed, and re-formed, its importance lay less and less with the specific groups who initiated it and more with the kinds of responses it made possible. Decentralization hid from many radical women the impact of their ideas as the experiences that had provoked and formed a feminist consciousness in the first place re-created themselves not only beyond the new left, but beyond the middle class as well. In thousands of consciousness-raising groups; in hundreds of health clinics, rape-crisis centers, shelters for battered women; in the proud assertion of lesbian community and culture; in feminist therapy collectives and the growing research on female sexuality from the female point of view; in magazines and newspapers addressed to women; in feminist caucuses and women's studies programs; in feminist publishing houses; in the Conference of Labor Union Women (CLUW) and the National Black Feminist Organization (NBFO)—the process repeated and renewed itself as questions and possibilities deepened and spread.*

Like many suburban housewives Jan Schakowsky felt isolated in 1968 and 1969. She had few female friends and saw little chance to find help and support from other women. "I felt real different; my kids were both in diapers; I felt totally trapped." Then she began to hear and read about the women's movement, "about the injustices, and I started reading, you know, even women's magazines, and watching the talk shows." Her days became consumed not only with diapers but also with news of feminism. "By the time my husband walked in the door all hell would break loose. He was responsible for all the evils of the world and especially

---

* See Richard F. Hamilton, *Class and Politics in the United States* (New York: Wiley, 1972), pp.151-9, 214-25, on definitions of class in the United States that are helpful in clarifying the original class base of the women's movement. He argues that the most significant break in attitudes lies between the upper-middle and lower-middle classes rather than between lower-middle and working classes. The women's movement, in these terms, was organized by women of the upper-middle class, but such women articulated problems experienced especially by women in the clerical and sales jobs of the lower middle class and in-service blue-collar jobs. On CLUW, see Patricia Cayo Sexton, "Workers (Female) Arise!" *Dissent*, 21 (Summer 1974), 380-95; on NBFO, see "Black Feminism: A New Mandate," *Ms.*, 2 (May 1974), 97-100. See also William Chafe, "Feminism of the 1970s," *Dissent*, 21 (Fall 1974), 508-17.

responsible for keeping me trapped. What kind of person was he? Didn't he understand?" Throughout this crisis in her life and marriage Jan Schakowsky drew constant support from "all those unseen people" about whom she had read. "I knew that if I ever met Gloria Steinem we would be best friends. I felt real close. *Ms.* magazine, I read it totally uncritically. I didn't care what kind of bullshit articles were in there, it was my magazine." Knowing of no local groups related to the women's movement, she and her friends formed a consumer group as their own feminist gesture. "We talked about how the problems that we faced related directly to the fact that we were women, and the kind of changes as women that we had to go through in order to face those things." From that experience she went on to become a prominent leader of the Citizens Action Program in Chicago and later a staff member of Illinois Public Action Council.[14]

In sharp contrast, women whose initial refusal to participate in the prescribed life patterns had forced them to the periphery of American culture also found in the new ideas a handle on change and visibility. Lesbians entered the women's movement only to find that they had to struggle there, too, for autonomy and recognition. In the process, they sparked not only a movement for gay rights but also the development of a self-affirming lesbian culture. As one woman put it, "Without a sense that I go back further than my literal birth, I find it difficult to feel substantial and to resist various strains on my energy and self-respect caused by attitudes toward me both as a woman and as a lesbian." Links with other lesbians, "living next door or living years, even centuries before me," strengthened her ability to struggle for selfhood. The knowledge that her story follows the patterns of other, older ones "lets me believe in my ability to survive and accomplish." Battling alone against the dominant culture leads to a sense of hopelessness. So, "to remain isolated from the mainstream of contemporary culture may not be such a bad thing; to remain isolated from my own lesbian culture for one more day delays beyond all acceptable limits my coming into my own strength and power."[15]

The movement galvanized women who had always felt deviant and invisible (lesbians) as well as those who followed "normal" paths but also felt invisible (housewives). It also reached into the lives of the mass of women in "women's jobs"—groups considered "unorganizable" by the labor unions. Darlene Stille had worked her way through college against her parents' wishes and got a job in an insurance company in 1965. Her starting salary, lower than that of her male counterparts, was $85 a week. "I worked in a great bullpen with a lot of other people. It was noisy; it was uncomfortable; it was gloomy; it was depressing. I just couldn't believe that after all those years of effort, this is what it had come to." That "first great anger" grew as she was rejected for a supervisory post because of her sex, but it had nowhere to go. "The great anger I felt just sort of stuck there." It stayed on through other jobs ("I just had this notion that I could pull myself up by my bootstraps. And my bootstraps kept breaking.") until April 1973. Stille had avoided women's meetings, fearing that they would be just gripe sessions, but when some friends in NOW suggested that she come to an action protesting the differential treatment of women employees by Chicago businesses, she went. "I came away from that action feeling that something could be done . . . that I had seen something done, that I had seen these men sign an agreement. . . . It was the first time I had seen something accomplished other than griping." Two days later she was on a picket line· at the Kraft Food Plant, demanding equal treatment for women. "It was wonderful feeling that all this anger that had been backing up inside me now had a release, that I could bark back somehow . . . that I could find my voice in a larger community of women." Subsequently Stelle was elected chairperson of Women Employed, the organization of female employees in Chicago that had called these demonstrations.

Women Employed (WE) grew out of conversations among activists in the Chicago Women's Liberation Union who wanted to reach working women. With help from the Chicago YWCA they began to build on the insights of feminism to organize clerical employees with an eye not only to seeking equal pay and benefits, but also to the humiliating subtleties of sexism on the job. According to WE organizer Liz McPike, the success of such organizing revealed dramatic changes in consciousness among clerical workers who realized that their treatment on the job reflected their position as women. When a legal secretary was fired for refusing to make coffee, Women Employed instigated a nationally televised demonstration to protest the stereotypic assumptions involved. The woman—who announced that she made coffee at home in the mornings and had no intention of doing it again at work—was quickly rehired.

A similar organization in Boston, "9 to 5," developed out of a YWCA workshop in which a group of women sought ways to organize as office workers, teachers, homemakers, and students. Ellen Cassedy, one of the originators, pointed out that most of the women who joined 9 to 5 would preface their entrance with: "Well, listen, I'm not one of those women's libbers, but . . . ," which she interpreted as a sign that "the women's movement was very much on their minds, and they really did see this as kind of stepping into fighting for their rights, [but] didn't want to have to look different or sleep around or something to be involved." They saw themselves joining a movement, "and were kind of nervous about it."

Such nervousness persists. Change continues to be difficult and frightening. It produces reaction, backlash, but remains the only impelling choice. When the U.S. Congress offered to subsidize a national convention of women in a gesture to the 1976 International Women's Year, few understood the depths of experience, sophistication, and passion among women waiting to be tapped. The media had lost sight of the feminist movement as its impact dispersed through the society, and it focused instead on conflicts between feminist leaders and conservative women.

Yet when the national women's meeting convened in Houston, Texas, in November 1977, it demonstrated a new level of maturity and breadth in the feminist upsurge. In a hall of several thousand women, one-third of whom represented minorities, union representatives and professionals joined with old and young women; Asian American, Native American, Afro-American, and Chicana women; deaf, blind, and wheelchair-confined women. A growing note of respect crept into the news reports as seasoned political reporters marveled at the skill with which the convention was organized and run. What had been widely envisioned as a likely debacle turned out to be a dramatic statement of the changes wrought in the last decade, injecting renewed vigor and unity into the movement.

Minnesota delegate Anne Truax, like many others, had left home fearful that the convention might end up in a shambles. She returned convinced that she had lived through one of the greatest experiences of her life. The platform represented a molding of the spectrum of feminist demands from the Equal Rights Amendment and equality on the job to child care, abortion, and lesbian rights. As the meeting progressed, it became clear that the earlier divisions which had seemed so deep no longer held sway. The democratic spirit that had come out of early consciousness-raising groups now invaded a highly structured convention. A collective ethos dominated, despite the presence of many prominent women—political figures, magazine editors, three "first ladies." According to

Truax, "There was a whole lot of community [and] respect for individual viewpoints. . . . There was a great sense of democracy in that meeting." Women felt a necessity to support one another's issues in the "recognition that the rights of each of us as individuals was hanging on the unanimity with which we came to those votes. . . . Maybe some of it was sisterhood."

The women at Houston demonstrated that feminism had, in the space of a decade, generated a change that is still taking place. Today a widespread awareness that women are devalued in their traditional roles, that they receive lower pay for the same work, and that they have been used as sex objects allows millions of women to recognize their own situation and begin to assert themselves. They find strength for such self-assertion from the knowledge that other women before them have won victories: court rulings, laws against discrimination, changes in vocabulary, etiquette, and personal life. They are not alone.

Young women in the 1960s arrived at their feminist consciousness through an involvement in other causes. In the 1970s, thousands of women have become politicized first through the awareness of their own oppression. Within the women's movement they have gained strength and self-confidence and they have extended their social concerns into other arenas as well. As women move into other activities—running for political office, organizing unions and community groups, seeking new professions, agitating on issues concerning the conditions of their work, consumer protection or environmental quality—they bring with them a new level of self-awareness. Thus women are making feminism a central component of every other social concern. The new feminism has not abolished sexual discrimination and sexual divisions of labor. But it has fundamentally challenged the roles of the sexes. And sisterhood, powerful in its infancy, holds the potential to transform the future.

Appendix

SNCC POSITION PAPER (Women in the Movement)

(Name Withheld by Request, November 1964)

1. Staff was involved in crucial constitutional revisions at the Atlanta staff meeting in October. A large committee was appointed to present revisions to the staff. The committee was all men.

2. Two organizers were working together to form a farmers league. Without asking any questions, the male organizer immediately assigned the clerical work to the female organizer although both had had equal experience in organizing campaigns.

3. Although there are women in Mississippi project who have been working as long as some of the men, the leadership group in COFO is all men.

4. A woman in a field office wondered why she was held responsible for day to day decisions, only to find out later that she had been appointed project director but not told.

5. A fall 1964 personnel and resources report on Mississippi projects lists the number of people in each project. The section on Laurel, however, lists not the number of persons, but "three girls."

6. One of SNCC's main administrative officers apologizes for appointment of a woman as interim project director in a key Mississippi project area.

7. A veteran of two years' work for SNCC in two states spends her day typing and doing clerical work for other people in her project.

8. Any woman in SNCC, no matter what her position or experience, has been asked to take minutes in a meeting when she and other women are outnumbered by men.

9. The names of several new attorneys entering a state project this past summer were posted in a central movement office. The first initial and last name of each lawyer was listed. Next to one name was written: (girl).

10. Capable, responsible, and experienced women who are in leadership positions can expect to have to defer to a man on their project for final decisionmaking.

11. A session at the recent October staff meeting in Atlanta was the first large meeting in the past couple of years where a woman was asked to chair.

Undoubtedly this list will seem strange to some, petty to others, laughable to most. The list could continue as far as there are women in the movement. Except that most women don't talk about these kinds of incidents, because the whole subject is [not] discussable—strange to some, petty to others, laughable to most. The average white person finds it difficult to understand why the Negro resents being called "boy," or being thought of as "musical" and "athletic," because the average white person doesn't realize that *he assumes he is superior.* And naturally he doesn't understand the problem of paternalism. So too the average SNCC worker finds it difficult to discuss the woman problem because of the assumption of male superiority. Assumptions of male superiority are as widespread and deep rooted and every much as crippling to the woman as the assumptions of white supremacy are to the Negro. Consider why it is in SNCC that women who are competent, qualified, and experienced, are automatically assigned to the "female" kinds of jobs such as typing, desk work, telephone work, filing, library work, cooking, and the assistant kind of administrative work but rarely the "executive" kind.

The woman in SNCC is often in the same position as that token Negro hired in a corporation. The management thinks that it has done its bit. Yet, every day the Negro bears an atmosphere, attitudes and actions which are tinged with condescension and paternalism, the most telling of which are when he is not promoted as the equally or less skilled whites are. This paper is anonymous. Think about the kinds of things the author, if made known, would have to suffer because of raising this kind of discussion. Nothing so final as being fired or outright exclusion, but the kinds of things which are killing to the insides—insinuations, ridicule, over-exaggerated compensations.

This paper is presented anyway because it needs to be made know[n] that many women in the movement are not "happy and contented" with their status. It needs to be made known that much talent and experience are being wasted by this movement when women are not given jobs commensurate with their abilities. It needs to be known that just as Negroes were the crucial factor in the economy of the cotton South, so too in SNCC, women are the crucial factor that keeps the movement running on a day-to-day basis. Yet they are not given equal say-so when it comes to day-to-day decisionmaking. What can be done? Probably nothing right away. Most men in this movement are probably too threatened by the possibility of serious discussion on this subject.

Perhaps this is because they have recently broken away from a matriarchal framework under which they may have grown up. Then too, many women are as unaware and insensitive to this subject as men, just as there are many Negroes who don't understand they are not free or who want to be part of white America. They don't understand that they have to give up their souls and stay in their place to be accepted. So too, many women, in order to be accepted by men, or men's terms, give themselves up to that caricature of what a woman is—unthinking, pliable, an ornament to please the man.

Maybe the only thing that can come out of this paper is discussion—amidst the laughter—but still discussion. (Those who laugh the hardest are often those who need the crutch of male supremacy the most.) And maybe some women will begin to recognize day-to-day discriminations. And maybe sometime in the future the whole of the women in this movement will become so alert as to force the rest of the movement to stop the discrimination and start the slow process of changing values and ideas so that all of us gradually come to understand that this is no more a man's world than it is a white world.

SEX AND CASTE

A kind of memo from Casey Hayden and Mary King to a number of other women in the peace and freedom movements.

November 18, 1965

We've talked a lot, to each other and to some of you, about our own and other women's problems in trying to live in our personal lives and in our work as independent and creative people. In these conversations we've found what seem to be recurrent ideas or themes. Maybe we can look at these things many of us perceive, often as a result of insights learned from the movement:

Sex and caste: There seem to be many parallels that can be drawn between treatment of Negroes and treatment of women in our society as a whole. But in particular, women we've talked to who work in the movement seem to be caught up in a common-law caste system that operates, sometimes subtly, forcing them to work around or outside hierarchical structures of power which may exclude them. Women seem to be placed in the same position of assumed subordination in personal situations too. It is a caste system which, at its worst, uses and exploits women.

This is complicated by several facts, among them: 1) The caste system is not institutionalized by law (women have the right to vote, to sue for divorce, etc.); 2) Women can't withdraw from the situation (a la national-ism) or overthrow it; 3) There are biological differences (even though those biological differences are usually discussed or accepted without taking present and future technology into account so we probably can't be sure what these differences mean). Many people who are very hip to the implications of the racial caste system, even people in the move-ment, don't seem to be able to see the sexual caste system and if the question is raised they respond with: "That's the way it's supposed to be. There are biological differences." Or with other statements which recall a white segregationist confronted with integration.

Women and problems of work: The caste system perspective dictates the roles assigned to women in the movement, and certainly even more to women outside the movement. Within the movement, questions arise in situations ranging from relationships of women organizers to men in the community, to who cleans the freedom house, to who holds leadership positions, to who does secretarial work, and who acts as spokesman for groups. Other problems arise between women with varying degrees of awareness of themselves as being as capable as men but held back from full participation, or between women who see themselves as needing more control of their work than other women demand. And there are problems with relationships between white women and black women.

Women and personal relations with men: Having learned from the movement to think radically about the personal worth and abilities of people whose role in society had gone unchallenged before, a lot of women in the movement have begun trying to apply those lessons to their own relations with men. Each of us probably has her own story of the various results, and of the internal struggle occasioned by trying to break out of very deeply learned fears, needs, and self-perceptions, and of what happens when we try to replace them with concepts of people and freedom learned from the movement and organizing.

Institutions: Nearly everyone has real questions about those institutions which shape perspectives on men and women: marriage, child rearing patterns, women's (and men's) magazines, etc. People are beginning to think about and even to experiment with new forms in these areas.

Men's reactions to the questions raised here: A very few men seem to feel, when they hear conversations involving these problems, that they have a right to be present and participate in them, since they are so deeply in-volved. At the same time, very few men can respond non-defensively, since the whole idea is either beyond their comprehension or threatens and exposes them. The usual response is laughter. That inability to see the whole issue as serious, as the strait-jacketing of both sexes, and as so-cietally determined often shapes our own response so that we learn to think in their terms about ourselves and to feel silly rather than trust our inner feelings. The problems we're listing here, and what others have said about them, are therefore largely drawn from conversations among women only—and that difficulty in establishing dialogue with men is a recurring theme among people we've talked to.

Lack of community for discussion: Nobody is writing, or organizing or talking publicly about women, in any way that reflects the problems that various women in the movement come across and which we've tried to touch above. Consider this quote from an article in the centennial issue of *The Nation:*

> However equally we consider men and women, the work plans for husbands and wives cannot be given equal weight. A woman should not aim for "a second-level career" because she is a *woman;* from girlhood on she should recognize that, if she is also going to be a wife and mother, she will not be able to give as much to her work as she would if single. That is, she should not feel that she cannot aspire to directing the laboratory simply because she is a woman, but rather because she is also a wife and mother; as such, her work as a lab technician (or the equivalent in another field) should bring both satisfaction and the knowledge that, through it, she is fulfilling an additional role, making an additional contribution.

And that's about as deep as the analysis goes publicly, which is not nearly so deep as we've heard many of you go in chance conversations.

The reason we want to try to open up dialogue is mostly subjective. Working in the movement often intensifies personal problems, especially if we start trying to apply things we're learning there to our personal lives. Perhaps we can start to talk with each other more openly than in the past and create a community of support for each other so we can deal with ourselves and others with integrity and can therefore keep working.

Objectively, the chances seem nil that we could start a movement based on anything as distant to general American thought as a sex-caste system. Therefore, most of us will probably want to work full time on problems such as war, poverty, race. The very fact that the country can't face, much less deal with, the questions we're raising means that the movement is one place to look for some relief. Real efforts at dialogue within the movement and with whatever liberal groups, community women, or students might listen are justified. That is, all the problems between men and women and all the problems of women functioning in society as equal human beings are among the most basic that people face. We've talked in the movement about trying to build a society which would see basic human problems (which are now seen as private troubles), as public problems and would try to shape institutions to meet human needs rather than shaping people to meet the needs of those with power. To raise questions like those above illustrates very directly that society hasn't dealt with some of its deepest problems and opens discussion of why that is so. (In one sense, it is a radicalizing question that can take people beyond legalistic solutions into areas of personal and institutional change.) The second objective reason we'd like to see discussion begin is that we've learned a great deal in the movement and perhaps this is one area where a determined attempt to apply ideas we've learned there can produce some new alternatives.

"WE STARTED FROM DIFFERENT ENDS OF THE SPECTRUM"

by Cynthia Washington

In 1963, Cynthia Washington, an engineering student at George Washington University, became a member of SNCC. Within a year she was director of a freedom project in Mississippi, registering voters, organizing in the community, and holding mass meetings. She went on to head the Atlanta Center for Black Art. She was a Fellow at the Institute for Policy Studies and editor of its newsletter, The Link, *when the following excerpt from a letter to* Southern Exposure *about her experiences in the civil rights and women's movements was published in the winter of 1977. She is now a Colleague at the Public Resource Center in Washington, D.C.*

During the fall of 1964, I had a conversation with Casey Hayden about the role of women in SNCC. She complained that all the women got to do was type, that their role was limited to office work no matter where they were. What she said didn't make any particular sense to me because, at the time, I had my own project in Bolivar County, Miss. A number of other black women also directed their own projects. What Casey and other white women seemed to want was an opportunity to prove they could do something other than office work. I assumed that if they could do something else, they'd probably be doing that.

I remember driving back to Mississippi in my truck, thinking how crazy they were. I couldn't understand what they wanted. As far as I could see, being a project director wasn't much fun. I didn't realize then that having my own project made a lot of difference in how I was perceived and treated. And I did not see what I was doing as exceptional. The community women I worked with on projects were respected and admired for their strength and endurance. They worked hard in the cotton fields or white folks' houses, raised and supported their children, yet still found the time and energy to be involved in struggle for their people. They were typical rather than unusual.

Certain differences result from the way in which black women grow up. We have been raised to function independently. The notion of *retiring* to housewifery someday is not even a reasonable fantasy. Therefore whether you want to or not, it is necessary to learn to do all of the things required to survive. It seemed to many of us, on the other hand, that white women were demanding a chance to be independent while we needed help and assistance which was not always forthcoming. We definitely started from opposite ends of the spectrum. . . .

I remember discussions with various women about our treatment as one of the boys and its impact on us as women. We did the same work as men—organizing around voter registration and community issues in rural areas—usually *with* men. But when we finally got back to some town where we could relax and go out, the men went out with other women. Our skills and abilities were recognized and respected, but that seemed to place us in some category other than female. Some years later, I was told by a male SNCC worker that some of the project women had made him feel superfluous. I wish he had told me that at the time because the differences in the way women were treated certainly did add to the tension between black and white women.

At a district meeting in Mississippi, I heard Stokely's comment that the only position of women in SNCC was prone—with the exception of women who either dressed or looked like men. I was standing next to Muriel Tillinghast, another project director, and we were not pleased. But our relative autonomy as project directors seemed to deny or override his statement. We were proof that what he said wasn't true—or so we thought. In fact, I'm certain that our single-minded focus on the issues of racial discrimination and the black struggle for equality blinded us to other issues. . . .

In the late 1960s, some black women were "producing children for the black nation," while others began to see themselves as oppressed by black men. For many, black women were the most oppressed group in American society, the victims of racism, chauvinism and class discrimination. Chauvinism was often seen as the result of forces acting upon all black people, and struggle between black men and women as an effective way to keep us from working together for our common liberation. On the other hand, my son by this time was three years old; I was divorced, and the thought that anyone would want to have a child to support by themselves seemed like a mean joke. If women were becoming pregnant to counter the charge that they took "manhood" away, then the position of black women, even in movement circles, seemed to have deteriorated. To me, it was not a matter of whether male/female oppression existed but one of priorities. I thought it more important to deal with the folks and the system which oppressed both black women and black men. . . .

The white people I talked with often assumed the basic necessities. That gave them the luxury of debating ideology and many things I felt would not change the position of black women. Abortion, which white women were fighting for, did not seem an important issue for black women. Women who already had children might need abortion in the future, but in the present they needed a means to support children other than welfare, a system of child care, decent homes and medical attention, opportunities for meaningful employment and continuing education. Again, we found ourselves in different circumstances with no program or tactic to begin building sisterhood.

Over the last two years, I find myself becoming more involved with women in Washington, discussing the impact of race, class, and culture on us all and concrete ways women can help each other survive. I also find that the same black women I knew and respected during the 1960s are in the process of re-forming a network. Most of us have now spent the greater part of our adult lives as single women involved in movement activities. We have been married, divorced, some have children; we have gone from town to town, job to job, talking to each other. The problems of womanhood have had an increasing impact on us, and the directions of our own, of my own, involvement in the women's movement are still unfolding.

LIBERATION OF WOMEN

(New Left Notes, July 10, 1967)

The following analysis of women's role came out of the Women's Liberation workshop; as such it cannot be changed and is therefore not open to debate.

What is open to this body is the acceptance or refusal of programs designed to (1) free women to participate in other meaningful activities and (2) relieve our brothers of the burden of male chauvinism.

Analysis: In the world today there are three main divisions among people: those of the capitalist world, the Socialist world, and the Third World. The crisis of our time is the transformation from capitalism to socialism. The role of the Third World in this transformation is revolutionary, but an integral part of their fight is the necessity of their own independence.

As we analyze the position of women in capitalist society and especially in the United States we find that women are in a colonial relationship to men and we recognize ourselves as part of the Third World. Although we realize that our sisters in the Socialist world have problems with male supremacy, we feel that an analysis of their position would be different than ours and is not necessary for the purposes of this statement.

Women, because of their colonial relationship to men, have to fight for their own independence. This fight for our own independence will lead to the growth and development of the revolutionary movement in this country. Only the independent woman can be truly effective in the larger revolutionary struggle.

We call for all programs which will free women from their traditional roles in order that we may participate with all of our resources and energies in meaningful and creative activity. The family unit perpetuates the traditional role of women and the autocratic and paternalistic role of men. Therefore we must seek new forms that will allow children to develop in an environment which is democratic and where the relationships between people are those of equal human beings. These new forms will allow men to benefit from the experience of and responsibility for the protection and continuation of life. The following suggestions are programs which point in the direction of the new relationships which we are creating:

1) The creation of communal child care centers which would be staffed by the men and women and controlled by the staff and children involved in each center.

2) In order to help women in their struggle for independence we call for the right of women to choose when they will have children. This means (a) the dissemination of birth control information and devices to all women regardless of age and marital status, and (b) the availability of a competent medical abortion for all women who so desire.

3) Ultimately technology and automation will eliminate work which is now necessary for the maintenance of the home. Until this occurs every adult person living in the household will have to assume an equal share of the work.

People who identify with the movement and feel that their own lives are part of the base to bring about radical social change must recognize the necessity for the liberation of women. Our brothers must recognize that because they were brought up in the United States they cannot be free of the burden of male chauvinism.

1) Therefore we demand that our brothers recognize that they must deal with their own problems of male chauvinism in their personal, social, and political relationships.

2) It is obvious from this convention that full advantage is not taken of the abilities and potential contributions of movement women.

We call upon women to demand full participation in all aspects of movement work, from licking stamps to assuming leadership positions.

3) People in leadership positions must be aware of the dynamic of creating leadership and are responsible for cultivating all of the resources available to the movement.

4) All SDS chapters must recognize that campus regulations discriminate against women in particular and any program must include in its demands a call for women's rights. The above is also true of all programs conceived and initiated by SDS.

Educating people and generating discussion about the liberation of women shall be the responsibility of the internal education arm of SDS:

1) The editor of NLN [*New Left Notes*] shall solicit articles on the subject.

2) Bibliography and pamphlets on the subject shall be part of the program.

3) A committee shall be set up by the National Council to develop an analysis of the exploitation of women as producers and consumers in the American capitalist economy, and to present a report to the December NC [National Council] upon which concrete proposals of a programmatic nature can be based.

We seek the liberation of all human beings. The struggle for liberation of women must be part of the larger fight for human freedom. We recognize the difficulty our brothers will have in dealing with male chauvinism and we will assume our full responsibility in helping to resolve the contradiction. freedom now! we love you!

Notes

Chapter One

1. Philip Wylie, *Generation of Vipers* (New York: Holt, Rinehart and Winston, 1955), pp. 194–217; Marynia Farnham and Ferdinand Lundberg, *The Modern Woman: The Lost Sex* (New York: Harper & Brothers, 1947), pp. 114, 90–167, 355–77.

2. *Life* magazine (December 24, 1956), pp. 41, 46; Robert W. Smuts, *Women and Work in America* (New York: Schocken Books, 1971), pp. 149–50; Betty Friedan, *The Feminine Mystique* (New York: Dell, 1963), chapter 7; William Henry Chafe, *The American Woman: Her Changing Social, Economic, and Political Roles, 1920–1970* (New York: Oxford University Press, 1972), pp. 207–14; George Gallup and Evan Hill, "The American Woman," *Saturday Evening Post* (December 2, 1962), pp. 15–32; Peter Gabriel Filene, *Him/Her Self: Sex Roles in Modern America* (New York: Harcourt Brace Jovanovich, 1974), pp. 189–94; Robert S. Weiss and Nancy M. Samuelson, "Social Roles of American Women: Their Contribution to a Sense of Usefulness and Importance," *Marriage and Family Living*, XX, no. 4 (November 1958), 338–66; "The Fortune Survey: Women in America," *Fortune*, 34, no. 2 (August 1946), 10.

3. Stevenson quoted in Friedan, *Feminine Mystique*, p. 54; Marguerite M. Dixon, "Adolescent Girls Tell About Themselves," *Marriage and Family Living*, XX, no. 4 (November 1958), 400–1; Melvin B. Freedman, "The Passage Through College," *Journal of Social Issues*, XII, no. 4 (1956), 15–16.

4. Stevenson quoted in Friedan, *Feminine Mystique*, p. 53. For subsequent developments in the lives of the Smith College graduates to whom Stevenson spoke, see Robert Reingold, "Upheavals Among Smith Alumnae Illustrate Role Changes," *The New York Times*, November 30, 1977.

5. Ellen Keniston and Kenneth Keniston, "An American Anachronism: The Image of Women and Work," *American Scholar*, 33, no. 3

(1964), 371; Alva Reimar Myrdal and Viola Klein, *Women's Two Roles: Home and Work* (London: Routledge and Kegan Paul, 1956), p. 183; David Riesman, Nathan Glazer, and Reuel Denney, *The Lonely Crowd: A Study of the Changing American Character* (New York: Doubleday, 1953), pp. 332–3; Margaret Mead, "What Women Want," *Fortune*, 34, no. 6 (December 1946), 174–5; Friedan, *Feminine Mystique*, pp. 282–309; U.S. Department of Labor, *1969 Handbook on Women Workers*, Women's Bureau Bulletin No. 294 (Washington, D.C.: U.S. Government Printing Office, 1969), p. 33; Chafe, *American Woman*, pp. 181–95.

6. David Riesman, "The Found Generation," *American Scholar*, 25, no. 4 (1956), 431–2; Ashley Montagu, "The Triumph and Tragedy of the American Woman," *Saturday Review*, 41, no. 39 (September 27, 1958), 13–15, 34–5; Jerome Collins, "Changing Values in Ten Best Sellers of the 1930–35 and 1950–55 Periods" (unpublished Ph.D. dissertation, Harvard University, 1957), cited in Clyde Kluckholm, "Changing Values," in *The American Style: Essays in Value and Performance: A Report on the Dedham Conference of May 23–27, 1957*, ed. by Elting Elmore Morison (New York: Harper & Row, 1958), p. 170; see also John N. Brooks, *The Great Leap: The Past Twenty-Five Years in America* (New York: Harper & Row, 1966), pp. 200–1.

7. Smuts, *Women and Work*, pp. 64–5; Ravenna Helson, "The Changing Image of the Career Woman," *Journal of Social Issues*, 28, no. 2 (1972), 34; Chafe, *American Woman*, pp. 190–1, 222–4; Dean D. Knudsen, "The Declining Status of Women: Popular Myths and the Failure of Functionalist Thought," *Social Forces*, 48, no. 2 (1969), 187–8.

8. Knudsen, "Declining Status of Women," pp. 184–5.

9. Helen Hacker, "Women as a Minority Group," *Social Forces*, 30, no. 1 (1951), 68; Katherine Hamill, "Women as Bosses," *Fortune*, 53, no. 6 (June 1956), 219, 106–7.

10. Quotes from Alfred Kinsey et al., *Sexual Behavior in the Human Female* (Philadelphia: W. B. Saunders, 1953), p. 468; George Simpson, "Nonsense About Women," in *Sexual Behavior in American Society: An Appraisal of the First Two Kinsey Reports*, ed. by Jerome Himehoch and Sylvia Fleis (New York: W. W. Norton, 1955), p. 61.

11. Myrdal and Klein, *Women's Two Roles*; Smuts, *Women and Work*; National Manpower Council Reports, *Womanpower: A Statement with Chapters by the Council Staff*; *Work in the Lives of Married Women: Proceedings of a Conference on Womanpower Held October 20–25, 1957* (New York: Columbia University Press, 1957–8); Janet Zollinger Giele, "Introduction" to Viola Klein, *The Feminine Character* (Urbana: University of Illinois Press, 1971), pp. xxi–ix; Helson, "Changing Image," pp. 34–6.

12. "Young Wives with Brains: Babies, Yes—But What Else?" *Newsweek* (March 7, 1960), pp. 57–60.

13. Jean W. Campbell, "Women Drop Back In: Educational Innovation in the Sixties," and Joan Huber, "From Sugar and Spice to Professor," in *Academic Women on the Move*, ed. by Alice S. Rossi and Ann Calderwood (New York: Russell Sage Foundation, 1973), pp. 93–104, 125–35.

14. Judith Hole and Ellen Levine, *Rebirth of Feminism* (New York: Quadrangle, 1971), pp. 16–81; Lois W. Banner, *Women in Modern America: A Brief History* (New York: Harcourt Brace Jovanovich, 1974), pp. 231–3.

15. Jo Freeman, *The Politics of Women's Liberation: A Case Study of an Emerging Social Movement and Its Relation to the Policy Process* (New York: McKay, 1975), pp. 44–71.

16. See Keniston and Keniston, "An American Anachronism," pp. 355–75; and Alice Rossi, "Equality Between the Sexes: An Immodest Proposal," in *The Woman in America*, ed. by Robert J. Lifton (Boston: Houghton Mifflin, 1965), pp. 98–143.

17. NOW's formation and its early activities are described in great detail in Hole and Levine, *Rebirth*, pp. 81–95; Banner, *Women in America*, pp. 233–5; Freeman, *Politics of Women's Liberation*, pp. 71–102.

18. "Wives with Brains," reader response, *Newsweek* (March 21, 1960), pp. 2, 8; see also Filene, *Him/Her Self*, pp. 192–3.

Chapter Two

1. Angelina E. Grimke, quoted in Gerda Lerner, *The Grimke Sisters from South Carolina: Pioneers for Woman's Rights and Abolition* (New York: Schocken Books, 1971), p. 183.

2. For an examination of the link between race and sex in southern society, see Gunnar Myrdal, *An American Dilemma: The Negro Problem and Modern Democracy* (New York: Harper & Brothers, 1944), II, Appendix 5, pp. 1,073–8; Winthrop Jordan, *White Over Black: American Attitudes Toward the Negro, 1550–1812* (Baltimore: Penguin Books, 1968); Lillian Smith, *Killers of the Dream* (New York: W. W. Norton, 1949); Wilbur Joseph Cash, *The Mind of the South* (New York: Knopf, 1941); John Dollard, *Caste and Class in a Southern Town* (Garden City, N.Y.: Doubleday, 1957); and Jacquelyn Dowd Hall, "Revolt Against Chivalry: Jesse Daniel Ames and the Women's Campaign Against Lynching," Ph.D. dissertation, Columbia University, 1974, to be published in 1979 by Columbia University Press.

3. Anne Firor Scott, *The Southern Lady: From Pedestal to Politics,*

1820–1920 (Chicago: University of Chicago Press, 1970), pp. 10–13, 48–52, 136–45; Grimke quotes from Lerner, *Grimke Sisters*, pp. 193, 161–2; see also pp. 155, 157, 186; Hall, "Revolt Against Chivalry," pp. 88–112, quote from p. 89.

4. Anne Braden, *The Wall Between* (New York: Monthly Review Press, 1958), p. 230.

5. Quotes from *motive*, XIX, no. 4 (1959), 2, 6; XIX, no. 1 (1958), 33, 1.

6. See Hall, "Revolt Against Chivalry," pp. 124–6, for similar revelatory experiences in interracial meetings among women in the 1920s and 1930s.

7. Smith, *Killers of the Dream*, pp. 27–8.

8. Stembridge quoted in Howard Zinn, *SNCC: The New Abolitionists* (Boston: Beacon Press, 1964), p. 33; Clayborne Carson, Jr., "Toward Freedom and Community: The Evolution of Ideas in the Student Nonviolent Coordinating Committee, 1960–66" (unpublished Ph.D. dissertation, University of California at Los Angeles, 1975), pp. 58–78; "Statement of Purpose in 1960" section of the SNCC Constitution (1960, 1962), State Historical Society of Wisconsin Manuscript Collection, Madison, Wisconsin (hereinafter cited as SHSW), Carl and Anne Braden Papers (hereinafter cited as Braden Papers), Box 60. The SNCC statement of purpose is also quoted in Cleveland Sellers, *The River of No Return: The Autobiography of a Black Militant and the Life and Death of SNCC* (New York: William Morrow, 1973), p. 39.

9. Zinn, *SNCC*, p. 38.

10. Robert Coles, "Social Struggle and Weariness," *Psychiatry*, 27, no. 4 (1964), 313; Zinn, *SNCC*, pp. 38–9; Lucretia Collins quoted in James Forman, *The Making of Black Revolutionaries: A Personal Account* (New York: Macmillan, 1972), pp. 150–1.

11. Carson, "Toward Freedom and Community," pp. 18, 68–70; Anne Braden, "News from SCEF," a typed report, April 30, 1962, and "Statement by Diane Nash Bevel," issued April 30, 1962, in handwritten draft, SHSW, Braden Papers, Box 47.

12. Interviews with Nan Grogan and Cathy Cade; [Myrna Wood], "Ruby Doris," *New Left Committee Bulletin*, 1, no. 1 (November 1967), 8, in Jo Freeman's files.

13. Forman, *Making*, pp. 235, 238–9; Sellers, *River*, p. 53; interviews with Mary King, Jean Wiley, and Gwen Patton; see *The New York Times*, October 10, 1976, for a story on the SNCC reunion in 1976.

14. Judith Brown to Anne Braden, personal letter, September 19, 1968, SHSW, Braden Papers, Box 82.

15. Ron K. Parker, "The Southern Student Organizing Committee" (unpublished paper, January 5, 1965, in author's possession); inter-

views with Anne Braden, Sue Thrasher, Nan Grogan, Dorothy Burlage, and Gene Guerrero.

16. Anne Braden to a friend, carbon of personal letter, November 1, 1960, SHSW, Braden Papers.

17. Brown to Braden letter; Jane Stembridge to Anne Braden, personal letter, November 14, 1960, SHSW, Braden Papers, Box 62.

18. John O'Neal, "Report of Week's Activities," report to SNCC office, October 12–15, 1962, SHSW, Braden Papers, Box 47, for an example; Charles Sherrod quoted in Forman, *Making*, p. 276; interviews with Dorothy Burlage, Mary King, and Sandra Cason.

19. Richard Haley, "Statement to CORE-SED on Patricia Stevens Due," n.d., SHSW, CORE Papers, Series 5, Box 52; Sellers, *River*, p. 69; Forman, *Making*, p. 260. For an account of other young women leaders, see also the unidentified personal letter from Albany, Georgia, October 18, 1962, to the SNCC office, and the typed article entitled "Police Brutality in Southwest Georgia," 1963, SHSW, Braden Papers, Box 47.

20. "Job Description: Mary King Communications," carbon copy, n.d., Mary King's personal files, Washington, D.C.

Chapter Three

1. Elizabeth Sutherland, ed., *Letters from Mississippi* (New York: McGraw-Hill, 1965), pp. 22–3.

2. Mary Aicken Rothschild, "Northern Volunteers and the Southern 'Freedom Summers,' 1964–65: A Social History" (unpublished Ph.D. dissertation, University of Washington, 1974), chapter 2, offers a profile of the 1964 and 1965 Mississippi summer volunteers.

3. Quotes from Rothschild, "Northern Volunteers," pp. 177–8.

4. Dr. Sidney Silverman to Heather Tobis, personal letter, July 21, 1964, SHSW, Elizabeth Sutherland Papers; Heather [Tobis] to "my brother," Sutherland, ed., *Letters*, p. 110; Rothschild, "Northern Volunteers," p. 178.

5. Volunteer sheets nos. 1 and 69, 1965, SHSW, Mary Aicken Rothschild Papers (hereinafter cited as Aicken Papers); Stembridge quote from Zinn, *SNCC*, p. 7.

6. Peggy Dobbie to her parents, personal letter, June 23, 1974, SHSW, Sutherland Papers; Sandra Hard to her mother, personal letter, n.d., SHSW, Sandra Hard Papers; Avivia Futorian to unknown, personal letter, n.d., SHSW, Sutherland Papers; Sally Belfrage, *Freedom Summer* (New York: Viking Press, 1965), pp. 245–6.

7. Interview with Vivian Rothstein; see also Belfrage, *Summer*, pp. 137–61.

8. For accounts of the decision to include whites in the summer project, see Zinn, *SNCC*, pp. 181–9; Len Holt, *The Summer That Didn't End* (New York: William Morrow, 1965), pp. 35–7; Rothschild, "Northern Volunteers," chapter 1; Carson, "Toward Freedom and Community," pp. 211–27.

9. Interview with Heather Tobis Booth; Sutherland, ed., *Letters*, p. 15; Ruth Steward to her parents, personal letter, July 9, 1964, SHSW, Sutherland Papers.

10. Sutherland, ed., *Letters*, pp. 111–12, 229–30; Pam [Parker] to her parents, personal letter, August 12, 1964, Sutherland, ed., *Letters*, pp. 95–6; see also Rothschild, "Northern Volunteers," chapter 4.

11. Belfrage, *Summer*, pp. 66, 195; Jack Newfield, *Prophetic Minority* (New York: New American Library, 1966), p. 64; for other accounts of the lack of privacy and emotional strain, see Sutherland, ed., *Letters*, pp. 195–6; Sara Lieber, "Excerpts from My Letters from Mississippi," SHSW, Sutherland Papers.

12. Judy Yorke to her parents, personal letter, July 4, 1964, SHSW, Aicken Papers; Sutherland, ed., *Letters*, p. 150; Holt, *Summer*, p. 12.

13. Robert Coles and Joseph Brenner, "American Youth in a Social Struggle: The Mississippi Summer Project," unpublished paper quoted in Rothschild, "Northern Volunteers," p. 120; Mary Sue Gallaty to her parents, personal letter, August 28, 1964, SHSW, Sutherland Papers; Belfrage, *Summer*, p. 169.

14. Jan Louise Handke to unknown, personal letter, June 25, 1964, SHSW, Sutherland Papers; Zinn, *SNCC*, pp. 94–5; interviews with Jean Wiley, Gwen Patton, and Fay Bellamy.

15. Nancy to her mother, personal letter, July 8, 1964, in Sutherland, ed., *Letters*, p. 48; Jo to John and Cleo, personal letter, July 29, 1964, in Sutherland, ed., *Letters*, p. 45; for other accounts, see also Belfrage, *Summer*, pp. 234–5.

16. Peggy Dobbie to her parents, personal letter, July 1, 1964, SHSW, Sutherland Papers; Jan Louise Handke to her parents, personal letter, July 22, 1964, SHSW, Sutherland Papers; interviews with Vivian Rothstein, Heather Booth, and Mimi Feingold.

17. Interviews with Ella Baker, Fay Bellamy, Mary King, Cathy Cade, Nan Grogan, and Jean Wiley.

18. Joni Rabinowitz, "To: Student Nonviolent Coordinating Committee; From: Joni Rabinowitz, Southwest Georgia Project," April 8–21, 1963, memo, Joni Rabinowitz personal files, copy in author's possession; "another woman" quoted in Rothschild, "Northern Volunteers," p. 185.

19. Sandra Hard to Mom, John and Annette, personal letter, June 29, 1964, SHSW, Sandra Hard Papers; interviews with Staughton Lynd, Jean Wiley, Fay Bellamy, Mary King, and Betty Garman.

20. See Eldridge Cleaver, *Soul on Ice* (New York: Dell, 1968), for a

powerful and honest examination of the attitudes of black men toward white women.

21. Interview with Jimmy Garrett.

22. Interviews with Gwen Patton and Jean Wiley.

23. Interviews with Heather Booth and Pam Allen; see also Alvin F. Pouissant, M.D., "The Stresses of the White Female Worker in the Civil Rights Movement in the South," *American Journal of Psychiatry*, 123, no. 4 (1966), 401–5, for a hostile but useful analysis by a black psychiatrist.

Chapter Four

1. Interviews with Howard Zinn, Betty Garman, Jean Wiley, Gwen Patton, and Fay Bellamy.

2. Mary King to Sara Evans, personal letter, January 26, 1975.

3. "SNCC Position Paper (Women in the Movement)," mimeographed copy, Waveland, Mississippi, November 1964, in author's possession. I am grateful to Clayborne Carson, Jr., for sending this document to me. For an account of the Waveland meeting, see Carson, "Toward Freedom and Community," pp. 260–86. Interviews with Sandra Cason, Kathie Sarachild, Mary King, and Jimmy Garrett; [Myrna Wood], "Ruby Doris," *New Left Committee Bulletin*, 1, no. 1 (November 1967), in Freeman's files. See Maren Lockwood Carden, *The New Feminist Movement* (New York: Russell Sage Foundation, 1974), pp. 59–60; Robin Morgan, "Introduction," in *Sisterhood Is Powerful: An Anthology of Writings from the Women's Liberation Movement*, ed. by Robin Morgan (New York: Vintage Books, 1970), p. xxi.

4. Interview with Jimmy Garrett; Josephine Carson, *Silent Voices: The Southern Negro Woman Today* (New York: Delacorte Press, 1969), pp. 254–5.

5. Zinn, *SNCC*, pp. 186–8. See also Rothschild, "Northern Volunteers," pp. 26–7.

6. Sutherland, ed., *Letters*, p. 185; Belfrage, *Summer*, pp. 79–80.

7. Hamer quoted in Belfrage, *Summer*, p. 238; Forman, *Making*, pp. 395–6; Stokely Carmichael and Charles V. Hamilton, *Black Power: The Politics of Liberation in America* (New York: Vintage Books, 1967), p. 96. See also Carson, "Toward Freedom and Community," pp. 242–59.

8. Anne Moody, *Coming of Age in Mississippi* (New York: Dell, 1968), p. 384; interview with Jean Wiley and Betty Garman; Coles, "Social Struggle," p. 308.

9. Forman, *Making*, pp. 413–22; Pat Watters, *Down to Now: Reflections on the Southern Civil Rights Movement* (New York: Pantheon Books, 1971), p. 332; Newfield, *Minority*, p. 3.

10. Julius Lester, "The Angry Children of Malcolm X," in *Black Protest Thought in the Twentieth Century*, ed. by August Meier, Elliott Rudwick, and Francis L. Broderick (2d ed., Indianapolis: Bobbs-Merrill, 1971), pp. 477–9, 473; Forman, *Making*, pp. 441, 437–8; Debbie Louis, *And We Are Not Saved* (Garden City, N.Y.: Doubleday, 1970), pp. 208, 220–47; Carson, "Toward Freedom and Community," pp. 284–99; interview with Betty Garman.

11. Louis, *Not Saved*, pp. 239, 243.

12. Casey Hayden and Mary King, "Sex and Caste: A Kind of Memo," *Liberation*, 10 (April 1966), 35–6.

Chapter Five

1. See also Kirkpatrick Sale, *SDS* (New York: Vintage Books, 1973), pp. 40, 48n., 49n., 58n., 73–9, 82, 93n. Jim Monsonis was SDS national secretary in 1962–3.

2. Tom Hayden, "Student Social Action," from a speech delivered at CHALLENGE, University of Michigan, March 1962, reproduced by VOICE Political Party (New York: Students for a Democratic Society, n.d.); Sale, *SDS*, p. 35.

3. Kenneth Keniston, *The Young Radicals: Notes on Committed Youth* (New York: Harcourt, Brace and World, 1966); Richard Flacks, "The Liberated Generation: An Exploration of the Roots of Student Protest," *Journal of Social Issues*, XXIII (July 1967), 52–75; James Putnam O'Brien, "The Development of a New Left in the United States, 1960–65" (unpublished Ph.D. dissertation, University of Wisconsin, 1971), pp. 204–51, 83–4; Sale, *SDS*, pp. 17–22, 88–90.

4. Cason quoted in National Student Association, *Steps Toward Equality: A Report on Desegregation in the United States*, cited in O'Brien, "Development," p. 91. Cason described her spontaneous eloquence and the response it evoked as her "moment of glory." Newfield, *Minority*, p. 15.

5. Sale, *SDS*, pp. 88–9; interview with Anne Braden; SDS *Bulletin* (October and November 1963; January 1965); Literature Lists, 1965, SHSW, SDS Manuscript Collection, Series 2A (hereinafter cited as SDS-2A), Box 3.

6. Sale, *SDS*, pp. 35, 40, 49, 93; "Key List," January 18, 1963, Box 1; "Roster for the 1963 SDS Convention," Box 1; "Worklist," November 23, 1963, Box 1; SDS *Bulletin* (May 1964), Box 6; "SDS National Council Meeting Minutes," June 16, 1964, Box 2; C. Clark Kissinger, "Convention Report," SDS *Bulletin* (July 1964), Box 6; Delegate List, June 1964, National Convention, Box 2; "SDS Membership List—Boston Area," Summer 1964, Box 2; "SDS Worklist," Summer 1964, Box 2; "SDS-NC

Minutes," September 5–7, 1964, Box 2; "Worklist, New SDS members,"
Winter 1964–5, Box 7; Mailing Labels for New SDS Members, Summer
1965, Box 3; 1965 Convention Directory, Box 3, SHSW, SDS-2A.
   7. Interviews with Paul Booth, Steve Max, Sharon Jeffry, and Betty
Garman.
   8. SDS *Discussion Bulletin Supplement* (Spring 1964), SHSW,
SDS-2A, Box 6.

Chapter Six

   1. Casey Hayden, "Raising the Question of Who Decides," *New
Republic*, 154 (January 22, 1966), 9–10.
   2. O'Brien, "Development," pp. 275–6; Tom Hayden quoted in
Sale, *SDS*, p. 101; Todd Gitlin, "The Dynamics of the New Left," *motive*, XXXI, no. 2 (November 1970), 43.
   3. Tom Hayden and Carl Wittman, "An Interracial Movement of
the Poor?" (New York: Students for a Democratic Society, n.d.), pp.
17–18; "Port Huron Statement" (New York: Students for a Democratic
Society, 1962).
   4. O'Brien, "Development," p. 276; Sale, *SDS*, pp. 96–9; Richard
Rothstein, "Evolution of the ERAP Organizers," in *The New Left: A
Collection of Essays*, ed. by Priscilla Long (Boston: Porter Sargent,
1969), pp. 273–82; SDS *Bulletin* (March-April 1963).
   5. SDS *Bulletin* (October 1963); Sale, *SDS*, pp. 106, 113–15;
O'Brien, "Development," pp. 280–1.
   6. Andrew Kopkind, "Of, By and For the Poor: The New Generation of Student Organizers," *New Republic*, 152 (June 19, 1965), 18.
   7. Nanci Hollander, "Cleveland," SDS *Bulletin* (July 1964); Rothstein, "Evolution," p. 274; Tom Hayden, "The Politics of the 'Movement,' " *Dissent*, XIII, no. 1 (January 1966), 80.
   8. Sharon Jeffry to Dickie (Magidoff), personal letter, November
1964, SHSW, SDS Papers, Series 2B (hereinafter cited as SDS-2B), Box 9;
song lyrics from ERAP *Bulletin* (Summer 1965), SHSW, SDS Papers, also
quoted in Sale, *SDS*, pp. 131–2.
   9. Quotes from Jesse Allen, "Newark Community Union," *Studies
on the Left*, 5 (Winter 1965), 80; Casey Hayden interviewed in Richard
Rothstein, "Chicago: JOIN Project," *Studies on the Left*, 5 (Summer
1965), 123; Connie Brown, "Cleveland: Conference of the Poor," *Studies on the Left*, 5 (Spring 1965), 71.
   10. Casey Hayden, "Raising the Question," p. 9; Rothstein, "Chicago: JOIN," pp. 122–3; Kopkind, "Of, By and For the Poor," p. 19; "An
Introduction: Cleveland Community Project, Summer, 1966," SHSW,
Carol McEldowney Papers.

11. Allen, "Union," pp. 80–1; Kopkind, "Of, By and For the Poor," p. 16.

12. Sale, *SDS*, p. 137; Worklist Mailing, II, no. 13 (1965), SHSW, SDS-2A, Box 7; Kopkind, "Of, By and For the Poor," p. 18; interview with Mimi Feingold.

13. Nick to Ollie and Charlotte Fein, personal letter, July 29, 1964, SHSW, SDS-2B, Box 9; Kopkind, "Of, By and For the Poor," pp. 16–17.

14. Sale, *SDS*, pp. 99–101, 134–5. This analysis draws on interviews with participants in most of the longer-term ERAP projects and some of the briefer ones, as well as on my own experiences as a community organizer in Durham, North Carolina, in 1969.

15. Joan Bradbury, SDS *Bulletin* (September 1964); Rothstein, "Evolution," p. 275; Carol McEldowney to Greg Calvert, personal letter, December 5, 1966, SHSW, SDS Papers, Series 3 (unfiled; hereinafter cited as SDS-3); interview with Sharon Jeffry; CUFAW pamphlet, SHSW, Carol McEldowney Papers.

16. Patty Schneider, "A Progress Report on Mothers for Adequate Welfare," typed manuscript (n.d.), SHSW, SDS-3.

17. Interviews with Richie Rothstein, Leni Wildflower, and Alice Keller; Mike James, "Report on JOIN," *New Left Notes*, August 26, 1966; Casey Hayden quoted in Rothstein, "Chicago: JOIN," pp. 119–20.

18. Interview with Vivian Rothstein; Judi Bernstein interviewed in Rothstein, "Chicago: JOIN," pp. 124–5; Allen, "Union," p. 82.

19. Brown, "Conference," pp. 72–3.

20. *What Is JOIN?*, pamphlet (Chicago, 1964), SHSW, Carol McEldowney Papers; also interviews with Vivian Rothstein, Leni Wildflower, Sharon Jeffry, Paul Potter, and others.

21. Rennie Davis, quoted in Rothstein, "Chicago: JOIN," pp. 113–15.

22. Interview with Sharon Jeffry; Ronald Glick, "To the People: A History and Analysis of a Major Radical Left Organizing Effort of the Sixties" (second draft of an unpublished Ph.D. dissertation, University of California at Berkeley, 1973), pp. 150–1. On leadership composition, see George Brosi to Clark Kissinger, personal letter, June 26, 1964; ERAP letterhead; and National Council Minutes for June 16, 1964, SHSW, SDS-2A, Box 3.

23. Todd Gitlin, "Dynamics," p. 66; also interview with Paul Potter.

Chapter Seven

1. Sale, *SDS*, pp. 162–9; O'Brien, "Development," pp. 333–73; Hal Draper, *Berkeley: The New Student Revolt* (New York: Grove Press, 1965); Seymour M. Lipset and Sheldon S. Wolin, eds., *The Berkeley Stu-*

dent Revolt: Facts and Interpretations (Garden City, N.Y.: Doubleday, 1965).

2. Watters, *Down to Now*, p. 309; Sale, *SDS*, pp. 169–93, 246; O'Brien, "Development," pp. 408–12; "Report from the Editors: The SDS March on Washington," *Studies on the Left*, 5 (Spring 1965), 61–9. By December 1965 there were 4,300 members in the organization.

3. Carol McEldowney on the ERAP institutes, SDS *Worklist Mailing* (May 27, 1965), SHSW, SDS-2A, Box 7; Harriet Stulman to the national office, letter, May 4, 1965, 1965 Convention Folder, SHSW, SDS-2A, Box 7.

4. Interview with James Weinstein; Sale, *SDS*, pp. 203–16.

5. "SDS National Convention: Tentative Agenda," Kewadin, Michigan, June 9–15, 1965, SHSW, SDS-2A, Box 7; interviews with James Weinstein, Anne Froines, and Paul Booth.

6. Sale, *SDS*, pp. 216–48.

7. Interviews with Anne Froines, Paul Booth, Heather Booth, and Alice Keller.

8. Interviews with Steve Max, Heather Booth, and Paul Booth; Sale, *SDS*, pp. 248–52.

9. The account of the women's workshop is drawn from interviews with Heather Booth, Steve Max, Leni Wildflower, Vivian Rothstein, Sharon Jeffry, Cathy Barrett, Paul Booth, and Jimmy Garrett.

10. Sharon Jeffry and Carol McEldowney, "Notes," from the small group discussion on women and women's roles, SDS "Rethinking Conference," Champaign-Urbana, Illinois, December 1965, in Vivian Rothstein's files.

11. "On Roles in SDS," reprinted in *New Left Notes*, January 28, 1966.

12. "December Conference Impressions," *New Left Notes*, January 28, 1966.

13. See, for example, Larry Freudiger, "The White Revolution," *New Left Notes*, June 26, 1967.

14. On the sit-in, see also *New Left Notes*, May 13, 1966; Sale, *SDS*, pp. 256–63.

15. I worked with Lyn Wells in the summer of 1967 and was continually impressed by her audacity and organizing skill.

16. Greg Calvert, "In White America," speech reprinted in the *National Guardian*, March 25, 1967.

17. See Carl Davidson, "Toward a Student Syndicalist Movement" (Chicago: Students for a Democratic Society, n.d.); "The Teacher-Organizer Concept," handwritten paper, SHSW, SDS-3; Sale, *SDS*, p. 3; Davidson quote from *National Guardian*, April 8, 1967.

18. Marge Piercy, "Grand Coolie Damn," in *Sisterhood Is Powerful*, ed. by Robin Morgan, p. 424.

19. John Veneziale, "University of Washington: A Touchy Situation," *New Left Notes*, March 6, 1967; Bob Pardun, "Gentle Thursday," *New Left Notes*, February 3, 1967.

20. Piercy, "Grand Coolie Damn," p. 430; interview with Linda Dauscher.

21. Barrie Thorne, " 'Girls Who Say Yes to Guys Who Say No': Women in the Draft Resistance Movement," paper presented to the American Sociological Association, New Orleans, 1972, p. 1; Greg Calvert, "National Secretary's Report: From Protest to Resistance," *New Left Notes*, January 13, 1967; "We Won't Go—A Case Study of a Draft Resistance Union," *New Left Notes*, March 27, 1967.

22. Thorne, "Girls," p. 2; mimeographed letter, Wisconsin Draft Resistance Union, March 21, 1967, SHSW, SDS-3; "From Frustration to Affirmation: Developing Draft Resistance Unions in America," typed paper, Spring 1967, SHSW, SDS-3.

23. Thorne, "Girls," p. 5.

24. Heather Tobis, "A Reexamination of the 'We Won't Go' Conference," *New Left Notes*, January 13, 1966.

25. Francine Silbar, "Women and the Draft Movement," *New Left Notes*, March 27, 1967.

26. *New Left Notes*, April 22, 15; August 5; July 22; and November 18, 1966.

27. Jane Adams, "People's Power: On Equality for Women," *New Left Notes*, January 20, 1967.

28. Piercy, "Grand Coolie Damn," pp. 436–7.

29. *New Left Notes*, July 10, 1967.

30. This account of the convention meeting is based upon detailed handwritten notes by David Grunstein and someone else whose name does not appear on the copy, SHSW, SDS-3; Donald McKelvey, "Thoughts on the Convention," *New Left Notes*, July 10, 1967; and an interview with Beth Reisen.

Chapter Eight

1. Walter Goodman, "When Black Power Runs the New Left," *The New York Times Magazine* (September 24, 1967), 28–9, 124–8; William O'Neill, *Coming Apart: An Informal History of America in the 1960s* (New York: Quadrangle, 1971), p. 288.

2. Quoted from the typed transcript of the Sandy Springs, Maryland, Women's Conference, August 2–4, 1968, in author's possession; also interview with Freeman. The speaker here is probably Freeman.

3. Jo Freeman, "Origins of the Women's Liberation Movement,"

American Journal of Sociology, LXXVIII, no. 4 (1973), 792–811. Karl Mannheim, *Essays on the Sociology of Culture* (London: Routledge and Kegan Paul, 1956), pp. 91–2, describes insightfully the emergence of collective self-consciousness when a group finds itself in altered circumstances.

4. Judith Brown to Carl Braden, personal letter, August 27, 1968, SHSW, Braden Papers, Box 82.

5. "Memo: Carol Hanish to SCEF Women, Proposal for a Women's Liberation Program," August 10, 1968, SHSW, Braden Papers, Box 82. See Freeman, "Origins," for a description of the formation of the movement through the internal network.

6. Marilyn Webb to Heather Booth, personal letter, November 21, 1968, Correspondence Files for Thanksgiving Conference of Women, Lake Villa, Illinois, November 28–31, 1968 (hereinafter cited as Thanksgiving correspondence), in Charlotte Bunch's files; copy also in author's possession.

7. Judy Brown to Marilyn Webb, personal letter, August 8, 1968, Thanksgiving correspondence.

8. Interview with Heather Booth.

Chapter Nine

1. Eli Zaretsky, *Capitalism, The Family, and Personal Life* (New York: Harper & Row, 1976), describes this process in detail and with considerable insight into women's roles.

2. Susan Suthein, "Radical Women Protest Ugly Pageant," *National Guardian*, September 14, 1968; "No More Miss America!" leaflet in Jo Freeman's files; Beverly Grant to Pam Allen, personal letter, September 9, 1968, Pam Allen's files; Carden, *New Feminist Movement*, p. 32.

3. Kathie Sarachild, "A Program for Feminist Consciousness Raising," paper prepared for Thanksgiving Conference, Thanksgiving correspondence. The term "consciousness-raising" was, according to Sarachild, invented by Anne Forer. Shulamith Firestone to Jo Freeman, personal letter, March 1968, Freeman files.

4. See Pam Allen, "Free Space: A Perspective on the Small Groups in Women's Liberation" (New York: Times Change, 1970).

5. Mary Daly, *The Church and the Second Sex* (New York: Harper & Row, 1968) ; Mary Daly, *Beyond God the Father: Toward a Philosophy of Women's Liberation* (Boston: Beacon Press, 1973).

6. Kate Millet, *Sexual Politics* (Garden City, N.Y.: Doubleday, 1970), and Shulamith Firestone, *The Dialectic of Sex: The Case for Femi-*

nist Revolution (New York: William Morrow, 1970), initiated what was to be an avalanche of new books. See Carden, *New Feminist Movement*, pp. 162–3.

7. Neil J. Smelser, *Theory of Collective Behavior* (New York: The Free Press, 1962). William A. Gamson, *The Strategy of Social Protest* (Homewood, Ill.: The Dorsey Press, 1975), pp. 130–2, points out the extensive theoretical shortcomings in the collective behaviorist approach to the study of social movements. Mannheim quote from *Essays on the Sociology of Culture*, p. 91.

8. "The Harris Survey," May 20, 1971; December 11, 1975; December 8, 1975; "The Gallup Opinion Index," Report no. 92, February 1973; Report no. 113, November 1974; see also Cynthia Fuchs Epstein, "Ten Years Later: Perspectives on the Women's Movement," *Dissent*, 22 (Spring 1975), 170; "The American Woman on the Move," *Reader's Digest*, 108 (March 1976), 54. The Harris Poll records the continued ambivalence of women who support efforts to improve their lot but are not attracted by most women's rights organizations (December 11, 1975).

9. Carden, *New Feminist Movement*, pp. 33–7, describes women's changed perceptions as a "conversion process." See Jo Freeman, "The Tyranny of Structurelessness," *Berkeley Journal of Sociology: A Critical Review*, XVII (1972–3), 151–64; quote on lot system in Hole and Levine, *Rebirth*, p. 147.

10. Hole and Levine, *Rebirth*, pp. 133–4; quotes from Carden, *New Feminist Movement*, p. 36, and Morgan, ed., *Sisterhood Is Powerful*, p. xv.

11. See, for example, the discussion of Redstockings and the Feminists in Hole and Levine, *Rebirth*, pp. 136–47.

12. See Marabel Morgan, *The Total Woman* (Old Tappan, N.J.: Revell, 1975).

13. U.S. Bureau of the Census, *Statistical Abstract of the United States: 1975* (96th ed., Washington, D.C.: GPO, 1975), pp. 346, 347; "The Gallup Opinion Index," Report no. 107, May 1974; "The Harris Survey," December 11, 1975; December 8, 1975.

14. I am indebted to Harry C. Boyte for sharing the research from his forthcoming study of new forms of grass-roots organizing in the 1970s. His work demonstrates concretely the widespread impact of resurgent feminism.

15. Toni A. H. McNaron, "Finding and Studying Lesbian Culture," *Radical Teacher* (December 1977), p. 16.

Selected Bibliography

Books and Unpublished Dissertations

Ariès, Philippe. *Centuries of Childhood: A Social History of Family Life.* New York: Alfred A. Knopf, 1962.

Banner, Lois W. *Women in Modern America: A Brief History.* New York: Harcourt Brace Jovanovich, 1974.

Belfrage, Sally. *Freedom Summer.* New York: Viking Press, 1965.

Braden, Anne. *The Wall Between.* New York: Monthly Review Press, 1958.

Braverman, Harry. *Labor and Monopoly Capital: The Degradation of Work in the Twentieth Century.* New York: Monthly Review Press, 1975.

Brooks, John N. *The Great Leap: The Past Twenty-Five Years in America.* New York: Harper & Row, 1966.

Cantril, Hadley, ed. *Public Opinion: 1935–1946.* Princeton, N.J.: Princeton University Press, 1951.

Carden, Maren Lockwood. *The New Feminist Movement.* New York: Russell Sage Foundation, 1974.

Carmichael, Stokely, and Hamilton, Charles V. *Black Power: The Politics of Liberation in America.* New York: Vintage Books, 1967.

Carson, Clayborne, Jr. "Toward Freedom and Community: The Evolution of Ideas in the Student Nonviolent Coordinating Committee, 1960–66." Unpublished Ph.D. dissertation, University of California at Los Angeles, 1975.

Carson, Josephine. *Silent Voices: The Southern Negro Woman Today.* New York: Delacorte Press, 1969.

Cash, Wilbur Joseph. *The Mind of the South.* New York: Alfred A. Knopf, 1941.

Chafe, William Henry. *The American Woman: Her Changing Social, Economic, and Political Roles, 1920–1970.* New York: Oxford University Press, 1972.

Cleaver, Eldridge. *Soul on Ice.* New York: Dell Publishing Co., 1968.

Dahrendorf, Ralf. *Class and Class Conflict in Industrial Society.* Stanford, Calif.: Stanford University Press, 1959.

Daly, Mary. *Beyond God the Father: Toward a Philosophy of Women's Liberation.* Boston: Beacon Press, 1973.

————. *The Church and the Second Sex.* New York: Harper & Row, 1968.

Demos, John. *A Little Commonwealth: Family Life in Plymouth Colony.* New York: Oxford University Press, 1970.

Dollard, John. *Caste and Class in a Southern Town.* Garden City, N.Y.: Doubleday and Co., 1957.

Draper, Hal. *Berkeley: The New Student Revolt.* New York: Grove Press, 1965.

Farnham, Marynia, and Lundberg, Ferdinand. *The Modern Woman: The Lost Sex.* New York: Harper & Brothers, 1947.

Filene, Peter Gabriel. *Him/Her Self: Sex Roles in Modern America.* New York: Harcourt Brace Jovanovich, 1974.

Firestone, Shulamith. *The Dialectic of Sex: The Case for Feminist Revolution.* New York: William Morrow and Co., 1970.

Forman, James. *The Making of Black Revolutionaries: A Personal Account.* New York: Macmillan Co., 1972.

Freeman, Jo. *The Politics of Women's Liberation: A Case Study of an Emerging Social Movement and Its Relation to the Policy Process.* New York: David McKay Co., 1975.

Friedan, Betty. *The Feminine Mystique.* New York: Dell Publishing Co., 1963.

Fuchs, Victor. *The Service Economy.* New York: Columbia University Press, 1968.

Gamson, William A. *The Strategy of Social Protest.* Homewood, Ill.: The Dorsey Press, 1975.

Gilman, Charlotte Perkins. *The Home: Its Work and Influence.* New York: Charlton Company, 1910.

————. *Women and Economics.* New York: Harper & Row, 1966.

Gitlin, Todd, and Hollander, Nanci. *Uptown.* New York: Harper & Row, 1970.

Glick, Ronald. "To the People: A History and Analysis of a Major Radical Left Organizing Effort of the Sixties." Unpublished Ph.D. dissertation, University of California at Berkeley, 1973.

Hall, Jacquelyn Dowd. "Revolt Against Chivalry: Jesse Daniel Ames and the Women's Campaign Against Lynching." Ph.D. dissertation, Columbia University, 1974, to be published in 1979 by Columbia University Press.

Hamilton, Richard F. *Class and Politics in the United States.* New York: John Wiley and Sons, 1972.

Harrington, Michael. *The Other America.* New York: Macmillan Co., 1962.

Himehoch, Jerome, and Fleis, Sylvia, eds. *Sexual Behavior in American Society: An Appraisal of the First Two Kinsey Reports.* New York: W. W. Norton, 1955.

Hole, Judith, and Levine, Ellen. *Rebirth of Feminism.* New York: Quadrangle Books, 1971.

Holt, Len. *The Summer That Didn't End.* New York: William Morrow and Co., 1965.

Howe, Irving, and Coser, Lewis. *The American Communist Party: A Critical History.* New York: Frederick A. Praeger, 1957.

Howe, Louise Kapp. *The Future of the Family.* New York: Simon and Schuster, 1972.

Jordan, Winthrop. *White Over Black: American Attitudes Toward the Negro, 1550–1812.* Baltimore: Penguin Books, 1968.

Keniston, Kenneth. *The Young Radicals: Notes on Committed Youth.* New York: Harcourt, Brace and World, 1966.

Kinsey, Alfred; Pomeroy, Wardell B.; Martin, Clyde E.; and Gebhard, Paul. *Sexual Behavior in the Human Female.* Philadelphia: W. B. Saunders, 1953.

Klein, Viola. *The Feminine Character.* 2d ed. Urbana, Ill.: University of Illinois Press, 1971.

Lerner, Gerda. *The Grimke Sisters from South Carolina: Pioneers for Woman's Rights and Abolition.* New York: Schocken Books, 1971.

Lerner, Gerda, ed. *Black Women in White America: A Documentary History.* New York: Pantheon Books, 1972.

Lifton, Robert J., ed. *The Woman in America.* Boston: Houghton Mifflin Co., 1965.

Lipset, Seymour M., and Wolin, Sheldon S., eds. *The Berkeley Student Revolt: Facts and Interpretations.* Garden City, N.Y.: Doubleday and Co., 1965.

Long, Priscilla, ed. *The New Left: A Collection of Essays.* Boston: Porter Sargent, 1969.

Louis, Debbie. *And We Are Not Saved: A History of the Movement as People.* Garden City, N.Y.: Doubleday and Co., 1970.

Lynd, Staughton, and Ferber, Michael. *The Resistance.* Boston: Beacon Press, 1971.

Mannheim, Karl. *Essays on the Sociology of Culture.* London: Routledge and Kegan Paul, 1956.

Meier, August; Rudwick, Elliott; and Broderick, Francis L., eds. *Black Protest Thought in the Twentieth Century.* 2d ed. Indianapolis: Bobbs-Merrill Co., 1971.

Millet, Kate. *Sexual Politics.* Garden City, N.Y.: Doubleday and Co., 1970.

Mills, C. Wright. *White Collar: The American Middle Classes.* New York: Oxford University Press, 1951.

Mitchell, Juliet. *Woman's Estate.* New York: Vintage Books, 1971.

Moody, Anne. *Coming of Age in Mississippi.* New York: Dell Publishing Co., 1968.

Morgan, Marabel. *The Total Woman.* Old Tappan, N.J.: Fleming H. Revell Co., 1975.

Morgan, Robin. *Going Too Far.* New York: Random House, 1977.

Morgan, Robin, ed. *Sisterhood Is Powerful: An Anthology of Writings from the Women's Liberation Movement.* New York: Vintage Books, 1970.

Morison, Elting Elmore, ed. *The American Style: Essays in Value and Performance: A Report on the Dedham Conference of May 23–27, 1957.* New York: Harper & Row, 1958.

Myrdal, Alva Reimar, and Klein, Viola. *Women's Two Roles: Home and Work.* London: Routledge and Kegan Paul, 1956.

Myrdal, Gunnar. *An American Dilemma: The Negro Problem and Modern Democracy.* New York: Harper & Brothers, 1944.

National Manpower Council Reports. *Womanpower: A Statement with Chapters by the Council Staff.* New York: Columbia University Press, 1957–8.

————. *Work in the Lives of Married Women: Proceedings of a Conference on Womanpower Held October 20–25, 1957.* New York: Columbia University Press, 1957–8.

Newfield, Jack. *Prophetic Minority.* New York: New American Library, 1966.

O'Brien, James Putnam. "The Development of a New Left in the United States, 1960–65." Unpublished Ph.D. dissertation, University of Wisconsin, 1971.

O'Neill, William. *Coming Apart: An Informal History of America in the 1960s.* New York: Quadrangle Books, 1971.

Packard, Vance. *The Hidden Persuaders.* New York: David McKay Co., 1957.

Raines, Howell. *My Soul Is Rested: Movement Days in the Deep South Remembered.* New York: G. P. Putnam's Sons, 1977.

Riesman, David; Glazer, Nathan; and Denney, Reuel. *The Lonely Crowd: A Study of the Changing American Character.* Garden City, N.Y.: Doubleday and Co., 1953.

Rossi, Alice, ed. *The Feminist Papers: From Adams to de Beauvoir.* New York: Columbia University Press, 1973.

Rossi, Alice S., and Calderwood, Ann, eds. *Academic Women on the Move.* New York: Russell Sage Foundation, 1973.

THIS PAGE ONE LINE LONG.....

Rothschild, Mary Aicken. "Northern Volunteers and the Southern 'Freedom Summers,' 1964–65: A Social History." Unpublished Ph.D. dissertation, University of Washington, 1974.

Rowbotham, Sheila. *Women, Resistance, and Revolution.* New York: Pantheon Books, 1972.

Sale, Kirkpatrick. *SDS.* New York: Vintage Books, 1973.

Salper, Roberta, ed. *Female Liberation: History and Current Politics.* New York: Alfred A. Knopf, 1972.

Scott, Anne Firor. *The Southern Lady: From Pedestal to Politics, 1820–1920.* Chicago: University of Chicago Press, 1970.

Sellers, Cleveland. *The River of No Return: The Autobiography of a Black Militant and the Life and Death of SNCC.* New York: William Morrow and Co., 1973.

Smelser, Neil J. *Theory of Collective Behavior.* New York: The Free Press, 1962.

Smith, Lillian. *Killers of the Dream.* New York: W. W. Norton, 1949.

Smuts, Robert W. *Women and Work in America.* New York: Schocken Books, 1971.

Spectorsky, Auguste C. *The Exurbanites.* Philadelphia: J. B. Lippincott Co., 1955.

Stein, Maurice R. *The Eclipse of Community: An Interpretation of American Studies.* Princeton, N.J.: Princeton University Press, 1960.

Sutherland, Elizabeth, ed. *Letters from Mississippi.* New York: McGraw-Hill Book Co., 1965.

Thompson, E. P. *The Making of the English Working Class.* New York: Random House, Vintage Books, 1963.

U.S. Bureau of the Census. *Statistical Abstract of the United States: 1975.* 96th ed. Washington, D.C.: Government Printing Office, 1975.

U.S. Bureau of Labor Statistics. *The U.S. Economy in 1980:* Bulletin 1673. Washington, D.C.: Government Printing Office, 1970.

U.S. Department of Labor. *1969 Handbook on Women Workers.* Women's Bureau Bulletin No. 294. Washington, D.C.: Government Printing Office, 1969.

Ware, Celestine. *Woman Power: The Movement for Women's Liberation.* New York: Tower Publications, 1970.

Watters, Pat. *Down to Now: Reflections on the Southern Civil Rights Movement. New York: Pantheon Books, 1971.*

Whyte, William Hollingsworth. The Organization Man. New York: Simon and Schuster, 1956.

Wylie, Philip. *Generation of Vipers.* New York: Holt, Rinehart and Winston, 1955.

Zaretsky, Eli. *Capitalism, The Family, and Personal Life.* New York: Harper & Row, 1976.

Zinn, Howard. *SNCC: The New Abolitionists.* Boston: Beacon Press, 1964.

Articles, Periodicals, and Pamphlets

Allen, Jesse. "Newark Community Union." *Studies on the Left*, 5, Winter 1965, pp. 80–5.

Allen, Pam. "Free Space: A Perspective on the Small Groups in Women's Liberation." New York: Times Change, 1970.

"The American Woman on the Move." Article condensed from *U.S. News and World Report. Reader's Digest*, 108, March 1976, pp. 54–8.

"American Women's Dilemma." *Life* magazine, June 16, 1947, pp. 101–11.

Bell, Daniel. "Labor in the Post-Industrial Society." *Dissent*, Winter 1972, pp. 163–89.

"Black Feminism: A New Mandate." *Ms.*, 2, May 1974, pp. 97–100.

Boyte, Harry Chatten."The Textile Industry: Keel of Southern Industrialization." *Radical America*, March-April 1972, pp. 4–50.

Broverman, Inge K.; Vogel, Susan Raymond; Broverman, Donald M.; Clarkson, Frank E.; and Rosenkrantz, Paul S. "Sex-Role Stereotypes: A Current Appraisal." *Journal of Social Issues*, 28, no. 2 (1973), 59–67.

Brown, Connie. "Cleveland: Conference of the Poor." *Studies on the Left*, 5, Spring 1965, pp. 71–4.

Brown, Ray. "Our Crisis Economy: The End of the Boom." New York: Students for a Democratic Society, 1963.

Calvert, Greg. "In White America." Speech reprinted in the *National Guardian*, March 25, 1967, p. 1.

Chafe, William H. "Feminism of the 1970s." *Dissent*, 21, Fall 1974, pp. 508–17.

Coles, Robert. "Social Struggle and Weariness." *Psychiatry*, 27, no. 4 (1964), pp. 305–15.

Davidson, Carl. "Toward a Student Syndicalist Movement." Chicago: Students for a Democratic Society, n.d.

Dixon, Marguerite M. "Adolescent Girls Tell About Themselves." *Marriage and Family Living*, XX, no. 4, November 1958, pp. 400–1.

Epstein, Cynthia Fuchs. "Ten Years Later: Perspectives on the Women's Movement." *Dissent*, 22, Spring 1975, pp. 169–76.

Ferry, W. H.; Harrington, Michael; Myrdal, Gunnar; Theobald, Robert; Pauling, Linus; Heilbroner, Robert; and Seligman, Ben B. "The Triple Revolution." *Liberation*, April 1964, pp. 9–15.

Flacks, Richard. "The Liberated Generation: An Exploration of the Roots of Student Protest." *Journal of Social Issues,* XXIII, July 1967, pp. 52–75.

"The Fortune Survey: Women in America." *Fortune,* August 1946, pp. 5–6, 8, 10, 14.

Freedman, Melvin B. "The Passage Through College." *Journal of Social Issues,* XII, no. 4 (1956), pp. 13–28.

Freeman, Jo. "Origins of the Women's Liberation Movement." *American Journal of Sociology,* LXXVIII, no. 4 (1973), pp. 792–811.

————. "The Tyranny of Structurelessness." *Berkeley Journal of Sociology: A Critical Review,* XVII (1972–3), pp. 151–64.

"From Sisterhood to Priesthood: First Women to Be Ordained as Priests in the Episcopal Church." *Newsweek,* August 12, 1974, p. 52.

Fructer, Norman. "Mississippi: Notes on SNCC." *Studies on the Left,* Winter 1965, pp. 74–80.

Fusco, Liz. "Deeper Than Politics: The Mississippi Freedom Schools." *Liberation,* November 1964, pp. 17–19.

Gallup, George. "The Gallup Opinion Index." February 1973–November 1974.

Gallup, George, and Hill, Evan. "The American Woman." *Saturday Evening Post,* December 2, 1962, pp. 15–32.

Gitlin, Todd. "The Dynamics of the New Left." *motive,* XXXI, no. 2, November 1970, pp. 43–67.

Goodman, Walter. "When Black Power Runs the New Left." *The New York Times Magazine,* September 24, 1967, pp. 28–9, 124–8.

Graebner, Norman A. "Eisenhower's Popular Leadership." In *Twentieth Century America: Recent Interpretations.* Edited by Barton J. Bernstein and Allen J. Matusow. New York: Harcourt, Brace and World, 1969.

Hacker, Helen. "Women as a Minority Group." *Social Forces,* 30, no. 1 (1951), pp. 60–9.

Hamill, Katherine. "Women as Bosses." *Fortune,* 53, no. 6, June 1956, pp. 104–8.

Harris, Louis. "The Harris Survey." May 20, 1971–December 11, 1975.

Hayden, Casey. "Raising the Question of Who Decides." *New Republic,* 153, January 22, 1966, pp. 9–10.

Hayden, Casey, and King, Mary. "Sex and Caste: A Kind of Memo." *Liberation,* 10, April 1966, pp. 35–6.

Hayden, Tom. "The Politics of the 'Movement.'" *Dissent,* XIII, no. 1, January 1966, pp. 75–87.

————. "Student Social Action." New York: Students for a Democratic Society, n.d.

Hayden, Tom, and Wittman, Carl. "An Interracial Movement of the Poor?" New York: Students for a Democratic Society, n.d.

Helson, Ravenna. "The Changing Image of the Career Woman." *Journal of Social Issues*, 28, no. 2 (1972), pp. 34–6.

Johnson, Kathryn, and Sommers, Peggy. "The Political Economy of Sexism." Unpublished manuscript, Davenport, Iowa, 1972.

Keniston, Ellen, and Keniston, Kenneth. "An American Anachronism: The Image of Women and Work." *American Scholar*, 33, no. 3 (1964), pp. 355–75.

Knudsen, Dean D. "The Declining Status of Women: Popular Myths and the Failure of Functionalist Thought." *Social Forces*, 48, no. 2 (1969), pp. 183–93.

Komarovsky, Mirra. "Cultural Contradictions and Sex Roles." *American Journal of Sociology*, LII, November 1946, pp. 184–9.

Kopkind, Andrew. "Of, By and For the Poor: The New Generation of Student Organizers." *New Republic*, 152, June 19, 1965, pp. 15–19.

Ladies' Home Journal, August 1970.

Life magazine, December 24, 1956.

McNaron, Toni A. H. "Finding and Studying Lesbian Culture." *Radical Teacher*, December 1977, pp. 14–19.

Mead, Margaret. "Some Theoretical Considerations on the Problem of Mother–Child Separation." *American Journal of Orthopsychiatry*, 24, no. 3 (1954), pp. 471–83.

———. "What Women Want." *Fortune*, 34, no. 6, December 1946, pp. 172–5, 218–24.

Mezerik, Avrahm G. "Getting Rid of Women." *Atlantic Monthly*, June 1945, pp. 79–83.

Montagu, Ashley. "The Triumph and Tragedy of the American Woman." *Saturday Review*, 41, no. 39, September 27, 1958, pp. 13–15.

motive, 1954–60.

New Left Committee Bulletin, November 1967.

New Left Notes, 1965–9.

Norris, Louis William. "How to Educate a Woman." *Saturday Review*, November 27, 1954, pp. 9–10, 38–40.

Notes from the First Year, 1968.

Ollman, Bertell. "Toward Class Consciousness Next Time: Marx and the Working Class." *Politics and Society*, 3, no. 1 (1972), pp. 1–24.

Parker, Ron K. "The Southern Student Organizing Committee." Unpublished paper, New Orleans, Louisiana, 1965.

"Port Huron Statement." New York: Students for a Democratic Society, 1962.

Pouissant, Alvin F., M.D. "The Stresses of the White Female Worker in the Civil Rights Movement in the South." *American Journal of Psychiatry*, 123, no. 4 (1966), pp. 401–5.

Reingold, Robert. "Upheavals Among Smith Alumnae Illustrate Role Changes," *The New York Times*, November 30, 1977.

"Report from the Editors: The SDS March on Washington." *Studies on the Left*, 5, Spring 1965, pp. 61–9.

Riesman, David. "The Found Generation." *American Scholar*, 25, no. 4 (1956), pp. 421–36.

————. "The Saving Remnant: An Examination of Character Structure." In *Years of the Modern: An American Appraisal*. Edited by John W. Chase. New York: Longmans, Green and Co., 1949.

Robinson, Jo Ann. "Lillian Smith: Reflections on Race and Sex." *Southern Exposure*, IV, Winter 1977, pp. 43–8.

Rose, Arnold. "The Adequacy of Women's Expectations for Adult Roles." *Social Forces*, 30, no. 1 (1951), pp. 69–77.

Rothstein, Richard. "Chicago: JOIN Project." *Studies on the Left*, Summer 1965, pp. 107–25.

Sexton, Patricia Cayo. "Workers (Female) Arise!" *Dissent*, 21, Summer 1974, pp. 380–95.

Smith-Rosenberg, Carroll. "Beauty, the Beast and the Militant Woman: A Case Study in Sex Roles and Social Stress in Jacksonian America." *American Quarterly*, 23, no. 4 (1971), pp. 562–84.

Sontag, Susan. "The Third World of Women." *Partisan Review*, XL, no. 2 (1973), pp. 180–207.

Thorne, Barrie. "Girls Who Say Yes to Guys Who Say No': Women in the Draft Resistance Movement." Paper presented to the American Sociological Association, New Orleans, Louisiana, 1972.

Weiss, Robert S., and Samuelson, Nancy M. "Social Roles of American Women: Their Contribution to a Sense of Usefulness and Importance." *Marriage and Family Living*, XX, no. 4, November 1958, pp. 338–66.

Welter, Barbara. "The Cult of True Womanhood." *American Quarterly*, LVIII, no. 2 (1966), pp. 151–74.

What Is JOIN? Chicago: Students for a Democratic Society, 1964.

"Wives with Brains." Reader response. *Newsweek*, March 21, 1960, pp. 2, 8.

"Young Wives with Brains: Babies, Yes—But What Else?" *Newsweek*, March 7, 1960, pp. 57–60.

Manuscript Collections

Aicken [Rothschild], Mary. Papers, 1965–8. State Historical Society of Wisconsin. Madison, Wisconsin.

Allen, Pam Parker. Personal Files.
Braden, Carl and Anne. Papers, 1928–67. State Historical Society of Wisconsin. Madison, Wisconsin.
Bunch, Charlotte. Personal Files.
CORE. Papers, 1941–67. State Historical Society of Wisconsin. Madison, Wisconsin.
Evans, Sara. Personal Collection.
Freeman, Jo. Personal Files.
Halpern, Sydney. Personal Files.
Hard, Sandra. Papers, 1964–6. State Historical Society of Wisconsin. Madison, Wisconsin.
Jordan, Joan. Papers, 1966–72. State Historical Society of Wisconsin. Madison, Wisconsin.
King, Mary. Personal Files.
McEldowney, Carol. Papers, 1964–8. State Historical Society of Wisconsin. Madison, Wisconsin.
Rabinowitz, Joni. Personal Files.
Rothstein, Vivian. Personal Files.
Students for a Democratic Society. Papers, 1960–9. State Historical Society of Wisconsin. Madison, Wisconsin.
Schecter, Danny. Personal Files.
Sutherland, Elizabeth. Papers, 1964. State Historical Society of Wisconsin. Madison, Wisconsin.
Women's Liberation Collection. Arthur and Elizabeth Schlesinger Library on the History of Women in America, Radcliffe College, Cambridge, Massachusetts.

Oral Interviews

Allen, Pam Parker. San Francisco, California. July 17, 1973.
Baker, Ella. New York, New York. July 31, 1973.
Barrett, Cathy. San Francisco, California. July 17, 1973.
Baxandall, Rosalyn Fraad. Truro, Massachusetts. August 6, 1973.
Bellamy, Fay. Atlanta, Georgia. June 29, 1973.
Booth, Heather Tobis. Chicago, Illinois. November 5, 1972; July 9, 1973.
———. Chapel Hill, North Carolina. February 13, 1976.
Booth, Paul. Chicago, Illinois. July 13, 1973.
Braden, Anne. Louisville, Kentucky. June 10, 1973.
Braden, Carl. Louisville, Kentucky. June 10, 1973.
Brownmiller, Susan. New York, New York. July 27, 1973.
Bunch, Charlotte. Washington, D.C. June 21, 1973.

Burlage, Dorothy Dawson. Cambridge, Massachusetts. August 5, 1973.
Cade, Cathy. Berkeley, California. July 21, 1973.
Carcione, Linda. Washington, D.C. July 25, 1973.
Cason, Sandra (Casey). New York, New York. July 17, 1977.
Cassedy, Ellen. Somerville, Massachusetts. April 17, 1977. [Interviewed by Harry C. Boyte]
Chaffee, Lois. New York, New York. August 1, 1973.
Creamer, Day. Chicago, Illinois. April 28, 1977. [Interviewed by Harry C. Boyte]
Dauscher, Linda. San Francisco, California. July 19, 1973.
Densmore, Dana. Medford, Massachusetts. August 7, 1973.
Eagan, Andrea. New York, New York. August 1, 1973.
Easton, Barbara. Berkeley, California. July 5, 1973.
Feingold, Mimi. San Francisco, California. July 16, 1973.
Froines, Anne. Somerville, Massachusetts. August 6, 1973.
Fructer, Rachael. Brooklyn, New York. July 29, 1973.
Gabriner, Vicki. Atlanta, Georgia. June 29, 1973.
Garman, Betty. Washington, D.C. July 26, 1973.
Garrett, Jimmy. Washington, D.C. July 16, 1973.
Gordon, Linda. Somerville, Massachusetts. August 7, 1973.
Grogan, Nan. Atlanta, Georgia. June 28, 1973.
Guerrero, Gene. Atlanta, Georgia. March 25, 1978. [Interviewed by Harry C. Boyte]
Halpern, Sydney. Berkeley, California. July 20, 1973.
Hanish, Carol. New York, New York. July 28, 1973.
Hawley, Nancy. Cambridge, Massachusetts. August 7, 1973.
Jeffry, Sharon. Chicago, Illinois. July 12, 1973.
Jordan, Joan. San Francisco, California. July 19, 1973.
Keller, Alice. Chicago, Illinois. July 12, 1973.
King, Mary. Washington, D.C. July 24, 1973.
Kopit, Marcia. Washington, D.C. June 22, 1973.
Levenson, Marya. Cambridge, Massachusetts. August 4, 1973.
Lynd, Alice. Chicago, Illinois. November 4, 1972.
Lynd, Staughton. Chicago, Illinois. November 4, 1972.
McPike, Liz. South Bend, Indiana. August 20, 1977. [Interviewed by Harry C. Boyte]
Max, Steve. Chicago, Illinois. July 9, 1973.
Oglesby, Beth. Cambridge, Massachusetts. August 7, 1973.
Patton, Gwen. Washington, D.C. June 20, 1973.
Potter, Paul. San Jose, California. July 18, 1973.
Reisen, Beth. Boston, Massachusetts. August 7, 1973.
Robinson, Patricia. New York, New York. August 1, 1973.
Rothschild, Mary. Tempe, Arizona. February 3, 1977. [Self-interview]

Rothstein, Richard. Chicago, Illinois. July 12, 1973.

Rothstein, Vivian Leburg. Chicago, Illinois. July 10, 1973.

Sarachild, Kathie (Amatniek). New York, New York. July 27, 1973.

Schakowsky, Jan. Evanston, Illinois. April 30, 1977. [Interviewed by Harry C. Boyte]

Schecter, Danny. Somerville, Massachusetts. August 5, 1973.

Stille, Darlene. Chicago, Illinois. April 28, 1977. [Interviewed by Harry C. Boyte]

Thrasher, Sue. Atlanta, Georgia. June 30, 1973.

Truax, Anne T. Minneapolis, Minnesota. December 8, 1977.

Walton, Jean. Washington, D.C. June 21, 1973.

Weills, Anne. Berkeley, California. July 21, 1973.

Weinstein, James. Dekalb, Illinois. July 5, 1973.

Weisstein, Naomi. New Providence, New Jersey. July 30, 1973.

Wildflower, Leni. San Jose, California. July 18, 1973.

Wiley, Jean. Washington, D.C. July 26, 1973.

Wolfson, Alice. Washington, D.C. June 22, 1973.

Zagarell, Mike. New York, New York. August 1, 1973.

Zinn, Howard. Boston, Massachusetts. August 7, 1973.

Index

A Note About the Author

Sara Evans was born in McCormick, South Carolina, in 1943. She received both her B.A. and her master's degree from Duke University and her Ph.D. from the University of North Carolina at Chapel Hill. She has taught at the University of North Carolina and at Duke, and she is currently teaching women's history at the University of Minnesota in Minneapolis.

A Note on the Type

The text of this book was set on the computer in Caledonia, a typeface designed by W. A. Dwiggins. It belongs to the family of printing types called "modern face" by printers—a term used to mark the change in style of type letters that occurred in about 1800. Caledonia borders on the general design of Scotch Modern, but is more freely drawn than that letter.

Composed, printed, and bound by
American Book–Stratford Press, Inc.,
Saddle Brook, New Jersey.
Typography and binding design by Virginia Tan.